DEDICATION

To Anthony Canali, school guidance counselor and athletic coach extraordinaire; also my brother-in-law and friend, with whom I discussed the content that made it into this book on many occasions over the years. Anthony passed away in 2009 on his birthday after a heroic three-year battle with leukemia. I can visualize him reading this book, smiling, and nodding knowingly.

He touched many lives during his journey, mine among them.

Contents

Acknowledgments xix

Introduction xxi

Part I: Preparation 1

Chapter 1
How Job Seekers Really Find Their Jobs 3

Chapter 2
Knowing Who You Are . . . and What You Want 7

Chapter 3
Conquering Your Own Attitudinal Barriers 13
    Lack of Self-Esteem 13
    Wallowing in Self-Pity 15
    Bitterness and Negativity 16
    Lack of Interest and Enthusiasm 16
    Lack of Energy 17
    Hubris 18
    Disrespect 18

Chapter 4
Avoiding Self-Destruction 21
    Applying for Only One Job at a Time 21
    Applying with Tunnel Vision 22
    Applying for Jobs That Are Completely Unrealistic 22
    Not Working Every Connection 23
    Résumés That Stick Out for the Wrong Reasons 25

Chapter 5
Moving Down Parallel Paths Simultaneously 27

Chapter 6
Enhancing Your Career Credentials 31
   LL.M. and Certificate Programs 32
   State Specialty Certification Programs 34
      For More Information 35

Part II: Research 37

Chapter 7
What Employers Really Want 39
   Likeability 39
   Fit 40
   Intelligence 41
   Being a Quick Study 42
   Organizational Skills 42
   Persuasive Ability 43
   Well-Roundedness 44
   Accountability 44
   Career Progression 45
   Stability 45

Chapter 8
Expanding Your Horizons: Understanding Who Is Out There . .47
   Legal Job Market Demographics 48
   Mainstream Legal Careers 49
      Law Firms 49
      In-House Counsel Offices 51
      Government Law Offices 53
   Careers for Lawyers Outside the Mainstream 56
      Types of Non-mainstream Legal Careers 57
      Why So Many Law-Related Careers Exist 58
      What Makes Lawyers Attractive Candidates for
         Non-mainstream Positions? .59
      The Pluses and Minuses of Moving Out of the
         Mainstream 60

Chapter 9
The "Hidden" Legal Job Market: What It Is and How to Uncover It **63**
Profiling the Hidden Legal Job Market 64
Identifying Hidden Opportunities: Universal Strategies 65
Networking 65
Support Groups 65
Industry and Professional Contacts 66
Trends Analysis 67
Read ALL the Job Ads 68
Identify New Financings 69
Hunt for Profits 69
Examine Promotion and New-Hire Announcements ...69
Business Press Releases 70
Membership Organization Announcements 70
State, Local, and Specialty Bar Association Section and Committee Membership 71
Hidden Job Market Resources 71

Chapter 10
The Hidden Legal Job Market: Private Sector **75**
Law Firms 75
Expanding Existing Practice Areas 75
Rapidly Changing Practice Areas 76
New Practice Area Initiatives 77
"Spin-off" Practice Areas 79
Where the Law Firm Lawyers Are 81
Law Firm Hot Topics 81
Boutique Law Firm Trends 82
Skills Suddenly in Demand 83
Law Firm "Ancillary Businesses" (Subsidiaries) 84
Corporations 85
Hidden Corporate Legal Niches 85
Industry-Specific Corporate Legal Niches 87
New Product Announcements 88
Planned Business Expansions 89
Spin-offs 89
Emerging Companies 90

Chapter 11
The Hidden Legal Job Market: Public Sector **93**
   The Federal Government 93
      How the U.S. Government Hires Attorneys 93
      Unadvertised Government Jobs 94
      Federal Law-Related Jobs 95
      Monitor Major Legislation, Major Regulations, and
         Government Reorganizations 96
      Political Appointments at the Lower Levels 97
      Hidden Jobs in the Legislative Branch 98
      Federal Courts 100
   State and Local Government 100
      Executive Branch 100
      State Legislatures 101
      State Courts 102
      Other State and Local Government Hidden Legal
         Jobs 102
      Predicting the Near-Term Government Future 103
   Government Contracting and Subcontracting 104
      Federal Government 104
      State and Local Governments 105

Chapter 12
The Hidden Legal Job Market: Nonprofits **107**
   Trade and Professional Associations 108
   Academic Institutions 109
      Non-traditional Law School Teaching Positions 110
      Non–Law School Teaching Positions 110
      Identifying Non-traditional Academic Job
         Opportunities 111
      Professional Staff Positions on Campus 112
      The Higher Education Opportunity Act of 2008
         (Pub. L. 110-315) 114
   Healthcare Providers 115
   Public Interest and Advocacy Organizations 115
   Non-governmental Organizations (NGOs) 116
   Foundations and Other Charitable Organizations 117

Chapter 13
The Career Impact of External Phenomena 119
External Influences 119
Interest Rate Fluctuations 120
Energy Costs 120
Industry Reorganizations and Area Changes 121
Legislative or Regulatory "Threats" 121
Other Government Actions 122
Global Politics 123
Technological "Paradigm Shifts" 125
Invention and Innovation 126
Mergers and Acquisitions 127
Resource Shortages 128
Globalization and Legal Process Outsourcing 128
Dollar Depreciation 129
Bursting Bubbles 130
Unfortunate Coincidences 130
Professional Personnel Shortages 130
Interconnections 131

Chapter 14
Thinking a Few Moves Ahead 133
Steering Clear of Leaps of Faith .133
Transitional Strategies 135

Chapter 15
Flying Solo Without Crashing 139
Questions You Need to Ask and Answer 140
What Are My Goals and Objectives? 140
What Are the Components/Characteristics of My
Proposed Practice? 140
Are My Contemplated Practice Areas Growing? 142
Is This Practice Area Subject to Positive or Adverse
External Influences? 142
Where Should I Locate My Practice? 142
Are There Secondary Markets Where My Practice Area
Expertise Could Be Applied? 143
Are There Other Services That I Can Master and
"Cross-Sell" to Clients? 143
What Resources Will I Require? 144

How Should I Allocate My Time? 144
Who (and How Formidable) Is the Competition? 144
What Are My Strengths and Weaknesses, and How
    Can I Compensate? 145
Who or What Are the Primary Markets for This
    Practice? 146
What Is My "Value Proposition?" 146
How Do I Reach the Market? 147
How Can I Strengthen My Client Pitch? 148
How Do I Price My Services? 148
How Long Will It Take to Collect My Fees? 148
What Happens if My Business Fails? 148
Solo Practice Business and Marketing Plan 149
Why You Need a Business and Marketing Plan 149
Elements of a Good Business and Marketing Plan 149

Part III: Documents **153**

Chapter 16
Intelligent Preparation Before You Launch **155**
Time Management 155
Organization 156
Job Search Documents 157
Internal Documents (for your own reference) 157
Transferable Skills List 157
Dissecting Legal Job Ad Form 157
Networking Contacts Form 158
Networking Contacts Record 158
External Documents (for Your Contacts, References, and
    Prospective Employers) 158
Contacts Road Map 158
Résumé 159
Résumé Addendum 160
Representative Matters List 160
Deal Sheet 161
Résumé Substitutes 161
E-mailed Résumés 162
Video Résumés 162
KSA (Knowledge, Skills, and Abilities) Statements 162

Cover Letter (or Transmittal E-mail) 164
Transcript(s) 165
Writing Sample 165
Reference List 166
Letters of Recommendation 166
Annual Reviews and Performance Appraisals 166
Conflicts Check 167
Lining Up References 167
Invoking Your Contacts 167
Record-keeping 168

Chapter 17
Vulnerability Management: Mitigating Your Weaknesses 169
A Red Flag for Employers 170
The Most Common Résumé Weaknesses 170
Employer Reactions to Résumé Weaknesses 171
Antidotes 171
Weakness: Less-Than-Stellar Academic Performance . .171
Weakness: Gaps in Employment 173
Weakness: Current Unemployment 173
Weakness: A History of Job-Hopping 174
Weakness: Checkered Work History/Unremarkable
Career Progression 175
Weakness: Undistinguished Job Titles 175
Weakness: Too Much "Seasoning" 176
Weakness: Lack of a Life Outside of Work 176

Chapter 18
How an Employer Reads a Résumé .177
Private-Sector Employers 177
Government Employers 180

Chapter 19
How to Read and Respond to a Job Ad 183
Dissecting the Job Ad 184
Responding to the Job Ad 185

Chapter 20
**Identifying Your "Hidden" Skill Sets . . . and Matching
Them with Opportunities 189**
The Burnt-Out Litigator 190
The Panicked Real Estate Attorney 192

Chapter 21
Talking the Employer's Talk . . . Not Yours **201**
Translating Gobbledygook 202

Chapter 22
Getting Lost in the Ether . . . and Getting Found **205**

Chapter 23
The Critical Importance of Storytelling **209**
Why a Story? 209
Who Needs to Hear Your Story? 210
What Constitutes a Good Story? 212
The Boffo Gelato Transaction 212
How to Tell Your Story 214

Chapter 24
Identifying Winning Writing Sample(s) **217**
Writing Sample Evaluation Factors 218

Chapter 25
Overcoming "Ageism" **223**
Résumés 224
Opening Gambits 224
Handling Dates 224
Activities 225
Cover Letters and Transmittal E-mails 225
Interviews 226

Chapter 26
Coping with Disability **229**
Tilt the Odds in Your Favor 230
What Do You Say to a Prospective Employer . . . and
When Do You Say It? 231
How Do You Present It? 232
Prepare as You Would for Any Interview 233
Employer Concerns about Hiring and Working with
Disabled Employees 233
Countermeasures 233
Résumés 234

Cover Letters 234
Interviews 234
Accommodations 235
Special Hiring Programs 238
Federal Selective Placement Program for the Hiring of
Individuals with Disabilities .238
Disabled Veterans' Employment Program 239
Executive Order 13518, "Employment of Veterans
in the Federal Government" 240
Ten-Point Veterans' Preference .240
Comparable State Government Disabled Employment
Programs 240
Private-Sector Programs 241

Chapter 27
Legal Job Hunting Out of Town **243**
Economic Concerns 244
Paying for Travel to Interviews .244
Paying Your Relocation Expenses 246
Liability Exposure if the New Job Does Not Work
Out 246
Other Employer Concerns 247
The "Inconvenience" of Conducting an Out-of-Town
Search 247
Candidate Commitment to Relocating 248
Bar Admission Issues 248
Potential Employer Guilt if the New Job Does Not
Work Out 249
Additional Distance Job-Hunting Tips 249
Get the Jump on the Employer .249
Interview Strategies 250
Relocation Expense Strategies 250
Do's and Don'ts 250

Part IV: Contacts **253**

Chapter 28
**Managing Your References and Controlling the
Conversation** **255**
Timing: When to Find References 256
How Many References Do You Need? 258

Selecting Your References 259
    Identify Enthusiasts 261
    Dual-Use References 261
Who to Avoid 262
    Why Not a Letter of Recommendation? 263
The Unselected Reference 263
Initial Contact with Your References 265
    Keeping Your References Informed 266
Reference Lists 266
    When to Provide References 267
Employers That Do Not Provide References 268

Chapter 29
What Headhunters Do . . . and Don't Do **271**
Headhunting Defined 271
    Headhunters Are Not for Everyone 272
    Legal Headhunting Demographics 274
    What Are the Law Firms Actually Paying For? 274
The Legal Search Process 274
    Contingency v. Retained Searches 275
    A Three-Way Relationship 276
The Potential Value of Non-legal Headhunters 276
For More Information 277

Chapter 30
Networking Without Groveling **279**
Why Bother with Networking? 280
When to Communicate with Your Contacts 280
Whom to Contact 281
Building a Network from Scratch 281
What Your Contacts Need to Know About You 284
For Future Reference 285

Part V: Interviewing **287**

Chapter 31
Understanding What You Will Confront **289**
Categorizing Interviews 291
    Who Will Interview You? 291
    What Medium Is Used? 291

How Many Interviews? 292
What Type of Interview? 292
What Is the Employer Thinking During the Interview? . . .295

Chapter 32
What You Need to Accomplish **297**
Why You Are the Best Candidate for the Position 297
Your Energy Level and Enthusiasm 298
Your "Fit" with the Employer's Organization 298
Your Likeability 299
What Will Be the Next Step in the Recruiting
Process? 299
Leave the Interviewer(s) Wanting More 299
Do You Really Want to Work There? 299

Chapter 33
Handling the Tough Questions **301**
The Mother of All Tough Interview Questions 302
Other Tough Questions and Suggested Response Strategies . . 305

Chapter 34
Bridging the Power Chasm **313**
Great Questions to Ask 314

Chapter 35
When to Explain a Termination **319**

Part VI: Closure **323**

Chapter 36
Due Diligence: Scoping Out Your Prospective Employer **325**
Key Due Diligence Items 327
Internet Resources 328
Comparative Compensation Information 330
Questions for the Employer 331
Job Interview Due Diligence Questions 331
Post-Job Offer Due Diligence Questions 333
People You Should Talk To 335
A Word About Practice Area Due Diligence 337

Chapter 37
Negotiating the Employment Agreement **339**
    Employer Requests for Salary Requirements 341
        What Can You Negotiate? 341
    Finding Compensation Information 343
        General Information 343
        Law Firm Positions 343
        Corporations 343
        U.S. Government 343
        State and Local Government Jobs 344
        Colleges and Universities 344
        Trade and Professional Associations 344
        Nonprofits 344
        Other Useful Sources 344
        Strategic Knowledge for Employment Negotiations 344

Chapter 38
Epilogue: Connecting the Dots **347**

Appendix A
"Before" and "After" Résumés **351**

Appendix B
Maximizing Your Contacts **359**

Appendix C
Representative Legal/Law-Related Credential
    Enhancement Programs **361**

Appendix D
Résumé Addendum: Significant Highlights **371**

Appendix E
Selected Legal and Law-Related Networking
    Organizations **374**

Appendix F
Contacts Road Map **379**

Appendix G
Reference List 382

Appendix H
Interview Rating Scale 383

Appendix I
Networking Contacts Record 385

Appendix J
Sample Cover Letter/Transmittal E-mail 387

Index 389

About the Author 403

Acknowledgments

First, my wife, Anne Marie Canali Hermann, who makes it easy for me to pursue my dreams, reads my rough drafts and significantly improves them, keeps my feet to the fire, and corrects my butchering of the language.

Second, the next generation: my son David Hermann, daughter Elizabeth Hermann Smith, and their respective spouses, Jessica Bedoya Hermann and West Smith, for being so supportive of my writing.

Third, the many attorneys who have been my clients and who taught me so much about how—and how not—to manage a legal career.

Finally, my editor at ABA Publishing, Erin Nevius, whose enthusiasm for this project was infectious and whose insights and editing skills greatly improved the final product.

Introduction

Managing Your Legal Career: Best Practices for Success in the Law is the product of 30 years of counseling thousands of attorneys in career transition, ranging from matriculating law students to recent graduates to managing partners of major law firms who are looking for a change, all the way through chief legal officers of *Fortune* 500 corporations and government general counsels. In short, I have advised attorneys at all levels in every employment sector across many different industries. My clients have largely been attorneys practicing in this country, but have also included American lawyers working abroad (in every continent except Antarctica) and foreign attorneys seeking to work in the United States.

The legal career consulting universe too often imparts pedestrian, unimaginative, and unhelpful advice to attorneys in transition. It does not have to be this way. Over the course of my career, advising and assisting attorneys in career crisis, I developed and implemented an array of effective career transition and job-hunting techniques that I would like to make available to a wider audience. The result is this book, a distillation of what I learned and imparted to my clients. It encapsulates my own unique job-hunting strategies and tactics that have proven successful many times over.

Part I

Preparation

Chapter 1
How Job Seekers Really Find Their Jobs 3

Chapter 2
Knowing Who You Are . . . and What You Want 7

Chapter 3
Conquering Your Own Attitudinal Barriers 13

Chapter 4
Avoiding Self-Destruction 21

Chapter 5
Moving Down Parallel Paths Simultaneously 27

Chapter 6
Enhancing Your Career Credentials 31

Chapter 1

How Job Seekers *Really* Find Their Jobs

> Understanding how job seekers actually find their new jobs is critical base knowledge for anyone embarking on a job search or career transition. There is a great deal of misinformation about this topic, including "urban legends" and erroneous assumptions disseminated by career counselors who heard something that sounded good elsewhere and decided to pass it on.
>
> This chapter looks at both the empirical evidence and the experiences of the author's own legal career transition clients in an attempt to set the record straight.

Let's begin by debunking one of the hardest-to-budge myths about job hunting. The standard mantra you read in career books and hear from career management professionals is something like this:

> Ninety percent of job seekers get their jobs through networking.

Whenever I ask any of the purported "experts" where they came up with that figure, they draw a blank and quickly change the subject.

3

…vas an extensive study of how people find their … dated (read: pre-Internet) one (Mark Granovetter, …ge Their Jobs," Ph.D. thesis, Department of So-…rvard University, 1970, and Mark Granovetter, …Weak Ties," 78 *American Journal of Sociology* 1360–80 (1973)). The study roamed across all occupations, not just law. Here are the results:

- 56 percent of the survey respondents found their jobs through a personal connection, i.e., networking. Of this group:
  - 17 percent (9 percent of the total universe of job-seekers) found their job through a *close personal connection*;
  - 55 percent found their jobs through an *occasional connection* (31 percent of the total universe of job-seekers); and
  - 28 percent (16 percent of the total universe of job-seekers) found their jobs through *someone they did not know at all* when they began their job search, that is, a contact of a contact;
- 39 percent found their jobs through a published job ad; and
- 5 percent found their jobs through a headhunter (an executive search firm).

As you can see, networking was nowhere near the 90 percent solution but was still higher on the charts than any other job-finding mode. While this study still has some credibility because it was based on scientific polling, there have been a few unscientific surveys conducted by various organizations in the post-Internet era that are also revealing. Weddle's (*www.weddles.com*) most recent (unscientific) Annual Source of Employment Survey (March 2008) of more than 15,000 respondents found that networking was cited by only 10.6 percent of respondents (with only a marginal increase if you add in social media networks), less than the number (13.3 percent) who cited ads posted on Internet job boards, which was the number-one job-finding method.

There is no reason to believe that attorneys go about their job hunting any differently than the general professional population.

In addition to debunking the myth that 90 percent of job seekers find their jobs through networking, there are a number of additional lessons to be learned from these surveys:

1. Networking is important, but it is not all-important. It is still a good idea to comb through job ads and published vacancy announcements on the Internet and in newspapers and trade publications.
2. People do not necessarily get jobs through their friends ("a close personal connection"), but rather through their casual acquaintances as well as strangers. Why is that? Because weak ties are far more important to your job-hunting success than strong ties. The reason? Your friends occupy the same world you do. If you want to expand your possibilities, you have to do some probing beyond your own little world.

Two of my legal career counseling clients who got their jobs through networking bear this out. One of them was a man who, while unemployed and at home, became quite friendly with his postal carrier. One day his mailman asked him for permission to give his résumé to someone on his route who he thought might have an interest in it. My client was subsequently invited to interview for a position and wound up working directly for his postal carrier's other customer.

A second client gave her résumé to her beautician, thinking that her beautician ran across all sorts of individuals who were either prospective employers or individuals who might serve as potential intermediaries with prospective employers. The beautician asked my client a few questions to supplement her résumé and passed it on to one of her other clients, whose company then called my client in for an interview.

Casual acquaintances, you see, usually occupy very different worlds from your own. That makes them invaluable networking contacts.

Understanding how people find their jobs should serve as a guide to what you need to do for yourself when it comes to job hunting or career changing. The percentage breakdowns at the beginning of this chapter are indicators of where your efforts should be directed—at networking, both within and outside of your "circle"; at responding to job ads and vacancy announcements; and, if you have the requisite credentials, also using legal search (headhunting), which is discussed in more detail in Chapter 29, "What Headhunters Do . . . and Don't Do."

Chapter 2

Knowing Who You Are...
and What You Want

"Know thyself."

This exhortation, first uttered by the Oracle of Delphi around 1000 B.C., is one of the few pieces of Delphic advice that was not intentionally vague, hopelessly ambiguous, or capable of being interpreted to support any action ... or inaction.

Understanding who you are sounds easy, but in actuality is no walk in the park. Most of us spend the better part of our lives trying to figure ourselves out. Most of us never do.

However, that does not mean that you should forget about doing it. Going through the exercise is worth the effort, even if the outcome remains vague and somewhat unformed. The more you learn about yourself, the better you will be able to make good legal career decisions.

Making good career decisions has never been more important. Today's attorney is highly likely to have multiple jobs during his or her career. The era of graduating from law school, going to work

7

for a law firm, and retiring with a gold watch 40 years later is long gone. Moreover, only about one in 10 attorneys who begin their careers in a law firm wind up making partner in that firm.

Twenty years ago, the typical experienced attorney résumé that came across my desk described only one or two positions. A résumé that contained work experience at three or more employers was a rarity. Not any more. The situation has done a complete turnaround.

So adhering to the only sound advice ever to emanate from Delphi is extremely important.

What follows are 31 questions designed to help you know yourself and to organize your thoughts about what you want out of the legal job search and career transition process. Whatever you do, answer them honestly. This is more difficult than it sounds; we all tend to perceive ourselves as we would like to appear to others instead of confronting the unvarnished truth.

1. Who am I?
   - What is most important in life to me? Money? Family? Recognition? Time off from work? Love? Friends? Etc.?
   - What are my "essentials," the life aspects I will not do without?
2. Where have I been in my career?
   - legal positions
   - other positions
   - internships
   - summer jobs
3. Where am I now in my career progression?
   - Exactly where I want to be at this stage.
   - Not where I want to be.
   - Further along than where I thought I would be.
4. Where do I want to go from here?
   - my career goals
   - my financial goals
   - my work/life balance goals
5. What are my personal values?
   - ethics
   - lifestyle considerations

6. What are my workplace values?
7. What do I really want to do?
   - "mainstream" law
   - law-related work
   - something else
8. Do I want to work 9 to 5?
9. Am I a workplace loner, or do I crave interaction with colleagues, clients, etc.?
10. Am I more verbal than cerebral?
11. Why do I want a new job/career?
    - dissatisfaction with my duties and responsibilities
    - dissatisfaction with my employer
    - dissatisfaction with my supervisor(s)
    - dissatisfaction with my co-workers
    - lack of promotion opportunities
    - seeking a challenge
    - aligning with my background
    - aligning with my interests
12. Am I more comfortable if I have a lot of rules to follow?
13. Am I entrepreneurial/intrapreneurial?
14. For whom do I want to work?
    - private sector
      - law firm
        - large, midsize, or small
        - general or boutique
        - my own solo practice
      - for-profit corporation
        - *Fortune* 500, smaller, or startup
        - publicly traded or closely held
        - type of industry
        - domestic vs. multinational
      - consulting firm
        - general management consulting firm
        - legal/law-related specialized consulting firm
    - nonprofit sector
      - college/university
      - hospital
      - museum

- foundation
- public interest/advocacy organization
- trade or professional association
- labor union
- other
- public sector
  - federal, state, or local government
  - special district—e.g., Port Authority of New York & New Jersey, Washington Suburban Sanitary Commission, East Bay Municipal Utilities District
  - hybrid (public-private)—e.g., government-sponsored enterprise such as Fannie Mae,* Freddie Mac;* self-regulatory organizations, such as Financial Industry Regulatory Authority, stock exchange, and Public Company Accounting Oversight Board
  - international organization/multilateral development organizations, e.g., United Nations, World Bank, Pan American Health Organization, World Trade Organization

15. What kind of "trends analyses" do I have to do?
    - industry
    - type of employer
    - type of position
    - practice area
    - other

16. What circumstances beyond my control do I need to be concerned about?
    - economic uncertainties, e.g., interest rate fluctuations, energy prices, takeover risks
    - legislative/regulatory uncertainties
    - globalization, e.g., foreign competition, outsourcing potential
    - technology impact, e.g., product obsolescence, productivity threats

---

*As this book goes to press, the final status of Fannie and Freddie is uncertain.

17. Where (geographically) do I want to work?
    * preferred cities and countries, if applicable
    * places I want to avoid, period
    * my geographic mobility
18. What is my target date for securing new employment?
19. When do I need to begin my career transition planning?
    * immediately
    * after _____ (specific event)
20. What must I accomplish in order to get where I want to go?
21. Whom do I need to talk to?
    * friends
    * acquaintances
    * professionals in the field
    * trade/professional associations
    * alumni of certain organizations
    * career counselor(s)
    * colleagues
22. What information do I need to provide to these contacts?
    * documents
    * oral statements/"elevator speech"
23. Who are my contacts' possible contacts?
24. Who will be my professional references?
25. What do I need to provide to my references?
26. When do I need to initiate contact with my references?
27. What supplies/resources will I need for an effective career transition?
28. Am I executive search/"headhunter" material?
29. If yes, which headhunters should I approach?
    * legal
    * industry
    * type of employer
30. Should I pursue additional credentials?
    * LLM
    * certificate(s)
    * state specialty certification
    * a "transitional" position
31. If yes, what credentials make sense?

If you are able to answer most of these questions with sufficient detail, you should develop a clearer sense of (1) who you are, professionally and otherwise; (2) where you want to go with your career; and (3) what you need to do to get there. In essence, you will have created a personal business and marketing plan that you can apply to your career transition.

Chapter 3

Conquering Your Own Attitudinal Barriers

Attitudinal barriers are the intangible characteristics that can neutralize all of the positive objective traits, skills, abilities, and knowledge that you may bring to a prospective employer, as well as to all of the intermediaries along the way who might be in a position to help you. Fortunately, overcoming or at least sublimating these barriers is not nearly as difficult as covering up a serious objective, substantive deficiency. Dealing with these barriers is central to any successful employment search.

Making a positive impression on an employer is a prerequisite to receiving a job offer. If your attitudinal barriers get in the way, your opportunity to do that fades.

Lack of Self-Esteem

My legal-job-seeking clients, almost without exception, came into my office for our initial consultation looking as if they were carrying the weight of the world on their shoulders: unsmiling, less-than-vigorous handshakes, often shuffling their feet, and with a stooped posture. Many could not—or would not—make eye contact with me.

For job-seeking purposes, you can equate lack of self-esteem with lack of confidence. If you do not have it, it will be immediately apparent to everyone involved—prospective employers, networking contacts, references, support groups, etc. It will not only affect the way you present yourself to people, but may also seep into the key verbal and electronic communications you direct to them—telephone interviews, phone calls with references and contacts, résumés, cover letters, e-mails, etc. Lack of self-esteem can often be discerned in application documents and attendant communications. Résumés and other introductory documents seem unimaginative, unresponsive to the position being offered, and sometimes sloppily or carelessly constructed. Similarly, e-mails and cover letters can often appear lackluster and come across as a chore.

Your *affect* will affect key individuals' reaction to your "pitch" and, with respect to references and contacts, their effectiveness on your behalf. The reason is that self-esteem and self-confidence are infectious. People naturally gravitate to other people who manifest these traits (provided they are not "over the top"). They want to be part of their universe and want to help them. Conversely, they tend to shy away from individuals who lack self-esteem and self-confidence, and to be less than enthusiastic about helping them or even having them around.

The solution is, first, to remember who you are. You would not have made it through the competition at the many levels you have so far successfully traversed—college, law school, your jobs, extracurricular achievements—without being pretty exceptional. A large number of your contemporaries fell by the wayside along the way, while you kept going and achieved something.

Second, examine rationally why you are in this position. If you have been laid off from your prior employment, the reason probably has less to do with you than with the tenuous financial position of your previous employer, or of the legal or general economy.

Third, remember that you are not alone. You have plenty of company—attorneys and millions of others similarly situated who also are victims of the national, local, or organizational economy. In fact, in any economy there are always going to be winners and losers. A cursory glance at the companies that make up the Dow Jones Industrial Average (DJIA) today versus 20 years ago will show you that. The bluest of blue-chip companies constitutes this index of 30 stocks, and 17 of the companies—57 percent—that were part of the DJIA in 1990 are not there now.

Fourth, visualize incidents and moments in your life when you felt really good about yourself. If you experienced them once, you can certainly do so again.

If none of these suggestions work to pull you out of your funk, then fake it during your job search. You do not have to be "on" 24/7, only when you are crafting your application documents or communicating and meeting with your references, contacts, and employers. The rest of the time, you can gripe, droop, and shuffle to your heart's content.

Wallowing in Self-Pity

Let's stipulate that there are a lot of good reasons for attorneys to feel sorry for themselves: Being an attorney means representing clients who bring a lot of emotion along with their legal matters, being constantly put in adversarial situations, having to be alert and on your toes almost all of the time, demanding work hours, high stress levels, etc. The danger is that if you let self-pity overwhelm you, it will get in the way of strategic and tactical career thinking and planning and positive behavior. Like lack of self-esteem or self-confidence, self-pity comes across immediately and negatively to the people you will have to interact with in order to advance.

One of the biggest mistakes job interviewees make is to share their "woe is me" attitude with potential legal employers. They are not interested. They are not there to soothe your feelings or act as your sounding board for life's unfairness. The only things they are interested in are whether you can perform the job and whether you are the kind of individual that they want to have around.

No one responds positively to a whiner. Don't expect anyone to empathize or sympathize with you. People have their own problems, and most believe that they have overcome them or found other coping mechanisms.

What is true for employers is also true for networking contacts and references.

If "nobody knows the troubles you've seen," good. In the hiring realm, nobody need know. Nobody wants to know. Keep them to yourself.

Bitterness and Negativity

I once interviewed someone I thought was a very capable attorney for a position in my office. By the end of the interview, I was sufficiently impressed that I was prepared to offer her the position on the spot. Then she said, "By the way, I may need some time off for depositions because I am suing my current employer. He is a real bastard and is cheating me out of a promised raise." She proceeded to launch into a tirade against both her current employer and employers in general. I tried to maintain a poker face while listening to this diatribe and yearning to hustle her out of my office.

You never want to express any bitterness or negativity about current or past employers when interviewing for a position. You may believe that the injustices done to you by bosses will gain the interviewer's empathy, but you will be dead wrong (emphasis on "dead" with respect to the immediate job opportunity).

Employers identify with other employers, not with job candidates. What you will have accomplished by your outburst will be to prompt the interviewer to believe that you might be a danger to his or her organization at worst, or a disruptive and discomfiting individual to have around the office at best. Either reaction will result in rejection.

Lack of Interest and Enthusiasm

The universe of rejected candidates is littered with job seekers whose presentations were marked by a lack of interest or enthusiasm. This is easy to spot at an interview, though a bit more difficult to discern in résumés, cover letters, e-mails, and other application documents. That is a vital reason why you have to take great care and spend a good deal of time on your résumé and cover letters, and invest considerable "sweat equity" in crafting the best possible set of documents to properly manifest your interest in the position and your eagerness to get going. Both the structure and content of your documents contribute to sending the right message (see Appendix A, Before and After Résumés).

Similarly, when you are being interviewed, a lack of enthusiasm for work or for the specific position will be painfully obvious to an employer and just as off-putting as the other attitudinal barriers discussed in this chapter. Every employer believes that his or her position is the cat's meow and that you should be salivating at the thought of working for his or her august organization. One of the worst ways to show a lack of interest or enthusiasm is by not asking any questions of the interviewer. I always concluded that a job candidate with my company who responded to my query "Do you have any questions?" with "No, I think you have answered any questions I might have had" was not very interested in working for me. Consequently, incurious candidates did not receive a job offer.

Perhaps the most important reason for waxing enthusiastic is this: Enthusiasm is infectious. Virtually everyone responds positively to it: employers, contacts, references, others. I once managed a large outplacement of more than 100 attorneys who were being terminated by one employer. Three of them competed for a single position with the general counsel's office of a high-profile company. Two of the three had stellar academic and employment backgrounds; one did not. However, she had incredible enthusiasm, which translated into a vibrant, sunny personality. You could not help but like her and enjoy her company. She got the job.

Lack of Energy

It takes considerable energy to be an effective lawyer. The hours are typically longer than for most of the American work force, and the demands are high and unforgiving. Consequently, vigor is a highly valued trait among legal employers.

You need to demonstrate energy during a job interview. You do this not only by the way you behave—alert, stimulated, interested—but also by the words and expressions you utilize.

A judicial acquaintance of mine used to pose the following question to prospective clerks: "If it was the day before Thanksgiving and I were to request that you stay after work until you revised a draft opinion for me, what would you say, knowing that you might miss Thanksgiving dinner?" Candidates who exhibited surprise at the question or even just hesitated a bit too long before responding were out of luck. The judge told me that the best response he ever received was "Your Honor, whatever it takes!" He offered the position to this candidate on the spot.

Hubris

Hubris, arrogance, or overconfidence have no place in your job search or career considerations, much less your life.

I once interviewed an attorney for a position in my office who came in with all of the proper paper credentials. My initial impression of him was positive. He was well-dressed and well-groomed, looked me in the eye, smiled, appeared confident, and shook hands vigorously.

I motioned him to a seat on the opposite side of my conference table, which is when it all came tumbling down. As I began with some ice-breaking small talk, he removed his watch from his wrist and placed it on the table in front of him so that he could see the watch face. I was so stunned that I completely lost my train of thought. All I could conclude was that he did not believe that the interview or the job with my company was very important to such a busy man.

I felt the same: I did not want to waste my time. I sprinted through the interview formalities and moved him out as quickly as possible.

Another way that hubris manifests itself is when a candidate tells the interviewer how to improve his or her organization. This happens enough that it merits mention as an interview taboo. The interviewer's likely reaction, upon hearing from an untrained, uninformed novice about how to improve performance, is going to be, "Goodbye and good luck."

Disrespect

Admittedly, it is difficult to go from what you perceive as the top of the food chain—say, working for a major national law firm—to competing for a position that you feel is significantly lower in the legal pecking order, such as working for the government. It is equally tough to find yourself being judged, via your paper credentials and at an interview, by individuals who you feel are far less accomplished than you—graduates of lower-tier law schools, people who did not serve on a law review, etc.

The worst thing you can do during the job-hunting process is to show your lack of respect for the people who may hold your fate in their hands. It is imperative that you treat all human beings with respect and appropriate deference to their positions. Curb your desire to demonstrate how superior you are. Save that for cocktail parties and other one-upmanship milieus.

> Any one of these barriers can mean the difference between getting the job of your dreams and getting shut out. If you cannot rid yourself of them permanently, at least temporarily suspend your attitudinal barriers during your job search or career change.
>
> In short, get over yourself.

Chapter 4

Avoiding Self-Destruction

There are almost as many ways to self-destruct during a job search as there are job seekers. While I cannot honestly say that I have encountered them all, I have been exposed to enough of them to be able to draw a number of conclusions about which ones occur most frequently and which ones wind up in employer pantheons of classic job-hunting mistakes.

Applying for Only One Job at a Time

The more rapidly the terminated attorneys sent to us by our law firm, corporate, government, or nonprofit clients became reemployed, the more profit my outplacement company made. The longer they were out of work, the less profit we made. If these attorneys stayed unemployed for many months, we took a bath.

A major trade association sent us a lawyer who smashed the all-time record for remaining jobless and who, consequently, cost us a lot of money. He insisted that he could only focus on applying for one position at a time, then wait for the outcome before moving on to the next job opportunity. In his first 12 months with us, he applied for only three jobs as we sat helplessly watching his "slowsky" strategy. No matter what we said, he would not change his mode of operation.

It took him 18 months to find a new position. During that period, his severance payments from his prior employer ran out, his marriage almost collapsed, and he was disowned by his father. One other pertinent point: his job search took place during an economic boom.

Attorneys compete in a hugely competitive universe. Plodding leisurely down the path to reemployment is self-destructive in the extreme. You need to double and redouble your efforts, pursuing every realistic opportunity that comes your way. You need to provide serendipity with enough ammunition to strike you.

Applying with Tunnel Vision

If you find yourself in a situation where you have done only one type of legal work during your career, that does not mean that that particular practice niche is all you can do. Nor does it mean that you will be perceived by prospective employers as a candidate for only those types of positions.

To maximize the effectiveness of your job search, you need to expand your horizons and consider what else you could do with your particular background and skills in addition to what seems obvious. See Chapter 20, "Identifying Your Hidden Skill Sets . . . and Matching Them with Opportunities," for examples of how two attorneys could realistically flesh out their latent talents and abilities and look for opportunities in more than one practice area. Attorneys are among the most fungible of professionals. The expertise and skills they develop are marketable across a wide range of disciplines.

Applying for Jobs That Are Completely Unrealistic

This is not the same as applying for jobs for which you are not qualified per the job requirements cited in the employment ad. You may be highly qualified for a position, for example, that requires three years of experience although you have only two years of experience. A job that is completely unrealistic, in contrast, is one where you know that you lack the knowledge or background to do the job competently, and that it is unlikely that you can acquire it quickly enough to become secure in the position.

One of my outplacement candidates was a senior partner in a large law firm who lost her job when her "rabbi" in the firm, who was also the managing partner, retired and was replaced by a new managing partner. Suddenly, she was "exposed." She had risen in the firm's ranks largely through her friendship with the former managing partner, who took her under his wing because she was the daughter of one of his best friends. The problem was that she had never been given any real responsibility for her own cases and, thus, had not learned very much about lawyering. She had never litigated, taken or defended a deposition, been involved in negotiating or even documenting a transaction, drafted a brief, or done much legal research. To be perfectly blunt, she had developed neither much legal knowledge nor many legal skills.

Nevertheless, she insisted that she had to apply only for positions "at a comparable level," despite the painful fact that she could not possibly perform up to the demands of any of these positions. I was put in the delicate position of having to explain her deficiencies to her and redirect her efforts down several levels to where she might have an opportunity to succeed. I was able to do this only after over a year of rejections that left her feeling very frustrated and defeated.

Going into a job search, you should know your strengths but also your weaknesses. You will have more luck finding a job quickly if you apply only for those jobs you know you can do, and do well.

Not Working Every Connection

One of my law firm clients sent me a terminated associate who had been with the firm for just over one year, long enough for the firm managers to realize that he could not perform up to expectations and likely never would. His résumé was a disorganized disaster, his personality gave new meaning to the term "bland," his appearance was unprepossessing, his writing sample was in a language that only remotely resembled English, and he was not exactly articulate. Following my initial meeting with him, I was resigned to having him as a client until my own retirement. I saw no hope that anyone would hire him, or that I could transform him sufficiently to give him a decent shot at a legal job.

Two months later, he was hired as a third-year associate by the headquarters office of a huge national law firm in another city. How did he do it?

During one of our early conversations, I suggested that we sit together and make a list of every possible contact he had ever encountered who might be positioned to assist him. I fed him prompts such as "family," "family friends," "personal friends," "friends of friends," "professors," "classmates," "fellow alumni of his schools," etc. (see Appendix B, Maximizing Your Contacts). We prepared a hierarchical list of people he felt were his best contacts.

When we hit "roommates," his eyes lit up (the first and only time he ever emoted):

Candidate: One of my law school roommates from my first year is a possibility.
Me: Tell me about him.
Candidate: We got along pretty well. We used to go out for pizza and beer together all the time.
Me: That's it?
Candidate: No. He once told me that if I ever needed a favor, I should turn to him.
Me: That's a strange statement. What could he possibly do for you?
Candidate: Well, he works for a big law firm in the town where I grew up. I'm thinking of returning there.
Me: Would he put his job on the line, his legal reputation with the firm, to advocate for them hiring you?
Candidate: Don't know. But that not's important.
Me: Why not? Isn't that the favor?
Candidate: Not exactly. I wouldn't necessarily have to work at his firm.
Me: I don't quite get it.
Candidate: Well, his grandfather is the reputed head of a "family" out there, if you get my drift.
Me: Oh. I think I see where you're going with this.

The candidate got in touch with his former roommate and shared his employment aspiration with him. A week later, he flew out for three interviews with major firms. He received a job offer from all of them. I did not follow up with him after he began working, but I suspect that his lawyer deficiencies did not lose him his new job.

This candidate worked his connections as well as anyone possibly could. He maximized his possible networking contacts by viewing them not only for what they themselves could do for him directly, but also for the contacts they might have to whom they could refer him. While you may not have quite the same caliber of potential contacts, you may be quite surprised at your contacts' contact list.

Résumés That Stick Out for the Wrong Reasons

The essential principle to keep in mind should you wish to differentiate your résumé from the competition is that legal employers, regardless of political stripe, are all very conservative when it comes to assessing job applicants. It is not too extreme a statement to say that they are somewhere to the right of Ethelred the Unready. This is as true of the American Civil Liberties Union as it is of the National Rifle Association.

Here are the résumé "stick-out" factors that legal employers have told me are the ones that irritate them the most:

- *Résumés that spared no expense.* An expensively printed legal résumé is unnecessary. Employers focus on content and, to a lesser extent, structure and format. Don't waste your hard-earned money on ornamentation.
- *Bound résumés with cover sheets.* This is another total waste of money. Moreover, having to deal with bindings and additional pages will only irritate an employer, something you definitely do not want to be your first impression.
- *Résumés on paper other than white or off-white (such as cream or ivory).* Remember, legal employers are conservatives. Eschew colors.
- *Résumés with unusual typefaces.* Stick to Times Roman, Arial, Verdana, or another mainstream typeface. Fancy typefaces are just a distraction.
- *Résumés on unusually sized paper.* There is no advantage to submitting a résumé on paper that's a size other than the standard 8½" x 11".

- *Résumés that make it difficult to find key information.* Employers will not take the time to dig for the hidden gems in your résumé. It should be easy to find the key information about you.
- *Résumés that are "self-serving."* Employers tend to discount subjective statements about your capabilities. They want to see objective, verifiable information about you.
- *Résumés that stretch the truth.* Legal employers today are very sensitive to applicants who exaggerate or outright lie on their résumés. Résumé-checking companies are thriving, and legal employers are more skeptical than ever with respect to what they read in résumés.

There are countless ways to conduct a poor, unproductive job search, ranging far beyond the most frequent ones that I have observed in my legal career counseling practice and described in this chapter. All of them can be avoided by the injection of common sense into your job-hunting campaign. One of the best ways of "bootstrapping" yourself into exercising good common sense is to pose the question, What would I want to see if I were the employer?

Chapter 5

Moving Down Parallel Paths Simultaneously

> For virtually all attorneys, there is more than one possible career path to pursue. Paths may include employment sectors—private practice, corporate in-house, government; diverse industries; multiple practice areas; mainstream law and law-related jobs; and so on. The important thing is to know what options your particular skill set gives you, and how to explore each of these options.

Very few people can do only one thing at a time. Among attorneys this limitation is even rarer, thanks to the depth and breadth of both legal training and the rigorous, multifarious demands of law practice. Lawyers almost always have to become expert in a variety of substantive practice areas overlain by a complex matrix of procedural and evidentiary laws and rules, as well as formal and informal legal and administrative rules and regulations, systems, and procedures. Moreover, they are almost never able to focus exclusively on just one matter for any length of time. They must juggle numerous matters and consider multiple issues daily. Lawyers, consequently, become highly adept at what, in popular parlance, is called "multitasking."

This ability lends itself very well to job hunting and career changing. The wide variety of opportunities generally available to attorneys, often in practice areas and employment sectors that are different from those in which they are currently working, as well as the ability to pursue multiple opportunities and career paths simultaneously, call for a certain amount of dexterity.

The following example (the fact situation was provided by a legal career counseling colleague; the recommended career paths derive from my analysis of the case) is included to demonstrate the central importance of going down parallel paths simultaneously.

Sam Searcher graduated from one of the country's top law schools in the late 1980s with a J.D. and mediocre grades. One of Sam's assets was that his father was a well-known Washington-area lawyer—and for Sam this has been both a plus and a minus. Sam was not able to find a job upon graduation from law school and, after many false starts, decided to return to obtain an LL.M. in tax at another law school. Eventually, LL.M. degree in hand, he found a job with a small general practice firm that had a business practice. However, after a few years with that firm, Sam was told by his boss that it was time for him to move on.

Sam was quite discouraged and decided to leave the practice of law entirely. Again, he went back to school—this time for a master's in civil engineering. Then, armed with his engineering degree, he secured a position with one of the Washington, D.C., area's largest construction companies. He was doing well, but was anxious to find a way to combine his engineering and construction background with law.

I strongly recommended that Sam pursue all of the following possibilities concurrently:

- *Joining the American College of Construction Lawyers (ACCL)* (*www.accl.org*), if he was not already a member. The ACCL provides year-round networking opportunities. See Chapter 30, "Networking Without Groveling," for a discussion of the utility of this kind of networking.
- *Contacting non-legal headhunters,* namely those that operate solely within the construction industry and those whose practice includes the construction industry. However, even

if Sam elicited headhunter interest, he should not put all of his eggs in this basket. See Chapter 29, "What Headhunters Do . . . and Don't Do," for a discussion of non-legal headhunters.

- *Private practice.* While Sam did not have any portable business, he had more to offer a law firm now with his distinctive background and combination of disciplines. However, it would probably be in an "of-counsel" capacity.

  - *Boutique law firms.* Construction law boutique firms would be his best bet because they are not as tethered to traditional hiring modes and preconceived notions about potential employee backgrounds as large law firms. I identified eight construction law boutique firms in Sam's geographic area.

  - *Major firms with a construction law practice.* Although boutique firms were his best bet, large law firms with a construction law practice were also possible employers. Fifteen firms in his area had such practices.

- *Construction industry in-house counsel positions.* There were only a handful of construction companies in Sam's area large enough to have an in-house counsel office, but they were worth an effort.

- *U.S. government construction law practices with a civil engineering legal focus,* which included the general counsel offices at the Nuclear Regulatory Commission (NRC), Federal Energy Regulatory Commission (FERC), Defense Nuclear Facilities Safety Board, Department of Defense, Air Force, Army, Federal Bureau of Prisons, Appalachian Regional Commission, Architect of the Capitol, and National Capitol Planning Commission; the chief counsel offices at the Atomic Safety & Licensing Board Panel; the U.S. Army Corps of Engineers; the general counsel to the NRC Inspector General's office; the Justice Department's Civil Division; the FERC Office of Energy Projects; the Transportation Department's Federal Lands Legal Team; the General Services Administration's Real Property Division; and the Smithsonian Institution's Business Contracting Division, among others.

- *Alternative dispute resolution (ADR) providers to the construction industry.* ADR began in the construction industry and has thrived there for more than half a century. In addition to his construction and legal background, here was where Sam's tax background could also bolster his opportunities, because it meant that he had a facility with numbers and number interpretation and probably had exposure to tax accounting. Disputed issues often center on liability for delays and damages resulting therefrom (calculating costs and damages).
- *Consulting firms with construction lawyers on staff,* of which there were a handful of firms in the area dealing primarily with environmental permitting and water projects.
- *Trade associations with both a general counsel office and a construction law practice,* such as the National Association of Home Builders.
- *University risk management positions.* Issues handled in that position often involve campus construction.

When searching for new career opportunities, it's important to think through all the potential employers, however obscure. There are many hidden opportunities that can be uncovered if you think outside of the large-law-firm box. For more ideas on unearthing as many potential employers as possible, see Chapter 8, "Expanding Your Horizons: Understanding Who Is Out There."

> Sam is not unique. As I emphasized above, law is probably the most fungible profession. Lawyers must tackle many areas of human endeavor, and that positions them very well for a variety of jobs and careers where their legal education and background are valued. If Sam had pursued only one avenue at a time and exhausted it before moving on, he would have done himself a great disservice.

Chapter 6

Enhancing Your Career Credentials

I am often asked whether it makes sense to go back to law school for an LL.M. degree. My standard response is, "It depends." I then relate the sad tale of one of my legal career transition counseling clients. He spent over $50,000 to obtain an LL.M. in environmental law from a top-tier law school. When he graduated with the degree and began searching for an environmental position, he was asked by several employers:

Why did you go to that law school for your LL.M.? Didn't you realize that it's not a top school for environmental LL.M.?

My client was devastated to realize that the credential for which he spent so much money and invested so much time and effort was not much of a career builder. Had he done his "due diligence" research before matriculating and shelling out a fortune, he would have been a lot better off.

This chapter tackles this issue and how to make good decisions about further education.

31

LL.M. and Certificate Programs

Carefully consider the advice below *before* embarking on an LL.M. or any other educational program in the hopes of boosting your legal career:

- **An LL.M. can be a valuable addition to your credentials portfolio**, but you have to go into the academic program with your eyes wide open in order to maximize the utility of the degree. A bit of economic cost/benefit analysis and opportunity cost consideration is also a good idea. The benefits of and the opportunity afforded by earning an LL.M. degree had better be pretty fantastic if they are to outweigh the costs, given that the costs of most of the better degree programs are stratospheric. For example, Georgetown tuition for an LL.M. in 2009 was $43,750 per academic year. Throw in fees, books, and living expenses and you are looking at a total cost bordering on $60,000 per academic year. Other top schools cost even more. Even the least expensive programs are not cheap.
- **Examine certificate and comparable programs in addition to LL.M. and other degree programs.** Certificate programs offer an opportunity to obtain a credential—often a very strong credential—with far less investment of your time and money than an LL.M. Law schools in the United States currently offer more than 30 certificate programs in more than 25 topical areas that are open to non-degree candidates. Several of these programs are offered online.

In addition, many non–law school academic institutions, as well as other organizations such as trade and professional associations, also offer legal and law-related certificate programs, both on site and online. There are at least 400 such programs in approximately 60 practice areas that might be suitable for you, depending on your interests and career aspirations (see Appendix C, Representative Legal and Law-Related Credential Enhancement Programs). However, certificate programs warrant the same pre-enrollment scrutiny that you should undertake before enrolling in an LL.M. program.

- **Expand your survey of educational programs to include *law-related* ones.** Depending on your background and interests, and the state of the employment market, you may be better off in terms of enhancing your employability if you obtain a *law-related* graduate degree or a *law-related* professional certificate rather than an LL.M. There are, for example, superb law-related programs in fields such as contracting, international transactions, risk management, alternative dispute resolution, compliance, real estate, and insurance, to name just a few (see Appendix C).
- **Talk to individuals who have already earned the credential.** Get their opinions as to whether the credential made a difference in their careers, employability, promotion potential, and compensation. Ask them:
  - How difficult was it to find suitable employment after completing the program?
  - How much help—and what kind of help—did you receive with respect to finding employment from the granting institution's career and/or program office?
  - If you had it to do over again, would you still pursue the credential?
- **Talk to employers of individuals who have recently earned the credential.** Ask them:
  - Do you value the fact that your employee has the credential?
  - How does the credential benefit your organization?
  - Do you believe the credential is truly a career booster?
  - What is your opinion of the credential-granting organization?
- **Talk to current students.** Ask them:
  - Is the program worth the time, effort, money, and career interruption?
  - What do you intend to do with the degree or certificate?
  - How much, and what is the nature of, the career assistance you are receiving from the granting institution?
- **Talk to the career placement professionals and program directors at the sponsoring school or organization.** Ask them:

- Where can I expect to work once I successfully complete the program?
- What is the institution's track record when it comes to placing program graduates?
- Where do recent graduates work, and what career paths will be open to me?
- Please provide the specifics of what you can do for me during and after I complete the program.
- *The most important point of all:* If they stonewall you by saying they do not maintain such information or statistics, assert privacy or confidentiality reasons for not sharing this information, or become defensive, or if their answers are vague or otherwise unsatisfactory, say thank you, pocket your check or loan application, and walk away from the program.

State Specialty Certification Programs

Certification as a legal specialist in a particular practice area is a fairly recent development that is becoming increasingly important and interesting to practitioners. The American Bar Association (ABA) Standing Committee on Specialization establishes standards for the accreditation of certification programs. States that also accredit or otherwise approve programs for their bar members do not have to accept the ABA standards in lieu of their own, though many do. State approval is often the door opener that enables an attorney to advertise his or her specialty certification. Recognition by a state bar as an *attorney specialist* varies considerably from state to state. Similarly, state regulations regarding advertising yourself as an attorney specialist in a particular field also vary from state to state.

Certification by an ABA- or state-approved or -accredited specialty certification program can be a useful practice builder. Such certification does not preclude obtaining an LL.M., certificate, or other credential from elsewhere.

For More Information

- *Find a Certification Program,* ABA Standing Committee on Specialization (*www.abanet.org/legalservices/specialization/directory/home.html*)
- *Graduate Law Degree Program Directory,* fourth edition, Thomson Reuters (*www.attorneyjobs.com*)

Credential enhancement opportunities for attorneys are vast and do not have to be very expensive. There are academic and other certificate programs and state specialty certification opportunities that are available for virtually every legal and law-related practice area. Combined with a law degree, they can give your job prospects and career opportunities a significant boost.

However, you need to do a thorough due diligence investigation of any program, whether an LL.M. degree or a certificate, before handing over your hard-earned money and enrolling.

Part II

Research

Chapter 7
What Employers Really Want 39

Chapter 8
Expanding Your Horizons: Understanding Who Is Out
There 47

Chapter 9
The "Hidden" Legal Job Market: What It Is and How to
Uncover It 63

Chapter 10
The Hidden Legal Job Market: Private Sector 75

Chapter 11
The Hidden Legal Job Market: Public Sector 93

Chapter 12
The Hidden Legal Job Market: Nonprofits 107

Chapter 13
The Career Impact of External Phenomena 119

Chapter 14
Thinking a Few Moves Ahead 133

Chapter 15
Flying Solo Without Crashing 139

Chapter 7

What Employers *Really* Want

Put yourself in the potential employers' shoes—if the tables were reversed and you were the prospective employer, what would you would want? The candidate attributes that follow are discussed in very rough hierarchical order, from the most important to the least important. The order is based upon legal employer feedback to me over a period of several decades. However, every employer is unique and may have a preference for certain traits over others. Stay attuned to your interviewer's responses to you and try to determine what they seem to appreciate most.

Likeability

Three trademark attorneys competed for a very attractive job with NASCAR's general counsel office in Charlotte, North Carolina. Candidate #1 was a laconic gentleman, very bright, with an exceptional academic background, but rarely showed emotion and spoke in a monotone. Candidate #2 was a woman who could not keep her mouth shut and manifested a tremendous amount of nervous energy. Candidate #3 was a woman so upbeat and engaging that you wanted to take her home to Mama; the idealization of the Girl Next Door, but one who had gone to an undistinguished law school and was the poorest performer among the three candidates. Guess who got the job?

Getting an employer to like you is the most important goal you can achieve at a job interview. It does not assure you of a job offer, but if the employer does not like you, your stellar credentials will be irrelevant.

Being likeable is not difficult to achieve. Reduced to its essence, it means being polite and respectful, listening attentively when the other party is speaking, not interrupting, making eye contact, smiling when appropriate, nodding approvingly when you agree with a statement, and manifesting energy and enthusiasm without going overboard. Certain "pop" psychologists assert that if you "mirror" the posture and breathing patterns of your interviewer, you will win the likeability battle, but I don't think that's necessary; just be polite and engaged.

Fit

Do you align naturally with the employment situation? "Fit" is a function of both (1) congruence with the position for hire, and (2) your temperament compared to the rest of the office.

Fit is something that employers assess during job interviews. If they determine that fit might be a problem, it is unlikely that they will offer you the position, regardless of your other attributes.

Employers tend to probe for "fitness" by asking questions designed to elicit whether you align with their organizational culture and temperament. "Fit" questions include:

- Tell me about yourself.
- Are you a team player?
- What experience relevant to this position have you had?
- What do you know about our organization?
- Why do you want to work here?

See Chapter 33, "Handling the Tough Questions," for a discussion of how to respond to these questions.

Another, very effective way to get your fitness across to the employer is to incorporate examples of your fitness by referencing work experiences during your interview. See Chapter 23, "The Critical Importance of Storytelling."

Intelligence

Nice to have, but not the be-all and end-all, or even a perfect predictor of future success. The legal world is littered with graduates of non-elite law schools who made good. This is not to discount the importance of basic intelligence. However, intelligence is much more than doing well in school and on standardized tests. It also encompasses *creativity* and common sense, i.e., "street smarts."

Creative intelligence is the ability to confront a problem, devise a solution, pitch it effectively, implement it, and assess its outcome. The definition says it all about its importance in law practice. The best way to demonstrate creative intelligence on a résumé is via an addendum, where you have the space to elaborate on exactly how you attacked a problem. Your addendum should clearly explain how you got from point A to point B. See Appendix D, Résumé Addendum: Significant Highlights.

Common sense/street smarts is what I would call "situational intelligence," in contrast to innate intelligence. It is knowing how to react to specific situations that confront an individual in the course or his or her daily life.

Jimmy Carter probably scored higher on the SATs than any president. That would be wonderful for him if presidents were judged that way. He was a nuclear engineer, an alumnus of the Navy's hugely competitive and demanding nuclear submarine program. He was also a very good strategic thinker, recognizing the long-term implications of our energy dependency and coming up with a viable, long-term program to wean us off our energy profligacy. However, his presidency is generally not considered a roaring success—one often cited reason being his lack of common sense/street smarts.

Common sense is much harder to get across to an employer than either basic or creative intelligence. To some extent you can demonstrate it in a résumé addendum, as discussed, where it can intermingle with your manifestation of creative intelligence, but you should also try to demonstrate it during the interview.

Being a Quick Study

One of my legal career counseling candidates developed a reputation within her law firm for being the go-to person for new projects that no one had any experience in and that needed to be accomplished in a hurry. These capabilities gave her some protection from periodic downsizings that the firm endured. She very much needed this protection, as she was raising three young children and had to miss considerable work time as a consequence. Moreover, her billable hours were nowhere near what were expected of associates at her level.

When she left the firm to raise her children, she did so on her own terms.

This trait is one that you do not have to wait for an interview to demonstrate. You can do so in your résumé, and you can elaborate if necessary in a résumé addendum (see Appendix D).

If you think you need to hone this ability, put yourself into situations at work or in volunteer activities where you are forced to climb a learning curve quickly. The more experience you have tackling new and unfamiliar subject matter, the better you will be at it, and the more you will be able to say about it to a prospective employer.

Organizational Skills

There are many ways to get this "organizational skills" message across to a prospective employer. All of them should be utilized, given the importance of the message.

- *A reader-friendly and logically constructed résumé.* This is the first opportunity you have to impress an employer with your organizational skills. "Reader-friendly" means plenty of white space, bullets, and a less-than-overwhelming amount of type. You do not want the employer's first impression of your résumé to be that slogging through it is going to be an unpleasant experience.

- *An impressive reference list.* "Impressive" does not mean celebrity references. Rather, it means a reference list that contains information about (1) your relationship to your references, (2) when and how the employer should contact them, and (3) something that you did of which you are proud and that the reference can discuss with your employer (see Appendix G).
- *A writing sample cover sheet.* A cover sheet placing your writing sample in context will gain you a great many points with employers. Without one, they may spend most of their reading time wondering what your writing sample is all about and paying little attention to your writing and advocacy style (see Chapter 24, "Identifying Winning Writing Sample(s)."
- *Asking great questions at the interview.* This is where you "lock in" the message about your organizational skills. Employers like to hear great questions and award points for the forethought (read: organization) that went into preparing them (see Chapter 34, "Bridging the Power Chasm").

Persuasive Ability

When you strip away the veneer, persuasive ability is what practicing law is all about. Whether you are a litigator, a transactional attorney, a regulatory lawyer, or anything else that falls within the lawyering purview, you will win or lose on the basis of your ability to persuade others of your client's position.

Persuasive ability should be reflected in your résumé, primarily by crafting your statements about your duties and responsibilities in terms of your results. It is your outcomes, your accomplishments, that demonstrate persuasive ability. You can also supplement the necessarily more cryptic statements about your achievements in the body of your résumé with a highlights addendum where you can elaborate on them (see Appendix D).

Because persuasive ability is important, it is also a good idea to emphasize the point—again, objectively—in your cover letter or transmittal e-mail.

Well-Roundedness

Does your résumé imply that you are a drone who spent all your time in a law library carrel studying, or did you get involved in a variety of outside activities in law school? If you are an experienced attorney, does it indicate that all you do is work? If that is the case, then you are sending a regrettable message—that you are quite limited—to prospective employers.

Legal employers like to see that you have a life outside of the law, no matter how difficult that may be for you to attain. They have a good reason for wanting to see that you have more than one facet to your career personality. One of the ways you are likely to be judged is your capacity or potential to go out and develop business, keep clients satisfied, and/or interact comfortably with internal clients. A résumé that contains some indication of a community life in addition to a work life is one very good indicator of such potential.

Accountability

Accountability—taking responsibility for your actions—is unfortunately not something that society appears to value very much. Legal employers, however, value it very highly.

It is very difficult to ascertain if a job applicant has this admirable and increasingly rare quality. It is almost impossible to document on a résumé, and there is great hesitation on the part of candidates to admit to any glitches or screw-ups, even when posed the classic interview question: "What is your greatest weakness?" The only way that employers can even get close to an idea of an applicant's "accountability quotient" is through the job interview, and by asking astute questions of references and listening very carefully to their responses, including any "pregnant pauses" that might be very telling.

One way to get across the point that you are a responsible person is to develop one or more anecdotes that demonstrate this quality and that you can inject into your responses to questions at the job interview. See Chapter 33, "Handling the Tough Questions," for a more detailed discussion of this point.

Career Progression

Career progression in its purest form means that each move depicted on your résumé shows career advancement. Employers place a pretty high premium on career progression. However, the volatility of the legal job market makes this characteristic somewhat less significant with respect to hiring decisions than it used to be.

Nevertheless, you will earn points with prospective employers if you can demonstrate that the job changes that you made were motivated by the opportunity to advance your legal career; plus, it always looks good if other employers saw fit to promote you. See Chapter 17, "Vulnerability Management: Mitigating Your Weaknesses," for specific suggestions on overcoming the lack-of-career-progression problem on your résumé.

Stability

A decade ago, I would have viewed with concern an attorney résumé that indicated that the candidate had held three jobs in only 10 years. In the 1990s, I would have labeled such an attorney a "job-hopper," which is not a favorable term. Today that kind of career history is commonplace. In a complete attitudinal reversal, I might question the ambition of an attorney who remained with the same employer for a decade!

Despite an increasingly volatile job market (legal employment gurus say that a law school graduate in the twenty-first century will have eight jobs prior to retirement), employers still like to see applicants who have had a stable career. The one positive in this somewhat delusional employer concern is that stability now takes a back seat to many of the other attributes of the "ideal candidate." This should not, however, be viewed as a license to bounce around from job to job with disturbing frequency. That makes it difficult for an employer to feel good about a candidate.

Two candidate anecdotes are relevant to this discussion:

1.   One of my clients had the misfortune to have worked for no fewer than four law firms since graduating from law school 10 years prior to our counseling relationship. As I mentioned

above, this is not that unusual these days. However, in his case, each one of his firms had collapsed—gone belly-up. He reminded me of an Al Capp "Lil' Abner" comic strip character—Joe Btfsplk—who had the worst luck on the planet and walked around with a black cloud over his head.

My solution was to recommend that he add a very brief italicized statement under each job description in his résumé stating why he moved on to another position, such as:

Associate, Smith Jones & Brown LLC, Philadelphia, PA 2006-2008.
[Reason for leaving: Firm declared bankruptcy]

Despite his helter-skelter career and being unemployed, he landed a new position fairly quickly. This is a casual, subtle way of letting the prospective employer know you didn't leave any jobs due to poor performance.

2. Another counseling client held no fewer than seven jobs in 12 years, aggravating the situation by moving to a different city five times. I could recommend no easy solution for her plight, and she had an extremely difficult time finding a new position, despite being employed in a secure job and having done very well in each position she held. Even in the twenty-first century, employers don't want to hire someone, train them, and then lose that time and money a year later when they decide to move. Chapter 17, "Vulnerability Management: Mitigating Your Weaknesses," suggests ways to cope with a perceived absence of stability.

A candidate who can punch all of these tickets is a rarity, so do not be discouraged if you know that perfection will be difficult, if not impossible, to attain. Employers know this too. While they might dream dreams of the ideal candidate, they are generally realistic enough to know that if they can find one who satisfies most of these ideals, they will have made a good hiring decision.

Chapter 8

Expanding Your Horizons: Understanding Who Is Out There

This chapter is designed to give you an idea of the virtually limitless venues in which you can apply your legal training, along with the major variables that you need to consider in determining which opportunities you want to pursue.

Before you can position yourself for legal career and job search success, you have to identify the range of employers that might have an interest in what you have to offer. In addition to determining who they are, you need to go further and learn what they are all about.

This chapter looks first at legal market demographics, then divides and discusses the possible spectrum of potential employers and opportunities into two very broad categories: mainstream law and law-related careers. You should come away from reading this chapter with an understanding of the various types of legal and law-related careers and job opportunities: what they are; where they are; the key differences among them in terms of organizational culture, expectations, compensation, clients, and constituencies; pluses and minuses; where they are likely to be heading; and, perhaps most important, lifestyle considerations.

Our examination of law-related careers takes a more "macro" approach due to the large number of careers and jobs that fall within this category, as well as their tremendous diversity. It examines them from the standpoint of (1) types of non-mainstream legal careers, (2) the underlying reasons such careers exist, (3) what makes attorneys attractive candidates for these positions, and (4) the pluses and minuses of choosing an alternative path to utilizing your legal training.

Legal Job Market Demographics

The available statistics on attorney demographics paint a clear picture of legal market competitiveness:

- The American Bar Association (ABA) says that there are approximately 1.2 million licensed attorneys in the United States (up from 250,000 in 1975).
- There were approximately 200,000 full-time-equivalent law students in 2008–2009, including J.D., LL.M. and S.J.D. candidates, attending 200 ABA-accredited law schools, 55 California-accredited law schools, and three unaccredited law schools.
- The number of mainstream attorney jobs is 943,500 (per the Bureau of Labor Statistics [BLS]). "Mainstream" is defined as law firms, solo practitioners, corporate in-house counsel offices, government (at all levels—federal, state, local) general counsel and chief counsel offices.

- Approximately 171,500 lawyers work in approximately 49,000 U.S. law firms (BLS).
- Approximately 500,000 lawyers are solo practitioners (BLS).
- Approximately 115,000 lawyers work in 30,000 in-house corporate counsel offices (BLS).
- Approximately 112,500 lawyers work in 15,000 federal, state, and local government law offices (BLS).
- Approximately 35,000 lawyers work in 15,000 nonprofit organizations with legal offices (BLS). Nonprofits include trade and professional associations, advocacy groups, legal services providers, colleges and universities, certain hospitals, foundations, museums, and other organizations.
- Approximately 9,500 U.S.-trained attorneys work in the U.S. and abroad in international organizations, multinational corporations, law firms, and other organizations (BLS).

These are the salient facts that make law-related careers so attractive as an alternative. The number of law-related ("J.D. preferred") job opportunities is unknown, but is likely several million at a minimum. I define "J.D. preferred" to include positions for which a law degree is an asset but not necessarily a requirement. In other words, too many lawyers are competing for too few mainstream legal positions at any given time.

Mainstream Legal Careers

Three types of employers dominate the mainstream legal arena: law firms, in-house (corporate) counsel offices, and government general counsel and chief counsel offices. The analysis below should be read keeping in mind that these are rather broad generalizations.

Law Firms

Law firms can be categorized by:

- *Size*. This encompasses large, mid-size, small, and solo (meaning a single-attorney practice). Size categories are a highly variable construct. For example, the largest law firm in Spokane, Washington, has only 40 attorneys, which might not even be deemed mid-size in Los Angeles or New York.

- *Representation—plaintiff or defense.* As a rough "rule of thumb," virtually all large and most mid-size firms represent the defense; virtually all small firms and solo practitioners represent plaintiffs. There are, however, many exceptions. Large firms, for example, may represent individuals who hold prominent positions with their clients, such as the CEO of a *Fortune* 500 whose teenager is pulled over for drunk driving.

- *Specialty practice (or lack thereof).* Most firms do not specialize. Those that do might be designated "boutiques." A boutique practice can be either a substantive law area (e.g., bankruptcy or labor and employment law) or a type of practice (e.g., litigation, business transactions, or class actions), or a subspecialty of one of these (e.g., medical malpractice litigation, licensing, or shareholder derivative class-action lawsuits).

- *Subsidiaries:* Over 100 (generally very large) law firms have subsidiaries that provide law-related, quasi-legal, non-legal, or spinoff services.

- *Organizational culture:* You are likely to work harder and longer hours in a law firm than in any other law office environment. Forget what you've read in blogs and legal journals about the demise of billable hours. They are not going away. However, the traditional large firm "caste" system of "finders, minders, and grinders" is undergoing an evolution, albeit a slow one, toward less rigorous stratification and more overlap.

- *Expectations:* Demands are high. The law firm business model makes law firms less forgiving than other environments. Social Darwinism and survival of the fittest is still the rule.

- *Compensation/earning potential:* Both are generally higher in law firms than in other venues.

- *Clients and constituencies:* Business development and retention is becoming the business of every law firm attorney, not only "finders."

- *Where they are likely to be heading:* Look for more law firm mergers, including cross-border mergers. Globalization will have an increasing impact. Competition will increase as corporate clients demand more (often for less money) and will turn more to legal fee auditing. Law firms will continue to evolve from collegial, courtly, timeless relationships with clients into formulations more like bottom-line businesses.
- *Lifestyle considerations:* Work demands mean less time for family and outside activities, and more stress.

In-House Counsel Offices

Corporate counsel offices can be categorized by:

- *For-profit v. nonprofit:* For-profits break down into either publicly traded or closely held companies . . . an important difference, especially since Sarbanes-Oxley and the advent of closer regulatory scrutiny of corporate compliance of publicly traded, for-profit companies. Nonprofits come in very diverse forms: public interest, advocacy, trade and professional associations, academic institutions, philanthropic organizations, certain healthcare entities, and museums, among others.
- *Size:* In-house counsel offices span the entire size spectrum from very large (*Fortune* 1000 et al.) to just one lawyer. The smaller the office, the more likely an attorney is to handle a wider range of issues. Large offices often compartmentalize legal responsibilities and thus hire or develop specialists.
- *Location:* Companies may be local, regional, national, or multinational.
- *Nature of legal work:* In-house legal work focuses primarily on transactions, internal client counseling, and regulatory and compliance matters. Litigation is often farmed out to law firms, with in-house attorneys managing the relationship and partnering with outside firms to strategize cases and keep within budget. The biggest differences from law firms include:
  - no billable-hour requirement
  - no business development responsibilities

- • clients are largely internal line offices, such as Human Resources, Procurement, Accounting, etc.
- *Organizational culture:* You are likely to work fewer hours than in a law firm. Fewer and less-pressurized deadlines mark corporate practice. There is also likely to be less competitive pressure from peers. Corporate practice is often much more team-oriented than private practice.
- *Expectations:* In-house practice is generally less demanding than law firm practice due to diminished client pressures to perform. The emphasis on "winning" is less because in-house practice is generally not litigation-oriented. Transactional work is usually less adversarial and also often means that both sides "win" if a deal is consummated. In-house lawyers are expected to be sensitive to financial and bottom-line business matters and, in public companies, the concept of shareholder value and the counsel office's contribution to it. In-house practice is typically more structured than law firms and more bureaucratic.
- *Compensation/earning potential:* Attorneys are typically well compensated, but earning potential is not as great as in law firms. However, bonuses and deferred compensation are customarily larger.
- *Clients and constituencies:* In-house attorneys have, in essence, a single client: the company. However, they must also be attuned to their internal clients and external constituencies, i.e., shareholders and purchasers of the company's products and services.
- *Where they are likely to be heading:* Some of the same directions affecting law firm practice also apply to corporate practice. Mergers, acquisitions, strategic alliances, etc., are constant matters for legal work and job security concerns. Recent combinations demonstrate that no business is immune from a merger or takeover. Globalization affects companies more than law firms. After a generation of deregulation, the pendulum has shifted to what appears to be a lengthy era of re-regulation, which will heavily impact corporate practice.

- *Lifestyle considerations:* In-house practice usually means less time at work and more time for family and outside activities. Corporations are often in the forefront of family-friendly policies.

Government Law Offices

U.S. government law practice as a whole ranges over 112 practice areas in 3,000-plus law offices in the United States and abroad. Public-sector general counsel and chief counsel offices can be categorized by:

- *Level of government:* Attorneys work for either the federal, state, or local government. They may also work for special districts, quasi-governmental entities established for special purposes, such as transportation authorities, water and sewer authorities, and other functions that transcend jurisdictional lines.
- *Branch of government:* Government lawyers work for either the executive, legislative, or judicial branch of their respective jurisdictions.
- *Agency mission and impact on legal functions:* Government agency missions are established by legislation, regulation, or executive order. Agency legal office duties and responsibilities can be extremely narrow, such as the Office of General Counsel at the federal government's Election Assistance Commission, or extremely broad, such as the Department of Homeland Security Office of General Counsel. The scope of the agency's mission can thus limit the exposure of its attorneys to diverse practice areas and, correspondingly, their future marketability, i.e., the ability to move onward and upward.
- *Size:* Government law offices range in size from one or two attorneys to large cabinet departments with hundreds of lawyers. Depending on their legal needs, a large agency may have only a handful of lawyers, whereas a relatively small agency may have a fairly large legal office. The physical size of an agency may also be somewhat misleading. For example, it is also possible to serve in a tiny legal office that is part of a far-flung agency with thousands of lawyers. A

good example is the 9,000-attorney U.S. Department of Justice and its three-attorney Office of Tribal Justice, which has very little interaction with the rest of the lawyers in the department.

- *Nature of legal work:* This too can be extremely narrow, such as the Office of the Consumer Advocate at the Postal Rate Commission, where virtually the entire focus is representing the general public in hearings over whether to raise first-class postage rates (the public always loses), or extremely broad, such as the U.S. Commerce Department's Office of General Counsel, where responsibilities include almost everything that a private-sector company in-house counsel's office would do, plus many additional duties unique to the particular requirements of the department and its many unrelated subordinate units—the Patent and Trademark Office, National Institute of Standards and Technology, National Oceanic and Atmospheric Administration, International Trade Administration, Minority Business Development Agency, Technology Administration, etc. Again, an agency's legal work cannot always be known or understood by its name alone. The International Boundary and Water Commission has a very narrow mission, namely administering boundary and water treaties between the United States and Mexico. Its small Office of Legal Advisor, however, has vast responsibilities, including advising on treaty interpretation, litigation, administrative hearings, employment and labor law, appropriations law, contract law, environmental law, public international law, claims management, ethics, privacy law, and much more.

- *Organizational culture:* This is where you discover that government is by no means a monolith. There is as much variation among government legal offices at every level as one finds in private industry as a whole. Nevertheless, there are a few almost universally consistent truths about government legal employment, subject to certain exceptions:

  - Government attorneys are more likely to work regular hours than attorneys in any other employment sector, often no more than 35–40 hours per week.

- Government attorneys are much more likely than other attorneys to be offered flexible work arrangements, such as flex-time, flex weeks, telework, etc. One federal legal office with over 350 attorneys permits its staff to work from home and report into the office only two hours per month.

- There are no billable hour requirements. However, at least two federal government legal offices (the Trademark Office and the Board of Veterans Appeals) have "production quotas" that are quite demanding.

- Federal employment is probably the most secure legal employment extant. State and local government legal employment, in contrast, is not very stable, primarily because of the large number of states that are constitutionally required to balance their budgets every fiscal year. In years when this is a struggle (such as during the Great Recession), attorneys suffer furloughs, layoffs, and permanent job loss.

- *Duplication and overlap:* These are particularly unique to the federal government and open up many almost hidden possibilities. You might believe, for example, that the Environmental Protection Agency (EPA) is where you wish to practice environmental law in the federal government. However, if your job search stopped with EPA, you would then be missing out on the other 30-plus departments and agencies with environmental responsibilities that they have distributed among no less than 400 legal offices. This same phenomenon holds true for almost any other practice area that comes to mind. Be sure to look at government agencies that might have an office or an opening for someone with your legal specialty.

- *Expectations:* Government-wide, performance expectations are not as high as in the private sector. There are, of course, glaring exceptions to this blanket statement. The fact that some senior legal staff consists of political appointees can also make for widely varying expectations.

- *Compensation/earning potential:* Compensation and earning potential are both rather modest in comparison to the private sector. Federal government attorney compensation is better almost overall than state government compensation, and state government compensation is usually better than local government compensation. However, some local governments, principally those in large metropolitan areas, pay better than many states. And government benefits at virtually every level are quite good. Moreover, government employees can often retire at age 55 with maximum retirement pensions and benefits.

- *Clients and constituencies:* Theoretically, the client is the public, but it is an unseen, silent, and not always respected client for the most part. Consequently, the day-to-day client is the agency itself, and sometimes the political administration in charge in the jurisdiction. Like corporate in-house counsel offices, public-sector law offices often serve numerous internal clients.

- *Where they are likely to be heading:* At the federal-government level, look for more agencies, more legal offices, and generally more opportunities. Approximately 35–40 percent of the federal mainstream legal workforce will likely retire by 2013, opening up numerous opportunities. In addition, with re-regulation and reform on the upswing, the federal government is likely to be an excellent employer of lawyers for some time to come. The states and localities will hire and fire depending on their budget status in any given fiscal year.

- *Lifestyle considerations:* Exceptional from the standpoint of work hours, time off, and flexible work schedules.

Careers for Lawyers outside the Mainstream

There are hundreds of legal career alternatives to mainstream practice. They do not lend themselves to the neat categories into which mainstream careers can be divided—they are simply much too diverse and different from one another. Thus, the discussion in this section necessarily follows a format different from the discussion of mainstream legal careers.

Types of Non-mainstream Legal Careers

I wrote my first book about legal career alternatives (*JD Preferred: 600+ Things You Can Do with a Law Degree* (now the property of Thomson Reuters) in 1993. The 600-plus job titles were grouped under 30 broad topical areas:

- academic administration
- alternative dispute resolution
- banking and finance
- civil rights
- contracts, procurement, and grants
- court administration
- criminal justice and law enforcement
- energy and natural resources
- environment
- ethics and professional responsibility
- healthcare
- human resources
- human services
- insurance and risk management
- international affairs, trade, and investment
- intellectual property
- intelligence and security
- labor relations
- legal administration
- legal documents, information, and research
- legislative and regulatory affairs
- litigation management and support
- management and administration
- marketing and development
- media and entertainment
- real estate and housing
- taxation
- teaching—law school
- teaching—undergraduate and graduate
- transportation

When *JD Preferred* was published, readers were amazed at the large number of law-related careers identified as suitable for attorneys. With each passing year, the number has increased.

Why So Many Law-Related Careers Exist

My theory as to why there has been such a proliferation of law-related careers is that, with the passage of time, law tends to accrete and build upon itself, insinuating its tentacles into every nook and cranny of individual, group, and organizational behavior and activity. These non-mainstream careers, like cell division, tend to create new careers in new arenas.

The education sector is a great example of law-related career creation, one that is replicated in many other workplace environments. A combination of increased government regulation and more individual assertiveness (by teachers, administrative staff, and students) forced educational organizations to hire attorneys. Initially, colleges, universities, and school districts began hiring in-house counsel to deal with these matters. Then, as these matters became more complex and wide-ranging, they began establishing separate offices to focus specifically on certain issues that were taking too much of the general counsel office's time and attention. Consequently—and this is now well developed at the post-secondary level—you find attorneys working as judicial officers, planned-giving officers, real estate directors, ombudsmen, ethics officers, technology transfer specialists, contract and procurement administrators, risk managers, compliance officers, government affairs liaisons, and in other law-related campus capacities. Many job ads for these positions either require or prefer a J.D. degree.

New technologies also spawn new law-related careers. Space law, for example, was unheard of 50 years ago. The computer takeover of global communications has launched several new legal and law-related practices and job opportunities, such as in computer law, e-commerce law, Internet law, and e-discovery. Many new laws also give rise to new job opportunities in previously unknown or relatively quiet areas. The Sarbanes-Oxley Act, Pub. L. 107-204, for example, made corporate governance a huge practice area overnight.

Loopholes that shrewd minds find in laws can also foment new career opportunities. Hedge funds, derivative instruments, ratings agencies, and private equity are examples of financial products and services that, to date, are unregulated. Closing those loopholes through increased government regulation and stepped-up compliance and enforcement scrutiny is sure to provide new law-related job titles and employment opportunities in both the public and private sectors.

Threats and crises, be they political, military, environmental or otherwise, can also stimulate legal and law-related employment. Homeland security law is almost entirely the result of the 9/11 attacks on America. The idea of a carbon transactions manager is the unique consequence of the threat of global warming.

What Makes Lawyers Attractive Candidates for Non-mainstream Positions?

Attorneys have a tremendous background for moving into numerous law-related career fields outside of mainstream law, for the following reasons:

- They learn to think critically and analyze impartially.
- They come into contact with an incredibly wide range of human activities, problems, and emotions, and learn a great deal about how to handle and resolve them.
- They are trained problem-solvers and seekers of consensus, two skills of inestimable value to society and to almost any employer.
- They represent a proven, intelligent commodity, an asset to any organization, which is very important in an age when knowledge and information literacy are transferable commodities. They have demonstrated their ability to survive and succeed in demanding environments, such as law school, the courtroom, and the negotiating table.
- Their intellects and thought processes are challenged every working day.
- They have been "winnowed" many times over—college, law school, bar examinations, and practice.
- They are usually good at planning and organization.
- They have to be strategic thinkers.

- They are grounded in the fundamental rules governing society, which gives them a very powerful knowledge advantage.

These attractive traits are well known to savvy employers in many of these traditionally non-legal disciplines. This, in turn, gives attorneys an advantage when competing for such positions with non-lawyers.

Whether you seek a traditional alternative career, such as contracting, investigating, or teaching a legal subject, or one on the "cutting edge," such as technology transfer, risk management, or ethics and professional responsibility, your legal education and work experience are invaluable assets toward realizing that goal.

The Pluses and Minuses of Moving Out of the Mainstream

Like everything else in life, you need to balance the pros and cons of any decision. However, while such analysis is important in contemplating leaving mainstream law, it is of less importance with each passing year as the job market changes. Nowadays, maybe the best determinate is feedback from lawyers who have made such moves and from legal and law-related employers who have hired these career changers.

The positive sides of such a career move include:

- An easier path to professional employment.
- More civility in relations with individuals "on the other side" (to the extent another side exists).
- Much less rigorous and restrictive licensing requirements; consequently, fewer (if any) geographic constraints on where you can work.
- Possible opportunities to combine your non-legal education and work background with law.
- Better job security.
- No billable hours requirement.
- A reasonable work-life balance.
- Less stress.

The most important potential negatives include:

- Lower compensation.
- Reporting to and working with less-educated individuals.
- Less prestige.
- Possible stigma attaching to people who leave law.
- Possible obstacles to returning to mainstream law.
- Less career flexibility.

One of the biggest failings of legal job aspirants as well as the individuals and media that presume to advise them on their careers is lack of in-depth knowledge of (1) what it is like to work in different employment sectors, and (2) the array of possibilities open to attorneys. Without making the effort to acquire that knowledge, you will approach your career search from a disadvantage. You should always consider all possible professional opportunities, your career potential, and your economic well-being and career satisfaction.

Chapter 9

The "Hidden" Legal Job Market: What It Is and How to Uncover It

The current economic climate, marked by volatility, uncontrollable external factors, globalization, and constant uncertainty, makes it essential that you inject some creativity into the legal job–hunting process. What I call the "hidden legal job market" presents you with myriad opportunities to wax creative.

This chapter examines the hidden legal job market in general, followed by focusing on specific employment sectors—law firms, corporations, government, nonprofits—and law-related arenas. It is intended to (1) help you understand this hidden market and (2) exploit it to maximum advantage. If you are able to navigate the hidden job market, you will have a significant competitive advantage over job seekers who don't know of its existence or don't understand it.

The hidden legal job market means that you have to dig a little deeper to discover good job and career opportunities that might be out there for you. It is well worth the digging.

Profiling the Hidden Legal Job Market

The simplest definition of the hidden legal job market is job opportunities that are (1) not advertised, or not advertised through traditional means, or (2) not readily known to job seekers.

Whenever I allude to this sub rosa market, my clients ask me why an employer would purposely conceal the fact that his or her organization is hiring. Isn't it both counterintuitive and counterproductive? Employers do not purposely hide jobs. There are valid reasons why a position may not be advertised, or not be advertised at this particular point in time, or may be advertised in an unconventional way or via an unusual medium, or remain hidden from conventional job-seeking strategies. For example:

- *An established résumé bank, database, or register.* Many employers file résumés they receive (both solicited and unsolicited) for a fixed period of time, and then turn to that résumé bank or database when a position actually arises. At that time, they will either pull out the paper résumés they have received or retrieve the names and credentials of qualified candidates from the résumé database. If they have a fairly large collection of accomplished and recent résumés, they may not feel that they have to advertise open positions.

- *An online résumé bank.* Employers sometimes access online résumé banks compiled by outside companies that advertise job-placement services, such as Monster.com or Careerbuilder. However, this is a relatively rare occurrence with respect to attorneys.

- *Rapid organization growth.* If the employing organization is growing very rapidly, it may have no time to advertise openings. This is true of many high-tech companies, consulting firms, and even some law firms in hot fields during good economic times.

- *Promotion from within.* The organization has promoted someone from within, and not yet gotten around to recruiting a replacement for the vacancy created when the individual was promoted.

- *Saving time.* Some employers do not want to be compelled to review, and perhaps respond to, a ton of résumés from marginally qualified candidates. Consequently, they prefer to begin the recruitment process quietly by tapping into their own carefully cultivated networks. This could mean asking current employees to recommend possible applicants or going outside the organization to ask trusted advisors, acquaintances, or professional colleagues. If this method does not produce qualified candidates, the employer will then expand its efforts and advertise the position.
- *The job has not yet "jelled."* The employer knows that it will be hiring lawyers but has not yet taken the concrete steps to formalize the recruitment.

Identifying Hidden Opportunities: Universal Strategies

The following hidden job market identification strategies apply to most employment sectors and types of employer:

Networking

Networking is often the first, last, and only resort of many career counselors, as well as the job search element that job seekers fear the most (see Chapter 30, "Networking Without Groveling," which discusses how to network with confidence and without fear). Nevertheless, networking is one of the best ways to identify jobs that are not advertised. It is also the best way to get yourself seriously considered for a position, advertised or unadvertised—particularly if your intermediary endorses your candidacy and is well respected within the organization.

Support Groups

During a recent presentation I gave to a group of newly admitted attorneys, I had the attendees go around the room and state the law practice areas in which they were interested. One young woman expressed an interest in immigration law with a concentration on representing asylum applicants seeking refuge from domestic violence in their home countries. A second attendee advised her that he had recently completed an externship with a local Catholic Charities immigration law group that had received grant money to expand its domestic violence asylum representation program.

This situation is an excellent illustration of how your fellow job candidates who are not competing with you for the same positions can be immensely valuable sources of job-hunting intelligence. Alumni organizations, membership organizations, and other gatherings provide a forum in which non-competing job seekers can meet in order to share job leads and career insights. Information sharing among such candidates is non-threatening and can broaden the scope of your job search, expand your horizons, and bring new ideas and potential networking contacts to your attention, enabling you to leverage your job search. Moreover, while supporting your circle of job hunters, you are developing a network of professional colleagues for the future.

Industry and Professional Contacts

People who work in the industries in which you are interested are often "in the loop" concerning job opportunities. The best ways to find out who these individuals are and what they are up to professionally are as follows:

- Joining industry/practice area professional and trade organizations.
- Attending industry and professional meetings and conferences. For example, if you are interested in health law, attending meetings and events sponsored by the local chapter of the American Health Lawyers Association is one of the best ways to find out what is going on in the practice area, meet and cultivate relationships with health law attorneys in your geographic area, and develop strong information and intelligence sources.
- Reading industry and professional trade publications can help you monitor new initiatives and projects that could create job opportunities, as well as news of promotions that create vacancies.
- Seminars and CLE programs alert you to industry trends, major transactions, large new government and private-sector

contracts, the names and backgrounds of major players in the industry or practice area, and much more.

- Keeping abreast of news from local chambers of commerce, boards of trade, and economic development agencies can provide you with early intelligence about companies relocating to, or expanding within, your geographic area of interest. Very few people are aware that public utilities have extensive business attraction programs that seek to entice businesses to relocate to their service areas.

Trends Analysis

Every attorney should be doing this all the time, but analyzing societal, economic, business, and other trends is critical for legal job seekers and career changers. Trends analysis can tell you a lot about what is coming down the pike that could affect your personal circumstances, both positively and negatively.

Trends analysis means keeping up with both macro- and microeconomic and other tendencies and developments—internationally, domestically, and locally. You do this primarily by reading print and online newspapers and magazines, subscribing to blogs in your areas of interest, and monitoring trade and professional journals. Once you have established a solid and steady information flow, you need to sift the mass of information you are receiving through your own personal filter.

Here is an example: Eminem Domain is a central New York state real estate attorney in solo practice focusing on residential real estate closings. Thanks to the collapse of the housing market and the credit crunch, his practice is rapidly drying up. His trends analysis tells him that residential real estate transactions are not likely to recover anytime soon. Consequently, Eminem concludes that he needs to "reinvent" himself.

Among the many information tidbits that come his way is a series of articles about peak oil, renewed interest in natural gas, dramatic advances in natural gas deep drilling and extraction technology, and recent discoveries of large natural gas reserves, one of which—the Marcellus Formation—spans an area including central and western New York state, western Pennsylvania, western Maryland, and all of West Virginia. The confluence of this recent huge natural gas discovery, the Obama administration's energy independence initiatives, climate change legislative proposals, and the new deep drilling and extraction technologies that make the Marcellus Formation economically viable lead Eminem to conclude that gas companies that want to explore and drill in his region are going to have to obtain drilling rights from numerous landowners, and that his real estate background and knowledge might be of value. His subsequent natural gas industry research reveals that fossil-fuel energy companies refer to the individual who handle these tasks as a "landman."

Googling the term "landman" turns up an organization called the American Association of Petroleum Landmen (*www.landman.org*). While membership in the association is restricted to practicing landmen with several years of experience, a variety of home study courses are available to any interested individual on the association's Web site. Eminem signs up for "Environmental Awareness for Today's Land Professional," "Due Diligence for Oil and Gas Properties," and "Ethics for Land Professionals" and, upon completion, adds them to his targeted landman résumé. In addition, he constructs his résumé to make it clear to prospective gas company employers that he has the requisite background to perform competently as a landman by negotiating for the acquisition of mineral rights; negotiating agreements for the exploration for and development of natural gas; determining ownership in minerals through the research of public and private records; reviewing the status of title, curing title defects, and otherwise reducing title risk associated with ownership in minerals; managing rights and obligations derived from mineral ownership; and unitizing/pooling mineral interests. He then obtains a targeted list of regional natural gas exploration and development companies from the Internet and pursues landman positions with them.

Read ALL the Job Ads

Naturally, if you are seeking an attorney position, you want to see and read the job ads for lawyers in the newspapers, trade journals, and online. Limiting yourself to only attorney job ads, however, unnecessarily restricts your job search at the very time it needs to be expansive.

Don't limit yourself to just attorney ads. Look at all of the ads in order to detect patterns. For example, if you see job ads placed by employers hiring extensively across a variety of occupations, that is an indicator that their businesses are growing. They may not be hiring lawyers at present, but if they are expanding, there might soon be a need for legal talent.

Newspapers, particularly on Sundays, carry display ads in their employment sections. When you see a display ad seeking applicants for multiple positions, you may want to target that employer. Even if the company does not have an open position that suits you now, it will file your application and likely remember you when it comes time to hire for a legal position.

Identify New Financings

Newspaper business/financial sections and online financial Web sites often carry announcements of significant business financings. Such financings usually predate major expansions and a corresponding need for additional employees at many levels. A prime example of such ads can be viewed in *The Wall Street Journal*.

Hunt for Profits

Scan newspaper and online tables showing quarterly earnings reports for companies that have increased their profits by more than 5 percent from the preceding year. This growth rate often presages a need for additional employees.

Examine Promotion and New-Hire Announcements

As discussed, internal promotions usually mean that two positions opened: one for the person being promoted and another for the one taking his or her place, sometimes at an entry level. Promotion announcements and announcements of new hires often appear in a "People," "Job Moves," or similar column in the local newspapers, business journals, legal trade publications, and industry or sector trade publications (both print and online). You should focus on the position left open rather than the one that is the focus of the media attention. If the "promotee" is leaving a job you are qualified to perform, send your résumé to the company before it can get around to formally seeking a successor. Also, consider calling the human resources department at the company to find out if the vacated position is still open.

Business Press Releases

Businesses often issue press releases when they hire someone for a significant position in the organization. You can use these to pinpoint where the new hire previously worked and the position he or she vacated there. Press releases also provide information about new business initiatives, acquisitions, divestitures, etc., all of which can be important early alerts about hiring plans.

Businesses are not the only employers who issue press releases about new hires and business developments. Government agencies have extensive public relations arms that publish releases, often announcing promotions, new program initiatives, and projected budgets for the next fiscal year. All of these have an impact on agency hiring. Even law firms, now that they are compelled to promote their services like other businesses, issue numerous press releases and put them on their Web sites.

Membership Organization Announcements

Attorney membership organizations frequently announce their members' job changes. For example, the following such announcements have appeared on the Web site of a regional chapter of the Association of Corporate Counsel:

- An attorney was promoted to a senior vice president position at a large manufacturing company.
- An attorney left the general counsel's office at a communications company.
- An attorney was promoted to the chief legal officer position with a major government services contracting firm.
- An attorney left an education trade association for a private law firm.

- An attorney was promoted to a deputy general counsel position with an insurance company.
- An attorney is leaving a high-technology company.
- An attorney was promoted to an associate general counsel position with a health maintenance organization.

There are hundreds of attorney membership organizations (see Appendix E, Selected Legal and Law-Related Networking Organizations), virtually all producing a barrage of information about the comings and goings of their members. Often this information is accessible online whether or not you are a member of the organization.

State, Local, and Specialty Bar Association Section and Committee Membership

The next step after mining membership organization Web sites for "hidden" job opportunities is joining one or more of these organizations. Some of them restrict membership to certain experienced practitioners, but many do not; they are happy to take your dues payment.

Joining legal and/or law-related membership organizations provides you with an instant network of potentially valuable contracts, gives you access to useful information about practice area developments and trends, provides the opportunity to attend organizational events that enable you to meet and greet like-minded attorneys, and affords a platform for "connecting the dots" in order to hone your trends analysis. This strategy can be particularly beneficial if you join an organization that is growing. Legal and law-related membership organizations grow because their practice areas or areas of interest are growing. The National Employment Lawyers Association, for example, has experienced a substantial growth in its membership rolls because employment law is booming.

Hidden Job Market Resources

Sources of information about the hidden job market are many and varied. Here is a selection of some of the most valuable information sources.

- *Legal journals* can be valuable sources of information about new jobs. Commercial legal journals often cover favorable developments at law firms, corporate in-house counsel offices, and government law offices. They also monitor the comings and goings of lawyers who work for these organizations, thereby giving you a heads-up on possible openings.

- *Industry and commercial trade publications* often have columns that note personnel changes, plus a wealth of other useful information. For example, each issue of *Aviation Week and Space Technology*, *The Economist*, and *Government Executive*, to name only a few, contains valuable information about new initiatives, personnel changes, company fortunes, etc.

- *Trade and professional association publications and Web sites*, while a bit more circumspect than commercial trade publications when discussing companies and people, still contain useful information about where their industries are going and what might happen when they get there in terms of job opportunities. To cite an example, the Business Software Alliance (*www.bsa.org*), an advocacy organization representing the world software industry, currently focuses a lot of attention on the growing epidemic of software piracy and on what can be done about it, primarily from a legal standpoint. BSA's initiatives and research reports imply that there is an increasing number of jobs being created that focus on anti-piracy matters and that the kind of "soft" intellectual property expertise necessary to work in this field can be readily acquired by any lawyer even without a scientific background.

- *Investment newsletters* often report on new product initiatives, company plans for the near-term and long-term, potential acquisitions and divestitures, the impact of new and proposed legislation and/or government regulations on particular industries and employers, etc. Most investment newsletters charge an annual subscription fee.

- *Government annual performance plans and strategic plans* are relatively recent additions to the massive volume of public-sector information that can be mined for hidden job opportunities. For example, a recent U.S. Department of Justice Fiscal Year Annual Performance Plan indicated that the department wanted to increase the number of attorney positions devoted to prosecuting terrorist activities from 416 to 523 nationwide in the coming fiscal year. That kind of advance notice of hiring intentions can be invaluable to job-seekers who want to plan ahead and position themselves to take advantage of a promising opportunity before the rest of the legal world jumps on it.

- *"Technology corridors"* are centers of economic growth and, consequently, job opportunities. They are established with a view to concentrating high-technology businesses— software development, medical devices, biotechnology firms, genetic engineering companies, pharmaceutical companies, etc.—in a small geographic area in order to leverage economic development and identify synergies. Mining tech corridors for legal and law-related job opportunities can be quite productive. Major technology corridors include:
  - Silicon Valley, California
  - Research Triangle Area, North Carolina
  - I-495 Boston Beltway, Massachusetts and New Hampshire
  - Dulles Technology Corridor, Northern Virginia
  - I-270 Corridor, Montgomery County, Maryland
  - Silicon Alley, Manhattan, New York
  - Convergence Corridor, between Denver and Fort Collins, Colorado
  - Fort Bragg All-American Defense Corridor, Fayetteville, North Carolina

Technology companies are faced with complex legal and regulatory issues and require considerable legal expertise. There is often a central repository of corridor company information that makes targeting potential employers a lot easier. The Northern Virginia Technology Council (*www.nvtc.org*), for example, with more than 1,100 member companies, maintains a wealth of insightful information about its members.

The strategies and techniques recommended in this chapter have a long and successful history among my legal career counseling clients. There are several advantages to utilizing this sort of "backdoor" advice: namely, being able to apply for positions before any competitors become aware that positions exist, thereby impressing employers with your creative approach to job hunting.

Chapter 10

The Hidden Legal Job Market: Private Sector

Law firms and corporations are founts of hidden legal and law-related jobs, with additional ones being added all the time. For law firms, the spur is their evolution from courtly, collegial professional associations into bottom-line businesses, plus a much more Darwinian competitive environment. For corporations, the primary trigger is stepped-up government regulation.

Law Firms

Law firms, the bloggers and pundits tell us, have been the hardest-hit in the legal community by the Great Recession. Nevertheless, they are still interesting sources of job opportunities.

Expanding Existing Practice Areas

Law firms prefer to find ways to earn more revenue out of established practices than having to build entirely new ones, and the Great Recession has prompted a rush to extract even more revenue out of existing practices, which aligns very well with the torrent of government policy initiatives designed to ease economic pain. For example:

- The Internal Revenue Service (*www.irs.gov*) undertakes and publishes a large number of statistical studies every year of virtually every facet of its activities. One of the most revealing bits of information from recent IRS studies is the fact that the number of tax controversies—disputes between the IRS and taxpayers, both corporate and individual—is escalating rapidly, and now numbers in the tens of thousands annually. Moreover, as state budgets become more uncertain, state revenue departments are following the IRS's lead and going after perceived underpayers and non-filers much more aggressively.

  How does that translate into law firm job opportunities? Tax controversy practice, heretofore something of a quiet "backwater," is emerging as a growth opportunity—a specialty by no means glutted with practitioners.
- Similarly, the push for healthcare reform is prompting both large law firms and smaller boutique practices to bolster their existing health law practices, and, for those firms lacking a health law practice, to launch one.
- The bipartisan consensus that food and drug regulation slipped in the last decade and the infusion of funds from Congress to the Food and Drug Administration has generated a rush among large law firms to add a practice in this area.
- Energy law, which has seen more than its share of highs and lows over the past several decades, is very much on the upswing again, thanks to the Obama administration's related efforts toward U.S. energy independence and climate change legislation. Law firms whose energy practices were in hibernation for many years have revived them, and many law firms have launched alternative energy practice groups.

Rapidly Changing Practice Areas

Besides the evolution of new and expanded practice areas, many traditional legal practice areas are rapidly evolving, presenting attorneys with new and interesting opportunities in which to find a niche and make a mark. Dramatic changes in technology are outpacing the ability of legislators and regulators to keep up-to-date. For example:

- Securities and bank regulators are confounded by their inability to regulate the *international flow of capital*. Major financial market players and investors can move trillions of dollars around the world at the press of a computer key, rendering irrelevant any controls that national and international governing bodies thus far have been able to devise.
- *Telecommunications technology* has advanced with startling speed, creating new consumer products, services, and complexities that traditional regulatory schemes never contemplated and are finding difficult to handle.
- Even healthcare has been profoundly affected by technology. *Telemedicine*, the ability to treat patients—and even perform surgery—from a very long distance has presented the authorities with serious issues concerning the licensing of healthcare professionals, professional liability, etc. Should a Colorado physician be permitted, via telemedicine technology, to treat a fallen skier on a Utah mountaintop, if the doctor is a recognized expert in the surgery but not licensed in Utah?
- The ability of *infectious diseases to move around the world* limited only by the speed of air travel has brought into sharp focus the dated nature of healthcare regulation at the borders and even impacts profoundly on seemingly distant, unrelated practice areas, such as immigration law.
- *Trademarks and copyrights*—This formerly stodgy practice area has become quite lively, thanks to the Internet, Google, electronic filing, etc.

New Practice Area Initiatives

Business realities are forcing law firms to anticipate trends and become much more aggressive opportunity seekers. Within weeks of the September 11, 2001, terrorist attacks, many law firms announced the establishment of *homeland security* practices. And even before the enactment of the landmark Sarbanes-Oxley Act in 2002 responding to the corporate and accounting scandals that dominated the news, many law firms had positioned themselves to market their newly minted *corporate governance* practices.

The complacent days when law firms could rely on a handful of major, loyal clients and their recurring legal requirements are gone. Now, law firms have to behave like any other business, be agile enough to respond instantly to changing market conditions, and then market their services aggressively.

Law firms pay management consultants and corporate intelligence services big bucks to alert them to the emergence of new practice areas. The skill involved in this kind of prognostication is, however, not very difficult to acquire. All it takes is keeping abreast of the news and doing some trends analysis of your own. It did not take a rocket scientist to discern that there would inevitably be a government regulatory and enforcement reaction to the excesses of Enron, WorldCom, Tyco, Adelphia, Arthur Andersen, etc., and that the additional regulatory "overlay" would create numerous opportunities for attorneys.

Less obvious practice areas that have arisen in recent years include:

- *Tribal finance practice*—a reaction to the 448 Native American casinos now in 28 states and the tribes' newfound business clout.
- *Commodities finance practice*—advising financial institutions on commodity finance transactions. This practice is a response to the increasing global demand for commodities.
- *Art recovery practice*—assisting disputants concerning the hundreds of thousands of paintings, sculptures, books and manuscripts, musical instruments, artifacts, and other cultural property that now reside in countries other than their countries of origin. Looting of art was so rampant during and immediately after World War II that this period is still a focal point of art recovery practice 60 years after the fact. The U.S. art market was totally unprepared for the onslaught of looted art that began arriving during or soon after the close of the war and may have peaked in the 1950s. With

Europe in ruins and the U.S. postwar economy booming, it was natural for art to move in this direction. Also, many refugee art dealers reestablished their businesses in the United States during and after the war, bringing with them relationships with dealers who remained behind in Europe. Art recovery disputes often involve individuals, institutions such as museums, sovereign states, and international organizations. Both major law firms and boutiques practice in this area.

- *Carbon transactions practice*—triggered by national, state, and foreign climate change legislation. Consists of developing financial projects generating carbon credits, creating funds that can purchase credits for the account of third-party buyers, carbon transaction deal execution, lobbying governments to improve the investment climate, addressing barriers to carbon finance, and encourageing the use of emission-trading mechanisms.
- *Golf practice*—handles legal, business, and land-use issues affecting the golf industry.
- *Longevity law practice*—largely the province of small firms and solo practitioners. Combines traditional elder law with Medicaid and health benefits planning, conservatorship, and guardianship. The centerpiece is the drafting of explicit directives for aging in place, hospice care, and charitable trusts.

"Spin-off" Practice Areas

One of the most interesting developments in law firm practice in recent years is the division of traditional practice areas into subspecialties. A few years ago, for example, "executive compensation" spun off from "employee benefits." An excellent current example is what has been happening in intellectual property, especially in "soft" IP—trademark and copyright. Trademark and copyright law were, for years, fairly low-key areas of IP practice. Not anymore. Now they are becoming much more interesting—sexy, even—as IP owners attempt to cope with a flood of issues generated by the leapfrogging of technology over traditional soft IP practice.

Read any IP trade publication, or visit any major law firm Web site, click on "practice areas," then on "intellectual property," and what do you see? The practice is no longer broken down into just patent, trademark, and copyright. Today you are just as likely to see such subspecialties as:

- brand management
- anti-piracy and counterfeiting
- advertising and marketing
- royalty securitization
- intellectual property asset management

For example, as IP became an increasingly important asset (by some estimates, IP now constitutes more than 75 percent of the assets of U.S. companies), IP asset management emerged as a significant business employing attorneys, among other professionals. The business is both internal—companies, colleges, and universities that establish IP asset management units—and external, in consulting firms that are engaged to identify, marshal, value, protect, and market IP assets.

IP is by no means the only legal practice area that has spawned spin-off practice niches. Other mainstream practice areas that generate exciting spin-offs include:

- *Health law*—healthcare fraud, bioethics, research ethics, legal nurse consulting
- *National security law*—homeland security law, emergency management law, disaster relief law
- *Family law*—nontraditional family law, international adoption law
- *Environmental law*—climate change, environmental ethics, water conflict management
- *Employment law*—workplace mediation, executive compensation
- *International trade law*—international arbitration, anti-money-laundering law

Spin-off practices represent the emergence of something new and interesting, where there are job opportunities. For many of these spin-off areas, there are credentialing possibilities that can enhance your employability. See, e.g., Appendix C, Representative Legal and Law-Related Credential Enhancement Programs.

Where the Law Firm Lawyers Are

Take a look around and see where law firm attorneys are flocking. This is an indicator of where the future lies. Here, you have a number of easy-to-implement analyses you can execute:

- State and local bar association sections and committees can be very enlightening in this respect. What are section and committee membership numbers and trends? Which ones attract the most attention? *What new sections and committees have been added lately?*
- Membership in state bar sections on alternative dispute resolution, employment law, cyber law, entertainment and sports law, intellectual property, energy law, and health law, for example, have been growing impressively. New sections and committees addressing terrorism, mass disaster response, elder law, corporate governance, and privacy, to name a few, have been popping up all over the country.
- Specialty bar associations. Which existing ones are growing? Which ones are new? How are they doing in terms of number of members? The Association of Corporate Counsel, American Health Lawyers Association, American Immigration Lawyers Association, Association of Attorney-Mediators, International Masters of Gaming Law, Internet Bar Association, National Association of College and University Attorneys, National Employment Lawyers Association, Energy Bar Association, and the Food and Drug Law Institute, for example, are thriving.

Law Firm Hot Topics

Law firms are very open about what they deem the "hot" practice areas; law firm Web sites contain a wealth of information about where they think their business is going. They do this through newsletters, articles, white papers, seminars, webinars, events, and other publications and information offerings. Law firms are fast becoming mini-publishing outfits. The impetus for much of this is business development: promoting areas of their firm that they think will generate business and paying clients. A quick scan of what firms are writing about tells you what they think the major issues of the day are—and/or will be in the very near future. This kind of intelligence can be a strong indicator of where the law firm jobs are likely to be.

A quick survey of what 10 randomly selected major law firms are writing about can tell you a great deal about where law firms believe their businesses are heading.

Boutique Law Firm Trends

The creation (and disappearance) of boutique law firms specializing in only one or just a handful of related practice areas is an excellent indicator of where the action is. One place to look for this phenomenon in all of both its positive and negative manifestations is Washington, D.C. The nation's capital is the Mecca of boutique law firms for obvious reasons (nothing generates legal business like U.S. government actions). In the 1970s, for example, telecommunications and energy boutiques proliferated in Washington. Then Ronald Reagan was elected president and both telecomm regulation and federal energy intervention and initiatives came to a screeching halt. The telecom and energy boutiques closed up shop and disappeared. In the mid-1990s, Congress passed the Telecommunications Reform Act of 1996, Pub. L. 104-104, and the telecom boutiques were resurrected. Similarly, electricity deregulation and a number of international events—oil price rises, the likely arrival of "peak oil" (the point in time of maximum global oil production)—have prompted a return of energy practices.

The rise, demise, and resurrection of telecom boutiques and energy practices were eminently predictable. All one had to do was be aware of what was going on in Congress, the Federal Communications Commission, the Department of Energy, and the Federal Energy Regulatory Commission, and plan accordingly.

Most Popular Law Firm Topics—Fall 2009

- corporate governance
- health law
- food and drug law
- China practice
- intellectual property
- securities law
- compliance
- climate change
- energy law
- immigration law
- employment law
- banking and finance law
- executive compensation
- tax law
- biotechnology and life sciences
- privacy law
- outsourcing
- government contracting

In addition to the trends that you can glean from what law firms are currently writing about, other developments that could be important to your legal career choices include demographics such as the aging baby boomer wave, which is already rendering elder law, Social Security disability law, and Medicare appeals very attractive emerging practice areas; legislative and regulatory reaction to the Great Recession, which is pushing securities fraud, mortgage fraud, and other financial crimes to the forefront; and technology advances, which have made international securities and financial regulation, telemedicine regulation, cyberlaw, life sciences law, technology licensing, and surrogate parenting, for example, interesting and potentially rewarding fields.

Skills Suddenly in Demand

Lawyering skills are not static. In the past quarter century, attorneys have been dragged kicking and screaming into the computer age, forced to learn Internet skills and certain software programs, not to mention a whole new language. Practicing without resort to e-mail or computerized legal research is inconceivable today.

It probably will not be too long before practitioners will find it equally inconceivable to practice without being at ease with videoconference depositions, e-discovery, and voice recognition software. Those who are "first past the post" in learning how to utilize these technologies will clearly be ahead of the competition.

Law Firm "Ancillary Businesses" (Subsidiaries)

Many major law firms (and some smaller ones) have established subsidiaries in order to compete with CPA and other consulting firms that have been taking legal services market share from them for some time now. Subsidiaries also establish potential new profit centers for the firms, help retain clients by offering them services in addition to legal services, and attract new clients who might then engage the law firm for legal services. Subsidiaries are intended to supplement traditional legal services offerings with other professional services. They are often run by attorneys and closely linked to the parent law firm, but with plenty of disclaimers about not giving legal advice, etc. While subsidiaries are usually wholly owned subsidiaries of law firms, they can also be joint ventures or partnering arrangements with other law firms or other professional service providers.

Law firm subsidiaries run the gamut of activities from very logical offshoots of lawyering—litigation consulting (with a view to incorporating an appreciation of the business issues involved in preparing cases for trial), document management for litigation support, and alternative dispute resolution services—to areas somewhat farther afield, such as insurance planning and recovery for policy holders, insurance claims analysis and valuation, risk management services, employee relations consulting, diversity recruiting and retention, government relations and lobbying, public affairs consulting, crisis communications, medical records consulting, business performance enhancement, governmental permitting, electronic compliance, corporate training programs (including online tutorials in a variety of legal topics), and many other fields of opportunity.

Subsidiaries generally hire attorneys with skills and backgrounds not necessarily sought when a traditional law firm is hiring first-year associates. For example, if you have experience working for a trade or professional association, you might be a strong candidate for a position with a law firm subsidiary that provides government relations services. If you are a nurse-attorney, you might be seriously considered for a position with a law firm subsidiary that provides healthcare risk management consulting advice.

Look for law firm subsidiaries to grow rapidly in the next several years and to expand into other professional service areas heretofore largely untapped, such as literary and talent agenting, sports marketing, corporate human resources, and intellectual asset management.

Corporations

While major corporations employ a great many attorneys, legal employment levels among *Fortune* 500 companies have largely been static or declining for 30 years. The real engines of corporate legal hiring are smaller companies.

It is also important to note that public company thinking about legal staffing is changing dramatically, thanks to the evolving demands of the Sarbanes-Oxley Act of 2002, a rash of new regulations promulgated by stock exchanges, and reinvigorated federal and state efforts to scrutinize and regulate corporate conduct more closely.

Hidden Corporate Legal Niches

Attorneys in corporations do not work only in in-house counsel offices. At some corporations, the general counsel's office may not even be the largest corporate unit employing lawyers.

- Virtually every major company has attorneys performing its ethics function. More than 50 percent of *Fortune* 1000 companies have an ethics office independent of their in-house counsel office. Both the Organizational Sentencing Guidelines (*www.ussc.gov/orgguide.htm*) and Sarbanes-Oxley have increased the centrality and prominence of the corporate ethics function and have compelled virtually every publicly traded corporation that did not yet have one to establish an

ethics office, thus generating additional employment opportunities for attorneys. Sarbanes-Oxley also generated attorney hiring for separate corporate legal offices that advise
corporate boards and audit committees, a phenomenon almost totally unknown until the act became law.

- Most companies of any significant size now also have dis-
crete compliance/regulatory affairs offices that make sure
the organization is cognizant of, and in conformance with,
the torrent of federal and state regulations that affect corporate activities. The barrage of legislation accompanying the
policy redirection and initiatives resulting from the Great
Recession, healthcare reform, energy independence, financial re-regulation, education reform, climate change, etc.,
will only enhance the importance of compliance and regulatory affairs for the foreseeable future.

- A growing number of corporations now have risk-management offices that attempt to evaluate financial and other risks
companies face and minimize them through insurance purchases and other measures. Attorneys are taught to evaluate
and temper risk every day, and the risk-management industry clearly recognizes that: approximately 20 percent of the
risk managers in the United States have law degrees.

- Corporate tax departments are often separate entities, thanks
to the escalating complexity of the Internal Revenue Code
and its state counterparts.

- Attorneys can also be found in corporate government affairs departments at headquarters, in state capitals, and in
Washington, D.C.

- Finally, corporate contract and procurement offices also
sometimes hire attorneys.

One of the most interesting corporate legal employment trends
prompted by both Sarbanes-Oxley and the Great Recession and
their progeny is the embedding of lawyers in diverse corporate operating divisions and support offices so that advice and counsel
will be immediately available to assess whether the corporation is
doing anything "wrong." In other words, setting up satellite general
counsel offices throughout the company. For instance, the legal is-

sues affecting human resources departments in some companies are so diverse, complex, wide-ranging, vexing, and threatening that there is a trend toward hosting their own legal counsel to handle employee grievances and charges of management misconduct, including sexual harassment, terminations, reorganizations, etc.

Industry-Specific Corporate Legal Niches

Specific industries and employment sectors often structure their own particular legal employment opportunities to the unique circumstances of their corporate purposes and missions.

Banking and Financial Services. Trust and wealth management departments at banks and other financial institutions have employed attorneys (often recent law school graduates) for many years. The Financial Services Modernization Act of 1999, Pub. L. 106-102 (also known as the Gramm-Leach-Bliley Act), knocked down the firewall between commercial banking and investment banking and other financial activities (which proved to be not such a great idea), thus expanding opportunities for attorneys in *subsidiary businesses* that cross-sell their depositors on securities, insurance, real estate, etc.

Insurance. Litigation management (dealing with outside counsel, strategizing cases, coverage decisions, examining billings, etc.), *claims administration* (especially directors and officers liability, professional malpractice, environmental liability, HIPAA matters, and disability concerns), and even underwriting (especially environmental and professional liability underwriting) are all niches in which attorneys are perceived as "value-added" employees at insurance companies.

At the insurance agency level, attorneys contribute to closing complex policy sales. A typical scenario goes something like this: The insurance agent markets policies to a large employer, elicits interest, then calls upon the sales team attorney ("advanced marketing consultant") to explain the legal and tax considerations of the policy to the prospective client and advise and assist in negotiating the transaction and closing the deal.

Manufacturing. Manufacturing firms with labor problems such as union elections, union decertification, WARN Act issues, etc., almost always have distinct and sometimes quite elaborate labor relations departments staffed with attorneys.

Accounting. CPA firms (in particular, the "Big Four": KPMG, PricewaterhouseCoopers, Ernst & Young, and Deloitte Touche) have large and growing legal staffs at both their headquarters and numerous field locations. A number of CPA firms even have more than one type of office performing legal functions:

- *In-house counsel offices.* These can be interesting first career stops for recent law grads with some "value-added" credentials in addition to their law degrees (e.g., concentration or strong performance in tax courses while in law school or an LL.M. in tax; or initial steps along the multipart CPA examination path).
- *National tax offices.* Attorneys in these offices monitor tax activity in Congress, the Treasury Department, and the IRS, and advise field employees on the constantly changing federal tax laws and regulations.
- *Consulting practice groups.* These groups often employ attorneys as consultants. Among these might be found corporate governance, litigation management, regulatory compliance, tax compliance, tax controversy, procurement, human resources, corporate recovery, and real estate, to name a few.

New Product Announcements

Companies get a lot of mileage out of announcing new products. If they are destined to be winners in the marketplace, it is likely that significant hiring activity, including legal hiring activity, will follow.

Every new product could represent an opportunity. Some may have obvious legal or regulatory implications that call for additional legal talent—for example, pharmaceuticals, medical devices, or innovative financial products. If you are a good trends analyst, you will be able to spot these possibilities before your competition.

Another example is the financial services industry, which employs lawyers in nontraditional roles where they craft and review the documentation necessary to launch new financial products and to advertise them without running afoul of the securities laws and regulations. Naturally, these positions are usually located in the major money centers—New York, Boston, Chicago, and San Francisco.

Planned Business Expansions

Very few businesses expand without adding more employees, lawyers included. Legal staff expansion usually trails basic business expansion by a few months—which is actually an advantage, as it enables the savvy legal job seeker to get his or her foot in the door before an actual job advertisement hits the streets.

Chambers of commerce, boards of trade, industrial and economic development agencies, state and local business attraction agencies, and utilities are either actively involved in these initiatives or monitor them, or both. This makes keeping up with their activities an important hidden job market identification strategy. There are three principal ways of keeping up with these developments: first, by monitoring organizational publications and Web sites; second, by following the reporting by local business journals; and third, by becoming actively involved in membership organizations like chambers of commerce and boards of trade.

Spin-offs

Corporate mergers and acquisitions have adversely affected many attorneys in recent years. The classic example: Megacorp buys Minicorp and lets all of the latter's legal staff go.

A far less publicized corporate reorganization phenomenon that presents great opportunity for attorneys are business spin-offs that create new, independent organizations—the opposite of mergers and acquisitions. Companies must be agile to survive in a rapidly evolving global economy. Consequently, the shedding of corporate units is a growing occurrence. The reasons behind the growth in spin-offs are many:

- Company may wish to exit a particular market.
- Company decides to concentrate on its core business and divest itself of anything that does not "fit" that strategy.
- Company sheds an underperforming division.
- Government antitrust or other regulators may force a spin-off or divestiture.

For example, major CPA firms came under pressure from the Securities and Exchange Commission in the late 1990s regarding their provision of both auditing and consulting services to the same corporate clients. Their very public response was to spin off their consulting arms into independent entities. In every case, the spin-off resulted in additional opportunities for attorneys.

There are approximately 100 to 200 spin-offs per year among publicly traded companies. Some of the larger recent spin-offs are listed below.

- Expedia from InterActive Corp.
- Ameriprise from American Express
- CBS from Viacom
- Chipotle from McDonald's
- Hanes from Sara Lee
- Carefusion from Cardinal Health

Emerging Companies

Established companies are not the only ones that offer legal opportunities. Keeping track of new companies that come on the scene and blossom is a very valuable way to carve out a possible job opportunity.

Venture capital firms always announce seed or "mezzanine" investments publicly, through Web site press releases, in industry trade journals, and in business sections of newspapers. Such announcements give you advance notice of likely hiring activity. You can monitor venture finance activity that might have legal hiring implications at *www.vfinance.com* and the National Venture Capital Association's Web site (*www.nvca.org*).

University technology transfer offices license faculty and researcher inventions and research that can be commercialized, incubate nascent companies established to commercialize their patents, and structure new businesses—such as joint ventures with faculty members, partnership arrangements and strategic alliances with outside companies, etc.—and announce these initiatives on their Web sites. For example, the MIT laboratories have spawned hundreds of companies, including some that became huge success stories, such as 3Com and Lotus. One of the best sources of this information is the Web site of the Association of University Technology Managers (*www.autm.net*).

Government research and development (R&D) initiatives also create new companies, bolster emerging companies, and sometimes create whole new industries, thus generating legal and law-related employment opportunities. For example, note the following items and technologies invented by or developed for the space program:

- halogen lights
- sports domes
- pocket calculators
- satellite phones
- "blue blocker" sunglasses
- digital watches and thermometers
- kevlar
- fiber optics
- compact disks
- magnetic resonance imaging (mri)
- scanners
- electronic ignitions
- laser scanners
- juice boxes
- cellular phones and beepers
- cable television
- GPS navigation systems

NASA (*www.sti.nasa.gov/tto*) and hundreds of other federal entities document their technology initiatives and commercialization opportunities on their Web sites. The Federal Laboratory Consortium for Technology Transfer (*www.federallabs.org*) is another excellent resource.

You can also keep tabs on emerging government policy and commercialization initiatives likely to have a major impact on business by monitoring the activities and research reports of the White House Office of Science and Technology Policy (*www.ostp.gov*), the Government Accountability Office (*www.gao.gov*), the Congressional Research Service (*www.loc.gov/crsinfo/whatscrs.html*), and the National Technology Transfer Center (*www.nttc.edu*).

A recent example of monitoring emerging companies for insights into the hidden legal job market is an Office of Science and Technology Policy fact sheet on U.S. Commercial Remote Sensing Policy, a potentially multibillion dollar industry that subsequently received a major government funding boost. Today, several hundred companies are involved in the remote-sensing industry and its related business—photogrammetry and geographic information systems. And those companies are all likely to have in-house counsel.

> Government inroads into private-sector behaviors have given a big boost to the concept of hidden legal job opportunities. We are now at the beginning of another era of stringent regulation, after a generation marked primarily by deregulation. As these eras historically have lasted for 30 to 35 years, look for more hidden legal jobs to be forthcoming.

Chapter 11

The Hidden Legal Job Market: Public Sector

Government regulation's impact on the creation of hidden legal job opportunities affects not only regulated entities, it also has a profound impact on government itself, where legal job seekers can find a huge number and diversity of hidden job opportunities.

The public sector, especially the U.S. government, offers many hidden legal job opportunities. In fact, the government creates more legal and law-related positions than any other employer anywhere.

The Federal Government

How the U.S. Government Hires Attorneys

To understand how and where the federal government "hides" its jobs for attorneys, you first have to know how the government goes about hiring lawyers. First, the most publicized and obvious way is during recruiting season, when some government agencies join law firms on law school campuses in the late summer and fall. Most such appearances are in conjunction with agency honors programs, of which there are 11 or 12 in the government. These are not hidden at all and focus on soon-to-graduate law students.

Second, there is year-round hiring of attorneys, which is a far less structured process. U.S. government attorney positions are exempt from normal civil service rules. That means that federal departments and agencies and their many legal offices (more than 3,000 nationwide) have total discretion when it comes to hiring lawyers. Unlike almost every other profession that government employs, no uniformity exists among federal legal hiring organizations in how they recruit and hire attorneys. You cannot assume that government is a monolith and that procedures that apply to the office of the chief counsel of the Federal Transit Administration, for example, apply equally to the Office of Professional Responsibility at the Justice Department. Certain offices may want you to use one type of application document; other offices may prefer to see another; some may want you to apply online using their own unique application template; others may want you to apply via the U.S. Office of Personnel Management's proprietary online application system. One office may ask you to submit a narrative statement responding to specific "knowledges, skills, and abilities"; another may ask you to respond to a set of "ranking factors." A parallel legal entity in the same agency may want to see only a résumé; another may want a "federal format résumé." One legal office may do all of its initial evaluation of candidates through its department's human resources office; another may reserve this function to itself. You must be cognizant of these distinctions in order to respond effectively to them.

Unadvertised Government Jobs

Unlike virtually all other government job opportunities, there is no statutory or regulatory requirement that U.S. government attorney job openings be advertised. While most are, many are not.

Federal hiring offices are also not always consistent with respect to their attorney vacancy hiring policies. Certain offices may advertise a legal position when one vacancy arises, then not advertise a new position the next time. In the latter case, they tend to look at résumés that they have recently received, either in response to a prior vacancy announcement or unsolicited.

Consequently, a federal legal job applicant has to be both *reactive* and *proactive*—reactive meaning that you have to keep your eyes open for advertised job opportunities (you can do this through *www.attorneyjobs.com* or *www.usajobs.gov*) and proactive in taking affirmative steps to alert a prospective federal employer to your credentials.

Federal Law-Related Jobs

In addition to the approximately 26,000 federal attorney positions, more than 100,000 U.S. government jobs qualify as "law-related." Many of these are filled by lawyers. They qualify as "hidden" because they do not have a job title that contains the word "attorney" or "counsel" or anything comparable. More than 150 federal job titles qualify as "law-related"—a position in which a law degree is often directly related to the work involved, or where a law degree may be preferred or desired, but not necessarily required. Law-related positions such as regulatory analysts, legal researchers, contract specialists, civil rights analysts, etc., are found in every federal department and agency throughout the United States and abroad. And as new federal agencies and functions emerge, keep an eye out for new positions that qualify as law-related.

The application process that applies to law-related positions that do not fall within the federal attorney occupation career series—designated by a series number (0905 for attorney jobs) that is always cited in federal vacancy announcements next to the job title—is more uniform than the attorney application process. Law-related positions (such as Civil Rights Analyst, series number 0160; Mediator, series number 0241; Equal Opportunity Compliance Specialist, series number 0360; Land Law Examiner, series number 0965; or Contract Administrator, series number 1102) are in what is called the Competitive Service, subject to all civil service rules and regulations. Unlike attorney positions, hiring for Competitive Service positions is fairly inflexible. Agencies must follow the rules, and thus the hiring process is largely uniform across departments and agencies.

However, more uniformity in hiring procedures from one agency and office to another does not change the hiring process appreciably from the standpoint of you, the candidate. The documents you submit for law-related positions should, of course, be as thorough and professional as any you would use to apply for a federal attorney position.

Monitor Major Legislation, Major Regulations, and Government Reorganizations

You will want to keep your eyes peeled and your ears alert to any major legislation coming out of Congress and your state legislature, as well as any government reorganizations. Both often have a profound impact on attorney employment. I call this "Hermann's Corollary to Newton's Third Law of Motion":

> For every government action, there is an at least equal and usually greater private-sector reaction.

Example 1: 9/11. Congress acted quickly to enact legislation with far-reaching legal and law-related hiring implications that often went far beyond the obvious in creating job opportunities for lawyers in both the public sector (at every governmental level) and the private sector:

- The *USA PATRIOT Act,* Pub. L. 107-56, imposed new regulatory compliance requirements on insurance companies and other financial services firms that were previously exempt. These mandates stimulated attorney hiring for both in-house counsel and compliance positions.
- The *Aviation and Transportation Security Act,* Pub. L. 107-71, created the new Transportation Security Administration (TSA), a far-reaching new bureaucracy that has 40,000-plus employees, including several hundred attorneys, throughout the country. TSA activities, primarily in the employment and procurement arenas, generated some private-sector attorney hiring.
- The *Public Health Security and Bioterrorism Preparedness and Response Act*, Pub. L. 107-188, which imposes a host of new duties on "first responders," prompted many such entities at the state and local level to hire attorneys and seek outside counsel.

- The *Department of Homeland Security Act*, Pub. L. 107-296, created the largest new federal agency in over 50 years, transferred 22 existing agencies into the new department, and established several new legal offices within the department, not to mention around $40 billion per year in contracting authority, generating a host of legal matters for private-sector attorneys, both in-house and in law firms.

Example 2: Enron and Related Corporate Scandals. Congress also acted rapidly in response to the corporate accounting and reporting scandals of 2001–2002. As discussed, the Sarbanes-Oxley Act has vast implications for publicly traded corporations, accounting and auditing firms, attorney regulation, securities brokers and dealers, and a number of other professional groups and their regulators, as well as the Securities and Exchange Commission, the Department of Justice, the U.S. Sentencing Commission, the Department of Labor, the Pension Benefit Guaranty Corporation, and self-regulatory organizations such as the Financial Industry Regulatory Authority, a new Public Company Accounting Oversight Board, stock exchanges, etc. This sweeping law also generated hundreds of new public-sector opportunities for attorneys, many in regulatory capacities, as well as thousands of private-sector opportunities in mainstream legal venues and in compliance and risk management.

Political Appointments at the Lower Levels

One of the most well-hidden legal job markets is the spate of positions available to lower-level political appointees in the federal executive branch, including entry-level attorneys. This is in addition to the vast amount of hiring that goes on continuously for regular federal attorney and law-related positions. More than 2,500 lower-level political appointments fall under this appointing authority. They are known in "governmentese" as "Schedule C" positions.

The turnover rate in Schedule C positions is significantly higher than in non-political federal attorney jobs. That means that there are always quite a few available at any given time, not only when there is a change of administration. In addition, agency and divisional heads frequently create new Schedule C positions. Schedule

Cs are automatically revoked when an incumbent leaves a position; so technically, there is no such thing as a "vacant" Schedule C position.

There are no real threshold requirements to qualify for a Schedule C position. Unless imposed by the hiring official (almost always a political appointee), you do not have to be a graduate of an ABA-accredited law school or sometimes even a bar member. Schedule C positions also differ from regular attorney and competitive civil service jobs because of their *"confidential or policy-determining* character," a term of art that is a euphemism for a political appointment. For this reason, federal agencies may fill Schedule C positions *noncompetitively*. Since they are political appointments, Schedule C positions are usually filled on an other-than-merit basis—meaning that you have to know somebody. This does not necessarily mean the president, his close advisors, or a member of Congress. Intermediaries/promoters can be almost anyone who knows someone in the administration or on Capitol Hill. A decision to place a position in Schedule C is made by the Director, U.S. Office of Personnel Management (OPM), upon agency request. Requests can be made on a single sheet of paper and are almost never denied.

Most such positions are at grades 13, 14, and 15 of the Federal General Schedule ($70,000–$127,000 in 2009, plus "locality pay"). However, there are also quite a few each year at the GS-9 and GS-11 levels, the typical attorney entry levels ($41,000–$64,000 in 2009, plus locality pay).

The *Federal Register* publishes a list of new Schedule C positions, usually (but not always) on the fourth Tuesday of each month (*www.gpoaccess.gov/fr/index.html*).

Hidden Jobs in the Legislative Branch

There are thousands of hidden legal and law-related jobs in federal, state, and local legislative branches and their support agencies. The federal legislative branch legal opportunities include:

- Attorneys—with the job title "attorney"—serve on 206 congressional committee and subcommittee staffs (512 total majority and minority committee staffs).

- Attorneys serve on 538 personal office staffs of members of Congress.
- More than 2,500 legislative assistants and legislative directors serve on Congress members' staffs, and a large number are attorneys.
- Several hundred attorneys work for legislative branch agencies, support organizations, and caucuses (in both attorney and law-related positions). Five legislative branch agencies with 22 separate offices employ attorneys:
  - Library of Congress
  - Government Accountability Office
  - Government Printing Office
  - Architect of the Capitol
  - Congressional Budget Office
- Nine congressional support offices have attorneys on their staffs:
  - Office of Compliance
  - Senate Office of Legal Counsel
  - Senate Office of Legislative Counsel
  - Office of the Secretary of the Senate
  - House Office of General Counsel
  - House Office of the Legislative Counsel
  - House Office of the Chief Administrative Officer
  - House Office of the Law Revision Counsel
  - Office of House Employment Counsel
- Two-hundred and eleven congressional caucuses may have attorneys on staff. Caucuses are groups of members of Congress that pursue common legislative objectives. They are formally organized as Congressional Member Organizations, governed under the rules of the U.S. House of Representatives. They are not always called caucuses— coalitions, study groups, task forces, and working groups are other names for caucuses. Examples: Afterschool Caucus, Blue Dog Coalition, Congressional Caucus on Hellenic Issues, etc. The number of caucuses can vary and is almost never static. New ones arrive and old ones leave the scene all the time.

Federal Courts

Hundreds of permanent staff attorneys work for the federal courts, including the Supreme Court, circuit courts of appeals, U.S. district courts, and U.S. bankruptcy courts; Article I courts, such as the U.S. Tax Court, U.S. Court of International Trade, U.S. Court of Appeals for the Armed Forces, U.S. Court of Veterans Appeals, U.S. Court of Federal Claims, U.S. Court of Appeals for the Federal Circuit, District of Columbia Court of Appeals, Superior Court of the District of Columbia, and U.S. territorial courts; and court support organizations, such as the Administrative Office of the U.S. Courts, Federal Judicial Center, Judicial Panel on Multidistrict Litigation, U.S. Sentencing Commission, and federal defender organizations nationwide.

Positions with Article III courts, federal defender organizations, the Administrative Office of the U.S. Courts, and the Federal Judicial Center are often advertised on *www.uscourts.gov,* as well as on individual court Web sites. Article I court positions are generally advertised on *www.usajobs.com, www.attorneyjobs.com*, and on individual court Web sites.

State and Local Government

Executive Branch

Attorneys tend to view state and local government legal hiring with tunnel vision: They often look for legal employment at the state attorney general's office, period. If they seek a municipal job, their examination will often be limited to the local prosecutor's office, the corporation counsel's office, and, if the municipality has one, the public defender's office. This narrow search methodology is a big mistake.

While some states have a highly centralized legal structure, with virtually all of the state's attorneys working for the attorney general, that is not always the case. Many states employ attorneys in numerous departments and agencies other than the attorney general's office. To cite just one example, Arizona's attorney general's office provides legal advice to all state agencies *except those specifically exempted by statute*. The 10 exempt agencies include:

- Director of Water Resources
- Residential Utility Consumer Office
- Industrial Commission
- Arizona Board of Regents
- Auditor General
- Corporation Commissioners and Corporation Commission (other than the Securities Division)
- Advocate for Private Property Rights
- Office of the Governor
- Constitutional Defense Council
- Department of Public Safety

These exempt agencies are authorized to hire their own attorneys directly. They also hire attorneys under other job titles, e.g., research analyst and intelligence analyst.

Most state and local governments maintain generic job Web sites where they list all of the positions available in their jurisdictions. Variations on this standard model, however, are legion. It is always advisable, therefore, to look at all of the possible Web sites where jobs might be listed. For a state government, for example, that could include the general state government Web site, the Office of the Attorney General, specific state agencies, and the state civil service Web site, if any.

State Legislatures

Most large states have full-time legislatures and large staffs. The following states fall generally into this category: California, Michigan, New York, Pennsylvania, Illinois, Florida, Ohio, Massachusetts, New Jersey, and Wisconsin. The average legislator in these states has nine staff members on his or her personal staff. Many staffers are attorneys.

State legislatures also employ attorneys in other positions generally comparable to those at the federal level. The New York State Legislature, for example, has more than 100 committees and subcommittees, 13 legislative commissions, and 17 task forces and other entities. State legislators also often have district offices.

In addition, almost every state legislature has the following offices in which lawyers work:

- Legislative Reference Bureau or Legislative Council
- Counsel's Office (one for each house in bicameral legislatures)
- Bill Drafting Office (a.k.a. Revisor of Statutes)

Note: Organizational names are not uniform from legislature to legislature.

The National Conference of State Legislatures (*www.ncsl.org*) hosts a jobs clearinghouse on its Web site. However, it relies on submissions from states, and they never submit many of their positions. For more complete jobs information, you need to visit the state legislative Web sites in the states in which you are interested.

State Courts

Like the federal courts, many state courts have staff attorney offices at the highest level and the intermediate appellate courts, as well as some local courts, particularly in the larger jurisdictions.

The only central repository of state and local court job opportunities is maintained by the National Center for State Courts (*www.ncsconline.org*) and is very limited in terms of the number of listed positions. You also need to visit the specific state court Web sites for the courts in which you are interested in order to identify job opportunities.

Other State and Local Government Hidden Legal Jobs

Additional law-related positions also exist in state and local government—some in positions that share similarity with their federal counterparts, but some that are quite different:

- *State and local economic development agencies* focus a lot of attention and resources on attracting businesses to relocate or establish new facilities in their locales. These prominent entities—which are often both physically and functionally close to the governor's or mayor's office—are staffed by bright individuals from various disciplines, including lawyers. These lawyers lobby legislators and regulators, prepare legislation and regulations, devise and explain intricate tax and regulatory concessions, and negotiate and document complex transactions with the legal representatives of target businesses.

- A number of states have established *patient rights* bureaucracies at the state, local, and healthcare provider levels. Patient rights advocates protect the legal rights of patients in hospitals, nursing homes, and other healthcare facilities, including representing them before administrative forums.

Predicting the Near-Term Government Future

The U.S. government publishes a veritable ocean of information about its intentions, often including its intentions with respect to hiring in general, and occasionally the hiring of attorneys and law-related positions in particular. Two documents, mandated by the Government Performance and Results Act of 1993, Pub. L. 103-62, generally available on department and agency Web sites, are sometimes valuable sources of this kind of information:

- *Strategic Plans*—A "road map" for agencies to meet their goals and fulfill their missions. Plans include measurable long-term goals for the organization over at least five years and are revised at least every three years.
- *Annual Performance Plans* are required by Congress from each agency with budget requests. Plans include measurable annual performance goals linked to longer-term goals in the Strategic Plan. While the amount of detail can vary, some plans include individual plans for each organizational unit, including legal offices.
- Department and agency *budget documents*. Information about hiring plans, if it exists, is usually found in the budget appendices rather than in the budget documents themselves. Some federal organizations provide detail down to specific hiring plans for lawyers. Budget appendices can be found on the Office of Management and Budget Web site (*www.whitehouse.gov/omb/*) and sometimes on agency Web sites.

Government Contracting and Subcontracting

Federal Government

Each year, the U.S. government contracts for goods and services with more than 200,000 companies and nonprofits. A number of these contracts are for legal or law-related services and training, or have a legal services component. In addition, certain contracts lend themselves to, or require, subcontracting for legal services.

Legal services contracts include recurring requirements such as:

- Debt collection
- Real estate closings and foreclosures
- Legal research and writing, including drafting administrative decisions
- Legal consulting in specialty areas
- Advice and assistance to foreign governments and non-governmental organizations in developing countries and emerging democracies and market economies.

Certain agencies do more legal services contracting than others, such as the departments of Justice, Housing and Urban Development, Labor, Treasury, Agriculture, and Commerce, the Equal Employment Opportunity Commission, and the U.S. Agency for International Development. Lists of prime contractors are matters of public record, and some agencies and offices (but by no means all of them) make these available on their Web sites.

You can receive notice of U.S. government contracts at *www.fedbizopps.gov*. In addition, if you have an interest in government legal services contracting, you should register with the government's Central Contractor Registration (*www.ccr.gov*). In addition, prospective contractors should communicate directly with each agency of interest's procurement office and Small and Disadvantaged Business Utilization Office, which can be reached via each agency's Web site.

State and Local Governments

State and local governments also do a good deal of legal services contracting. In fact, several states do more outsourcing of legal services than the federal government and across a wider range of practice areas. This is principally due to the fact that they have to operate under far more stringent budgetary constraints than the U.S. government.

Requests for proposals (RFPs) and invitations for bid (IFBs) can be found on state, county, and city procurement Web sites. There is no uniformity in the way this information is published or in state contracting procedures. The states that tend to contract most often and most widely for outside legal services are California, Massachusetts, Illinois, Hawaii, Texas, and Colorado.

As society grows more complex, technology ramps up the pace of change, and as the core tensions that gave rise to the founding of the United States—balancing the relationships (1) among the three branches of government, upon which the United States was founded, (2) between the central government and its constituent states, (3) between the government and its individual citizens, and (4) between the United States and foreign nations—also become more complex, hidden legal jobs proliferate in government at all levels.

Chapter 12

The Hidden Legal Job Market: Nonprofits

"Nonprofit" is a very broad term that encompasses both a wide variety of organizational types and a multitude of organizations. The nonprofit sector has, for years, grown faster than the U.S. business sector or government. Approximately 1.5 million nonprofits are registered with the Internal Revenue Service (IRS), with the largest numbers categorized as charitable/religious, social welfare, labor/agricultural, business leagues, social/recreational clubs, benevolent life insurance associations, credit unions, and veterans' organizations. In addition, there are also academic institutions, legal services organizations, foundations, healthcare provider organizations, non-governmental organizations, and museums that employ attorneys in a variety of different capacities. There are more than 440,000 other nonprofits—chambers of commerce, fraternal organizations, and civic leagues—also registered with the IRS. These numbers do not include the more than 377,000 U.S. religious congregations. The number of nonprofits has grown by more than one-third in the last decade. The number of hidden legal jobs in nonprofits has grown even more.

From an attorney's perspective, the most important feature of nonprofit organizations is that they are corporations; consequently, they share many structural and organizational features with their for-profit counterparts. Lawyers who work in the in-house counsel offices of nonprofits have many of the same responsibilities as their for-profit counterparts, the most obvious exceptions being securities practice and mergers and acquisitions. Nonprofits have to confront many of the same issues that impact for-profit companies and, thus, structure their "hidden" legal functions in much the same way. Nonprofit attorneys can also be found outside in-house counsel offices in such areas as compliance, ethics, risk management, government affairs, and occasionally even tax. The 2009 change in the IRS Form 990 filing requirements has compelled an increasing number of nonprofits to set up separate tax departments, in addition to the existing ones in nonprofits that engage in certain for-profit activities.

Most hidden attorney and law-related jobs in nonprofits are found in the following types of organizations:

- trade and professional associations
- academic institutions
- healthcare providers
- public interest organizations
- non-governmental organizations
- foundations and charitable organizations

Trade and Professional Associations

A trade association is an organization comprised of businesses within the same industry, which provides professional development, represents the industry to government and the public, and monitors legislation and regulations that could impact the industry. A professional association performs the same functions, but for a group of professionals in the same profession.

There are more than 35,000 trade and professional associations in the United States. They are concentrated in the larger cities, especially seats of government and major business centers. The Washington, D.C. area is home to by far the most associations—approximately

11,000. New York, Chicago, and Los Angeles are the other largest association centers. The remainder are largely concentrated in state capitals, with most found in Sacramento, Albany, Austin, Tallahassee, Boston, and Columbus. There are even a healthy number in smaller states' capitals, such as Olympia (Wash.), Salem (Ore.), Cheyenne (Wyo.), Montpelier (Vt.), and Pierre (S.D.).

Approximately 10 percent of associations have in-house counsel offices. In contrast, virtually all of them have government affairs (or government relations) offices, the function most central to their mission. Government affairs staffs are responsible for lobbying, monitoring legislative and regulatory initiatives, reporting to their members on these issues, preparing testimony, and testifying before legislative and regulatory bodies. Association government affairs offices are often staffed by lawyers. Overall, many more attorneys work in government affairs for associations than in their general counsel offices.

Attorneys can also be found in professional association ethics offices, in order to provide a central authority where association members can turn for both general and specific ethics advice. Associations such as the American Bar Association, American Medical Association, American Dental Association, American Psychological Association, American Institute of Architects, American Institute of Certified Public Accountants, and the National Association of Realtors have strong ethics staffs.

In addition, a significant percentage of the senior executive positions (chief executive officer, chief operating officer) in associations are held by attorneys.

Academic Institutions

The nation's 4,200 colleges and universities (2,300 are four-year institutions) provide a richly diverse and expanding environment for lawyers, thanks to three parallel trends that have heavily influenced campus legal hiring and staff development over the last 20 years—one teaching trend and two professional administrative staff trends.

Non-traditional Law School Teaching Positions

Traditional law school teaching positions are growing in number, but very slowly. ABA-accredited law schools are a pretty mature industry, and very few additional ones crop up. Law schools that are not ABA-accredited are increasing in number, but most positions are not full-time.

Competition for law school teaching positions is intense. Thousands of highly qualified attorneys with stellar academic and practice backgrounds compete ferociously for the relatively few positions that open up each year. A typical successful competitor's résumé would manifest a top-10 law school, law review, Order of the Coif, a federal appellate judicial clerkship, and perhaps some experience with a large national law firm.

However, because law schools have begun to recognize that they have to offer a more diverse curriculum and better prepare their students for the harsher, more competitive, and more volatile practice world of the twenty-first century, they now pay more attention to basic legal skills (research, analysis, and writing) and also offer more clinics and special programs. Consequently, the growth area in law school teaching jobs is in non-traditional teaching positions. These are often open to individuals possessing other than exclusively "dream" résumés.

Examples of non-traditional teaching positions include:

- academic support instructor
- clinical program director
- clinical program instructor
- staff attorney in a clinical program
- legal research and writing program instructor

Non–Law School Teaching Positions

This is where to find the major growth in law teaching, thanks to the following factors:

- The "formalization" of what used to be called "pre-law" studies into an actual undergraduate major, most commonly called Legal Studies at the several thousand schools that offer this major.

- A strong and growing market for attorneys in other, more traditional undergraduate and graduate departments, such as business, accounting, criminal justice and law enforcement, real estate, insurance, and international affairs, among others.
- The rapid expansion of paralegal certificate programs. There are more than 260 ABA-approved paralegal programs and several hundred additional programs.

The credentials required to teach in these venues are not as rigorous as they are for traditional law school teaching positions. Many professors and instructors come directly from a broad range of practice backgrounds and have varying levels of experience.

Representative Non–Law School Teaching Job Titles
- paralegal program instructor
- business law professor
- criminal justice program instructor
- dispute resolution teacher
- environmental policy teacher
- ethics instructor
- labor relations instructor
- law and anthropology professor
- law and economics professor
- law and history professor
- law and psychology professor
- law and society professor
- law and natural resources professor
- legal administration professor
- legal studies program coordinator
- legal studies program instructor
- real estate instructor
- security assistance management instructor
- tax instructor

Identifying Non-traditional Academic Job Opportunities
Most such teaching positions are publicly announced on school employment Web pages (*www.academic360.com* has links to most such

pages), or in the *Chronicle of Higher Education* (*www.chronicle.com*), as well as on Web sites such as *www.higheredjobs.com*. You could get a leg up on the competition by tracking grants, contracts, and gifts to law schools and other academic department programs with a law orientation. The Foundation Center (*www.fdncenter.org*) monitors the grant-making activities of the thousands of foundations and other charitable organizations in the United States and abroad, including those involving legal and law-related projects, such as grants to law schools and undergraduate institutions for new legal instructional programs, endowed chairs, etc. Here are some examples from a recent *Foundation Center* report:

- An eastern law school—$4 million grant from a charitable trust, to be matched by funding from the university's endowment, to enhance public service and environmental programs and endow two chairs.
- A midwestern university—$5 million gift from an alumnus to endow a new program consisting of an endowed chair and three assistant professorships for the study of law and religion.
- The U.S. Department of Education's Urban Community Service Program—awarded a New England university's Law and Public Policy Institute a multimillion-dollar grant to fund legal services, legal aid functions, and academic studies.

Professional Staff Positions on Campus

The last two decades witnessed an enormous growth in the number of college and university in-house counsel offices and the consequent bringing onto campus of much of the legal work formerly farmed out to law firms. Today, there are very few post-secondary institutions that do not have their own campus legal office.

In a related development, the increasing complexity of campus life and increasing involvement with government and the courts has prompted a second lawyer "explosion" on campuses. Many legal and law-related staff functions that require more specialized attention than they could receive from an in-house counsel office have been separated and put in specialized campus offices. Such activities may include:

- compliance
- equal employment opportunity and affirmative action
- labor relations
- faculty and staff employment matters
- risk management
- intellectual property asset management
- technology licensing
- contract management
- ethics
- academic grievances
- student discipline
- environmental affairs
- legislative and regulatory affairs
- disabled student affairs
- foreign student administration
- campus security (including sexual harassment)
- real estate transactions
- privacy issues (primarily academic and health information)

The selected list of campus issues that follows strikingly demonstrates why there is growing legal presence in academe:

- grade appeals
- disabled students and employees
- affirmative action
- student discipline on and off campus
- operating summer camps on campus
- alcohol and drugs
- union organizing of faculty and graduate teaching assistants
- faculty tenure disputes
- Gramm-Leach-Bliley privacy safeguarding rules
- safety and security searches
- reductions-in-force (faculty and staff)
- HIPAA impact
- copyright issues (library, art museum, publications)
- campus violence
- college athletics and risk management

- Family Educational Rights & Privacy Act, 20 U.S.C. § 1232g & 34 C.F.R. Part 99
- campus security
- sexual harassment (employees and students)
- immigration issues since 9/11
- suicidal students
- study abroad—risk management
- acceptable uses of e-mail and the Internet
- intellectual property in the digital/electronic environment
- Family and Medical Leave Act, Pub. L. 110-181
- distance education
- investigators on campus
- USA PATRIOT Act
- student workers on campus
- Title IX
- transgender student issues

A Cautionary Note about Professional Staff Job Titles

Academic institution staff job titles vary widely from one campus to another. There is probably no other industry where job titles encompassing the same function differ so dramatically. For example, one institution may advertise a "judicial officer" position, the title of which alerts you immediately that this is a legal/law-related position, whereas another institution labels a job with the same or similar description "student affairs coordinator." Consequently, you need to examine the fine print in a campus job posting whenever you suspect that there may be a preference for a law degree.

The Higher Education Opportunity Act of 2008 (Pub. L. 110-315)

This law, which was enacted and signed under the radar in August 2008, is destined to have a profound impact on campus legal hiring. It imposes no fewer than 300 new compliance requirements on colleges and universities. The act, which began being implemented through regulations promulgated in 2009, has already generated a large increase in the number of compliance positions advertised on Web sites such as *www.chronicle.com, www.higheredjobs.com*, and *www.attorneyjobs.com*. While many of these newly created positions are for general compliance professionals, a substantial number are for "specialists" in disability compliance, athletics compliance, academic compliance, and other fields for which a law degree is either preferred or desired.

Healthcare Providers

More than 50 percent of U.S. healthcare provider organizations are nonprofits. Their businesses are becoming much more complicated, thanks to advances in technology and a barrage of legislation and regulation—their environments have become mazes of complexity, confusion, and occasional contradiction (just try to read and understand HIPAA, Stark I, II, or III, or the federal and state Medicaid regulations) demanding the attention of in-house counsel, hospital risk managers, regulatory compliance officers, ethics officers, contract and procurement officers, and patient safety officers, among others.

A very rough rule of thumb is that hospitals with 200 or more beds represent something of a "tipping point" when it comes to legal and law-related staffing. The 1,600-plus 200-bed hospitals in the United States represent a pretty large potential for attorney hiring and for establishing the specialized legal and law-related offices listed in the previous paragraph. One figure that is very interesting is that 25 percent of hospital risk managers have a law degree. Healthcare risk management jobs are advertised on hospital Web sites, as well as job boards maintained by the American Health Lawyers Association (*www.ahla.org*), American Society for Healthcare Risk Management (*www.ashrm.org*), and *www. healthcareernet.com*.

Public Interest and Advocacy Organizations

There are approximately 500 legal aid and legal services organizations, plus federal, state, and local public defender organizations in the United States. Many have legal researcher positions in addition to their mainstream attorney positions. Other public interest and advocacy organizations also have a substantial number of law-related positions that are frequently occupied by attorneys. Land trusts are an excellent example of such organizations. A land trust is a nonprofit organization that, as all or part of its mission, works to conserve land by undertaking or assisting in land or conservation easement acquisition, or by its stewardship of such land or easements. Land trusts work with landowners who are interested in protecting open space, and sometimes in cooperation with government agencies.

Land trusts solicit donations of land, conservation easements, or money to purchase land from individual, corporate, community, and government donors. There are 1,600 U.S. land trusts, and they can be found in every state. The best-known land trusts are the ones that are national in scope and have a number of regional and local offices, such as the Nature Conservancy, the Trust for Public Land, the American Farmland Trust, the American Land Conservancy, The Conservation Fund, The Great Outdoors Conservancy, the Humane Society of the United States Wildlife Land Trust, the National Park Trust, the Audubon Society, and the Wilderness Land Trust.

Examples of specific land trust positions appropriate for J.D.s include:

- director of land preservation
- director of project review
- executive director
- land conservation coordinator
- acquisition manager
- land steward

For excellent information about land trusts, go to the Land Trust Alliance (*www.landtrustalliance.org*).

Non-governmental Organizations (NGOs)

An NGO is a nonprofit corporation that operates development programs. Many NGOs have social objectives, while others serve particular constituencies. NGO activities range from research, information distribution, training, local organization, and community service to legal advocacy, lobbying for legislative change, and even civil disobedience. NGOs range in size from small community groups to huge organizations with national or international memberships. Most NGOs that work in the legal arena do so internationally, often under contract to the U.S. Agency for International Development (USAID), the World Bank, or another multilateral or government agency.

Since the collapse of the Soviet Union and the emergence of new democracies and market economies, there has been a surge in the number of U.S. NGOs that provide "rule-of-law" advice and counseling, as well as in the number of organizational and personal service contracts seeking this kind of expertise. These new nations still need a great deal of legal and law-related assistance in order to establish stable statutory, regulatory, and institutional bases, and they turn to U.S. organizations to provide it.

Prime contracts for rule-of-law projects often generate subcontracts for specific legal and law-related services. Major contracting organizations, such as USAID, periodically publish lists of contracts awarded. In addition, prime contractors often maintain rosters of prospective legal subcontractors to whom they can turn when projects arise. NGOs and contractors such as Chemonics International (*www.chemonics.com*) and the IRIS Center at the University of Maryland (*www.iris.umd.edu*) maintain such lists. In addition, visit the ABA Rule of Law Initiative (*www.abanet.org/rol*), the Carter Center (*www.cartercenter.org*), the Asia Foundation (*www.asiafoundation.org*), as well as the U.S. Commerce Department's Commercial Law Development Program (*www.cldp.doc.gov*) and the U.S. Treasury Department's Office of Technical Assistance (*www.treas.gov/offices/international-affairs/assistance/index.shtml*).

Foundations and Other Charitable Organizations

There are more than 50,000 foundations and charitable organizations in the United States. They operate in every state and in almost every area of human endeavor. You would think that giving away money is easy, but like everything else in this increasingly complicated world, it is not. And, of course, wherever there is complexity, there are lawyers.

Attorneys in foundations and charitable organizations serve in a variety of capacities. The largest organizations have in-house counsel offices, where they perform many of the same functions as their for-profit counterparts. Lawyers also work as grant administrators, compliance officers, and in executive capacities. Foundations that award grants to legal organizations or for legal or law-related projects often employ lawyers to evaluate such grant applications, participate in decisions about awards, administer the grants, and evaluate the success of the grant programs.

For more information, visit the Foundation Center (*www.fdncenter.org*), a national organization that catalogues information about foundations, grants, grantees, IRS filings, and much more.

> The hidden legal job market is vast, far-flung, and expanding all the time. It can and should be a valuable career research option for law students and practitioners. There are a lot of opportunities out there for the individuals willing to go after them. One great advantage of the hidden legal job market is far less competition for the positions.

Chapter 13

The Career Impact of External Phenomena

I cannot remember a single legal career transition counseling client of mine who, when determining whether or not to pursue a job or career opportunity or to accept a job offer, adequately considered the potential impact on his or her career of outside influences that they could not control. Of course, as a responsible legal career counselor, I undertook this component of the requisite due diligence for them.

Declining to consider external factors that may impact a job, a career, a practice area, and/or an employer is a huge mistake. This is one of the most important investigations you can perform, and one that you should undertake for every position you seriously consider. Ignoring this essential consideration can be a career killer.

External Influences

These days and in this economic climate, there are certainly more externalities that can both positively and adversely affect legal careers than ever before. The principal ones are addressed below.

Interest Rate Fluctuations

Interest rates have an enormous influence on job availability and job security. When interest rates rise, for example, anything associated with the real estate industry suffers. When interest rates decline, the real estate industry does better. Similarly, any employer that must rely on outside financing—and that means virtually every employer—is almost guaranteed to do less hiring when rates rise than when rates fall.

Of course, when the entire economy is in a deep recession, the hiring effect of interest rate fluctuations is muted by the general economic malaise. In other words, in times like the Great Recession (when interest rates are at or near historic lows), attorneys and others lose their jobs regardless of interest rates. But the potential impact on your job and career does not disappear.

If you work in a practice area where either your clients, your practice area, or your employer is likely to be affected significantly by interest rate fluctuations (such as construction, manufacturing, commercial finance, securitization, etc.), consider very carefully if you want to be hostage to their rise or fall.

Energy Costs

When the price of a barrel of Saudi Arabian light crude oil goes up, some industries prosper—namely the energy sector—while others, such as airlines, become strained. When energy prices decline, energy-intensive industries such as airlines and utilities do well.

Companies are not the only organizations affected by rising or falling energy costs. When oil prices rise, energy trade associations hire more staff; when prices decline, they lay people off. Government also feels the impact. The U.S. Department of Energy was established as a consequence of the first oil shock of 1973–74, and it revved up its legal staff again following the second oil shock of 1979. Now, prompted by this third and most profound long-term oil shock and the consensus policy shift toward energy independence, the department's 36 law and law-related offices are staffing up once more.

The Energy Department is not the only federal agency that is increasing the size of its legal staff due to energy costs. Increased attention to energy independence is also prompting more hiring at law offices in the Interior Department, Justice Department, Environmental Protection Agency, and Nuclear Regulatory Commission, for example. In the private sector, alternative energy industries including wind, solar, wave, biomass, and others are also beefing up their legal staffs.

Industry Reorganizations and Area Changes

The petroleum industry is a great example of one that has turned inside out in only the last several years. For most of the twentieth century, "Big Oil" meant the "Seven Sisters" companies—Exxon, Mobil, Chevron, Texaco, BP, Royal Dutch Shell, and Gulf. Not anymore. The new Seven Sisters are the huge, state-owned national oil and gas giants—Saudi Aramco, JSC Gazprom of Russia, China National Petroleum Company, National Iranian Oil Company, Petroleos de Venezuela, Petrobras of Brazil, and Petronas of Malaysia.

The implications of this oil industry upheaval for attorney careers are substantial. The new Seven Sisters now own over two-thirds of the world's oil reserves and climbing, while the private oil companies' reserves are rapidly declining. The legal job impact across the entire fossil-fuel energy industry in the United States will be profound. As companies become smaller, they will need fewer attorneys. There will be a "trickle-over" impact on refining companies, oil service firms, and energy supply companies, as well as on the hundreds of law firms that serve the oil industry. Attorneys contemplating a long career within the industry and its collateral firms may want to have a fall-back plan.

Legislative or Regulatory "Threats"

Congress, state legislatures, and federal and state chief executives can give a tremendous boost—as well as do a lot of damage—to a legal career. They have the power to create, and also eliminate, whole departments and agencies with the stroke of a pen, and have done so on numerous occasions. For example, the following U.S. government agencies disappeared overnight at the end of 1995: the Resolution Trust Corporation, the agency set up to resolve the savings and loan collapse, and its 400 attorneys; the Administrative

Conference of the United States, the agency that studied and recommended improvements to the administrative hearing process and procedures; the Office of Technology Assessment, the congressional "think tank" and futures organization; and the 108-year old Interstate Commerce Commission (ICC).

Legal career damage can go far beyond the public sector. Legislative and regulatory actions can also have a major effect on private industry. Congress's elimination of the ICC had a devastating impact on, among others, attorneys representing the trucking, railroad, bus travel, water carrier, freight forwarding, pipeline, and other associated industries. Deregulation became popular in the late 1970s and lasted for a generation. Loosening of regulatory restraints on the airline industry, telecommunications, and the financial sector, among others, cost thousands of attorneys their jobs. A simple adjustment in the amount of money that one generation could pass, estate tax–free, to the next has had a profound effect on trust and estate lawyers.

You need to do enough "trends analysis" to protect yourself to the extent possible against these potentially career-killing legislative and regulatory actions. That means keeping up with the news and current events in general while drilling deeper through attention to trade publications and Web sites that monitor policy shifts and directions.

Other Government Actions

Legislative and regulatory developments are by no means the only way that government affects legal employment. Policy shifts, agency program initiatives and non-regulatory actions, executive orders, and court and administrative decisions can all have a major impact on job opportunities. For example:

- The American Recovery and Reinvestment Act of 2009, Pub. L. 111-5 (a.k.a. the Stimulus Bill), allocated $11 billion to the U.S. Department of Energy for grants to companies engaged in an array of energy independence projects, including advanced water power technologies, solar cell development and extensive wind energy construction projects, among others. This creates several hundred new attorney positions at the federal and state government levels, in energy company in-house counsel offices, and in law firms that serve these industries.

- The Pentagon abandons a weapons system and thousands of defense workers lose their jobs, in addition to the collateral businesses and individuals who provided goods and services to the defense contractors.
- The Commerce and State Departments impose export controls on sensitive technologies and cause entire businesses that relied on these exports to disappear.
- The state environmental department bans strip mining, throwing an entire industry sector out of business.
- The local taxicab commission votes to permit anyone to apply for a hack license, thereby opening up a formerly restricted secondary market and putting attorneys who specialize in the transfer and sale of hack licenses on the streets.

The lesson here is that you have to be tuned in to the possibility that either good fortune or calamity may befall the industry or organization for which you want to work. That means you have to keep your fingers on the pulse of what is going on in Washington, D.C., the various state capitals, and even municipal government agencies.

Court decisions have also had a major impact on legal employment. When the Americans with Disabilities Act of 1990, 42 U.S.C. §§ 12101 et seq. (ADA) became law, a host of major law firms launched ADA practices, only to see them decline and ultimately disappear, thanks to a series of court decisions that stripped away much of the act's enforcement authorities.

Global Politics

The world has become a much smaller place, thanks to transportation and communication technology breakthroughs and the impact of the information revolution. This means that your analysis of external factors that may affect your legal career cannot stop at the U.S. border.

- The end of the Cold War prompted the demise of numerous industries and employers that made their living out of East-West tensions, ranging from arms dealers to think tanks devoted to studying and analyzing the Soviet Union to U.S. lawyers who, for 50 years, had made a comfortable living as expatriates in Europe representing the hundreds of thousands of U.S. troops charged with offenses under the Uniform Code of Military Justice.

- While the end of the Cold War generated a once-in-a-half-century sea change in a large number of business and industry sectors, global politics cause positive and negative effects on jobs all the time. For instance, whenever a country nationalizes an industry consisting of U.S. participants, U.S. workers suffer. The U.S. government is so cognizant of these regular adverse developments that it even has established a federal agency to provide "political risk insurance" to companies whose foreign investments are nationalized: the Overseas Private Investment Corporation. Political risk insurance, however, does very little to alleviate job loss.

- Even negative international happenings can generate positive opportunities for lawyers. The 9/11 terrorist attacks on the United States prompted the enactment of a series of complex new laws and regulations that required thousands of private- and public-sector organizations to turn to attorneys for counseling and interpretation, including the USA PATRIOT Act, Pub. L. 107-56; the Public Health, Safety and Bioterrorism Preparedness and Response Act of 2001, Pub. L. 107-188; and the Aviation and Transportation Security Act, Pub. L. 107-71, among others. Three major new federal government agencies were created—the Department of Homeland Security, which, in addition to absorbing 22 existing federal agencies and their legal offices, established five new legal and quasi-legal offices; the Transportation Security Administration, with 38 new chief counsel and regional counsel offices throughout the country; and the Office of the Director of National Intelligence and its Office of General Counsel.

The 9/11 legislative response generated a tremendous amount of "churn" in the private sector as well, as major law firms established Homeland Security Law practices and corporations hired attorneys to advise and assist with the impact of the new laws on corporate activities.

- Actions that emanate from London, Brussels, Geneva, Tokyo, Shanghai, and Moscow also affect U.S. legal employment. For instance, the advent of the European Union, the emergence of new democracies and market economies around the world, the extensive increase in trade between the United States and China, etc., have all created new legal jobs in the United States.

The significance of international developments for your career is only going to increase. That means that you have to be on top of these phenomena and develop your own "early warning" system. Reading English-language Web site information posted by the foreign press is one way to do this. There are also a number of Web sites that offer English translations of foreign newspapers and magazines (see, e.g., *www.worldpress.org*). Subscribing to *The Economist* and periodic visits to *www.economist.com* is a very effective way to keep in touch with foreign developments. I also recommend bookmarking *www.reuters.com*, which does a serviceable job of covering the globe.

Technological "Paradigm Shifts"

"May you live in interesting times," says the ancient Chinese curse. We surely do. And technological change has a great deal to do with it.

One of the surest of sure things is the march of progress and the corresponding inevitability of technological change and its economic disruptions. The emergence of the railroads in the mid–nineteenth century caused the transport of goods by canal to dry up. The advent of the automobile devastated the blacksmith industry. In our own time, the rise of the personal computer and the availability of tremendous and inexpensive computing power to virtually anyone has had a massive impact on almost every aspect of work and every industry. The proliferation of the cell phone and disappearance of hard-wired telephones, pay phones, and telephone booths; the rise of the Internet, online advertising, and the consequent decline of newspapers; e-mail and its impact on communicating; blogs; social networking sites; hundreds of cable channels; real-time news—all of these technological innovations have created whole new practice areas for attorneys while diminishing others.

In healthcare, to cite just one industry, telemedicine, e-prescribing, new medical devices, the combining of medical devices with biologics and other drug therapies, nanotechnological applications, and many other technological breakthroughs have prompted a sea change in health law practice, creating new and exciting opportunities for lawyers.

In addition to being attuned to technology shifts that might advance or stymie your legal career, you also have to be sensitive to the accelerating pace of technological change as new technologies proliferate and serve as platforms for additional innovation. Paradigm shifts in technology are coming at us constantly. You need to be aware of them if you are to secure your career, and to take advantage of the opportunities they present. Some of the most informative sources of information about new technologies and their industry and employment implications include MIT's *Technology Review* (*www.technologyreview.com*), *Scientific American* magazine (*www.scientificamerican.com*), and a Web site that attempts to predict the timing of new technologies coming online, *www.techcast.org*.

Invention and Innovation

When Drs. Salk and Sabin developed a vaccine in the 1950s that successfully liberated entire generations of children from the terrible and terrifying scourge of polio, the March of Dimes, one of the most prominent and successful charitable organizations of all time, with a legal staff to match, barely survived, having to change its focus overnight and find a new disease to fight (it selected birth defects). While it managed to continue forward, it became a pale shadow of the fundraising juggernaut it had been.

On the plus side, inventions and innovative processes are huge creators of attorney jobs and careers. Intermodal containerized shipping, for example, where standard containers can be loaded without opening them onto ships, railcars, trucks, and airplanes, generated an array of novel legal issues bearing upon transportation, risk of loss, and related matters, some of which are still being sorted through today, 50 years after the invention of the standard shipping container.

Many current areas of cutting-edge innovation are likely to produce legal job opportunities. Examples include nanotechnology, combination medical devices and biologics, maglev (magnetic levitation) transportation projects, ceramic materials development, and the many green technologies prompted by the drive for energy independence.

There are some rather creative ways to track innovation and invention. One obvious resource is the U.S. Patent and Trademark Office, which maintains a public Web site that lists patent filings. Similar information about filings by organizations outside the United States can be viewed at the World Intellectual Property Organization's Web site (*www.wipo.int*). The National Aeronautics and Space Administration (*www.nasa.gov*) publishes a great deal of information about space program innovations that are being commercialized. The National Technology Transfer Center at Wheeling Jesuit University (*www.nttc.edu*) also publicizes information about innovation available for commercial exploitation. One of the most innovative ways to obtain advance notice of innovation is to monitor federal Requests for Proposal and "Sources Sought" announcements on *www.fedbizopps.gov*.

Mergers and Acquisitions

When Carborundum Corporation was acquired by Kennecott Copper in 1977, the Carborundum attorneys lost their jobs. The same thing happened to Kennecott's attorneys when the company was taken over by Sohio in 1981. Eight years later, it was the Sohio attorneys' turn to walk out the door when British Petroleum (BP) acquired Sohio.

This is a classic example of the volatile and uncertain modern business environment. What we have learned in recent years is that no company is too big to be considered takeover-proof. There are many Web sites that track mergers and acquisitions. You can identify them by Googling "mergers and acquisitions," "M & A," and "takeovers."

Resource Shortages

The Arab and Iranian oil embargoes of 1973–74 and 1979, respectively, resulted in a great many oil and gas industry jobs disappearing, including not only jobs that were directly affected, but also "collateral" positions in support industries, such as the financial services institutions that lent to the energy companies. Consequently, thousands of professionals and blue-collar workers lost their jobs, thanks to the Middle East turning off the oil spigot.

Commodity price volatility is increasing, and there does not seem to be much that the existing regulatory mechanisms can do about it. The current frustrations of the U.S. Commodity Futures Trading Commission are witness to that futility. The situation is destined to get worse now that financial firms are increasingly able to manipulate global commodity prices and influence supply.

Globalization and Legal Process Outsourcing

The globalization phenomenon still has a long way to run before it plays itself out and stabilizes (assuming that, at some point, it will). However, the profound impacts of globalization are already making themselves felt in the legal employment economy.

- U.S. manufacturers have moved their plants offshore for years now in search of lower labor costs. Most of us have experienced dealing with call centers in Bangalore and Mumbai when we have a computer problem. That costs jobs in the United States. Offshore outsourcing has now trickled over into professional services.
- The major legal research companies increasingly outsource their legal research requirements to Indian attorneys located on the subcontinent, the premise being that India is also a Common Law country. That means fewer research positions for U.S. attorneys.

- A presentation at a June 2009 conference at Georgetown Law Center asserted that law firms and corporations are also outsourcing legal research, as well as contract, memo, and brief drafting, and the preparation of patent applications. The presenters predicted that legal process outsourcing could be a $640 million business by the end of 2010.
- Outsourcing in the future will not be limited to litigation, contracts, and intellectual property. Look for certain aspects of due diligence to be outsourced.
- There are more than 150 firms in India and the Philippines alone that now offer legal outsourcing services at a fraction of the cost of hiring U.S. lawyers to perform these functions onshore.

If you contemplate employment with an organization for which you would perform legal tasks that could potentially be performed offshore, you should at least go into that position with your eyes open and a fallback plan in place.

Dollar Depreciation

Currency movements can have a sudden effect on jobs. The Euro's sharp rise against the U.S. dollar in the first years of the twenty-first century was a bonanza for U.S. exporters and retailers. American goods became cheaper than their European competitors, causing U.S. companies trading internationally to reap strong profits, while U.S. retailers saw an influx of European shoppers. Companies that do a large business abroad saw their earnings increase.

A chronically cheaper dollar may ultimately compel the oil-producing countries to denominate oil in currencies other than the dollar, since sticking with the dollar causes them to lose revenue. This and similar kinds of policy changes will put an added strain on the U.S. economy, causing a rise in interest rates and an increase in inflation, among other difficulties, and have a negative impact on employment. A depreciating dollar also makes U.S. companies more attractive acquisition targets.

Bursting Bubbles

Whether it be dot.coms or housing prices, when "irrational exuber-ance" peaks and bubbles inevitably pop, jobs are lost in droves. The Bureau of Labor Statistics reports that more than 9 million Ameri-cans lost their jobs between the beginning of the Great Recession in December 2007 and December 2009. However, job loss was not confined to the United States. Global interdependence meant that the effects of the housing market collapse and the resulting credit freeze caused tens of millions of jobs to disappear around the globe—yet another example of some of the more negative effects of glo-balization.

Forget about the "end of history" and the facile prognosticators who proclaimed a new economics. Bubbles *always* burst. Take great care to make sure you are not sitting on top of one as it expands beyond sustainability.

Unfortunate Coincidences

Some readers may remember being inundated with television ads for a breath mint called "AIDS." AIDS was, by far, the best-selling bad-breath product on the market and one of the most successful consumer products extant—until the early 1980s, when Acquired Immune Deficiency Syndrome was labeled "AIDS" for short.

AIDS, the breath mint, could not survive the misfortune of its name and quickly disappeared from grocery and drugstore shelves. Its personnel infrastructure followed shortly behind.

Unlike almost every other external influence on your legal ca-reer, it is extremely difficult to see these kinds of coincidences com-ing. The best you can do in any job is to keep your résumé, references, and networking contacts updated at all times so that you can be prepared to hit the ground running if necessary.

Professional Personnel Shortages

America has always been a beacon for ambitious foreign profes-sionals seeking more opportunity and a better life. That is evolving, however, into something ominous for a number of U.S. industries and employers. Increasingly, foreign professionals are staying home as their home country economies grow and provide more local opportunities, and those who come to the United States to study often now return home after they are awarded their degrees.

If U.S. hospitals, for example, experience doctor shortages, eventually they have to cut back or even close their doors. When they do, their employees—administrators, nurses, risk managers, accountants, attorneys, compliance professionals, ethicists, contract and procurement officers, etc.—lose their jobs.

Interconnections

Before closing this chapter, we need to touch upon the fact that there is rarely just one factor that threatens job security. As the world becomes more intertwined and complex, the number of factors that play off each other grows. Consequently, when planning your career and job moves, you need to take interrelated phenomena into account.

For example, rising oil prices will affect not only the energy industry but also the housing industry, because commuting from the suburbs to the city becomes very expensive. The decline of the dollar affects international trade and investment, the trade deficit, the level of borrowing by the federal government, and much more. Legislative action on climate change may dramatically alter the prospects of many industries as well as their legal representatives inside and outside of companies. Deeper analysis will show that climate change legislation will have a considerable impact on energy prices, which in turn could reengineer people's daily lives and habits. You need to determine how such interconnections can advance or jeopardize your career.

> This chapter is all about things—both good and bad (primarily bad)—that can happen to you that are out of your control. In an interdependent world where an insignificant occurrence thousands of miles away can have an impact on your job and career, you simply cannot ignore the necessity of factoring such issues into your career planning.

Chapter 14

Thinking a Few Moves Ahead

Legal job searches and career changes need to be approached as if you were a chess grandmaster. These fiercely competitive individuals do not move a chess board figure without considering all of the implications of the move and all of the possible moves they could make in countering their opponent's next move. You need to apply this same strategy to your legal career path.

You want to avoid getting stuck in a dead-end position, practice area, organization, employment sector, or industry. This is especially important in a volatile economy and uncertain job market, but is no less important in good times as well. Since the only constant in the twenty-first century is change, you need to think *career*, not just job.

Steering Clear of Leaps of Faith

One of my clients was offered a position with a small and fairly obscure U.S. government agency's legal counsel office and presented me with the terms of the offer, requesting my advice about the merits of the position. I warned him that, unless he intended to make this office his career, this might not be the best opportunity for him. He responded, "Look, Mr. Hermann, this is the first job offer I have received after two months of very active job searching. I feel I have to take it. What if nothing else comes along?"

I said that two months was hardly any time at all and that he should be pleased that he had a job offer in hand after such a relatively short time in the job market. I repeated my concern that he ran the risk of being pigeonholed and typecast by future employers if he went into this office with its very narrow, esoteric practice, one that did not offer much in the way of opportunities elsewhere.

Feeling uncertain about his prospects for securing another offer, he went ahead and accepted the position. Four years later, he contacted me and asked me for assistance in finding him another job. He felt that he had learned all that was possible at this agency, was unlikely to receive further promotions because staff turnover was almost nonexistent, and wanted out. He was still unemployed almost a year later, and finally had to settle for a quasi-legal position that represented a significant drop in both compensation and prestige.

The moral of this story is this: You need to perform a careful examination of two things when you are presented with a job offer—the job itself, and its future ramifications.

You need to think in fast-forward when a job offer comes your way, which means thinking a few moves ahead. You must ask yourself these questions:

1.   How is this job going to look on my résumé to future employers?
2.   Will my practice in this job position me for future jobs and career advancement?
3.   What kind of options will I have down the line if I take this job?

The answers to these questions need to be factored into your decision whether to accept or reject a job offer. A hasty acceptance could put you in "career gridlock," a situation that you want to attempt to avoid at all costs.

Transitional Strategies

It may not be possible to segue seamlessly and directly into the job or career of your dreams. I have had numerous clients who wanted to switch careers directly from something in which they had considerable experience and were earning a very nice living and move laterally into something entirely different. This was particularly true of (1) litigators who had reached the point where they felt like they were burned out, and (2) attorneys who had spent their careers up to that point in rather quiet waters—such as tax planning or drafting ERISA documents—and were looking for something a bit more dynamic. It has also been true of lawyers whose practices declined or dried up.

My advice, upon concluding that they would have a difficult time reinventing themselves in a new practice area, was often to think in terms of what they needed to do to position themselves for a successful transition, including thinking about the transition as more than a one-step process. I often recommend that, while taking an intermediate step, clients pursue a credential enhancement to strengthen their competitive case for the eventual move into the dream career.

For example, one of my clients had been a trusts and estates attorney whose practice was severely affected by Congress's increasing the estate tax exemption. He needed to find something else with a more solid future and was intrigued by government contract and procurement law. Government contracting for goods and services was a huge, growing, and far-flung endeavor, with hundreds of thousands of very diverse employers ranging from large law firms to corporations of all sizes to the government itself. Moreover, there were tens of thousands of law-related positions that did not carry the job title "attorney," but required legal knowledge. Government contracting and procurement certainly harbored excellent long-term prospects, given the enduring need of government at all levels to acquire goods and services, ramped up by a whole new set of threats to national and homeland security.

The only problem with his otherwise sophisticated reasoning was that no one was going to hire my client at the compensation level that he was seeking (and needed) without any government contract law experience. Consequently, I suggested that he think about obtaining an LL.M. in government contract law from the only local law school that offered such a program. The school also offered the program in its evening division, thus making it possible for my client to continue working full-time. Unfortunately, two factors made my recommended strategy a non-starter: (1) my client could not afford the LL.M. program price tag, and (2) he was no longer earning enough to continue his solo practice. Another option was required.

My next suggestion was that he look for employment where he might have a competitive edge based on his trusts and estates expertise while simultaneously obtaining a less-expensive government contracting credential. The only thing my client could think of was teaching trusts and estates or estate planning in a law school or other academic institution. I pointed out that such law school teaching positions were extremely rare and very difficult to get, and that teaching non-law graduate or undergraduate students in business, legal studies, accounting programs, etc., is often the province of adjunct professors who are paid very little.

What I suggested instead was a position such as a "planned giving" or "charitable giving" officer in a college, university, hospital, museum, or other development (read: fundraising) office. These positions required strong knowledge of estate planning and trusts and estates law, as well as the ability to work closely with the legal and financial representatives of prospective wealthy donors. While institutions generally preferred candidates with fundraising experience, my client's volunteer activities including serving on boards and committees that raised money for community organizations. Development office positions pay quite well because they are central to the survival of the organization, and successful officers (this is one of those positions where it is easy to measure success) often are eligible for bonuses.

After several months, my client was able to land a job as a planned giving officer with a local university. At the same time, he joined the National Contract Management Association ($65 fee) and enrolled in its online Certified Federal Contracts Manager course ($150 plus $95 examination fee), intending to enroll in its online

Certified Commercial Contracts Manager course ($150 plus $95 examination fee) upon completion of the first course. Both certification programs permitted self-study from home at one's own pace.

My client remained with the university development office for two years. He completed both certifications during that time and also attended several association educational conferences where he both bolstered his knowledge and networked with contract professionals. He then began applying for contracting positions and eventually secured one with the U.S. government as a mid-level contract administrator.

> Attorneys are often tempted to opt for immediate job security over their longer-term career interests. I cannot tell you not to do this, because earning an income and job security are clearly of paramount importance. However, before you make such a decision, be sure that you have considered the key question: "Where do I go after this job?"

Chapter 15

Flying Solo Without Crashing

Deciding to open a solo law practice is a huge decision that should never be taken lightly. The U.S. Department of Labor's Bureau of Labor Statistics (BLS) says that 500,000 attorneys—more than 40 percent of the entire U.S. lawyer population—are in solo practices. What the BLS cannot tell us is how many of those practices thrive and how many survive. My admittedly non-scientific, anecdotal evidence gathered over three decades of legal career counseling tells me that the failure rate is significant.

When I first contemplated launching my business, I attended a U.S. Small Business Administration class, "Starting and Managing a Business." The instructor walked into the classroom and asked for a show of hands: "How many of you want to go into the food business?" My hand was the only one that did not go up. The instructor then pointed at me and said: "You stay. The rest of you should leave right now. I'm doing you a favor."

He went on to point out that going into the food business required more than just a great recipe that your family and friends rave about. You need to understand ordering, spoilage, health department requirements, recruiting, personnel management, inventory management, marketing and sales, publicity, etc.

A similar admonition could just as easily be applied to launching a solo law practice.

Questions You Need to Ask and Answer

The following questions and issues are key to assessing your solo practice inclinations and opportunities and your likelihood of success. All of them may not be readily answerable, depending on your own unique characteristics, motivations, and attitudes. However, you should try to answer as many of them as you can, and be as objective about your answers as possible.

What Are My Goals and Objectives?

This is perhaps the most important threshold question. Why do you want to go solo? What do you want this practice to become? Where do you see yourself in five years?

Every business needs benchmarks, or measuring sticks. These should not be mere general statements, such as "I want to be successful and have a profitable practice." That is not good enough. *You need to document specific measurable objectives that you can compare your performance to at stated intervals.* If you meet your targets, great. If you do not, your benchmarks should prompt you to consider certain mid-course corrections.

You should think about this document as a work in progress, one that can change to meet your revised expectations based on your widening knowledge base as your practice evolves.

Measurable objectives could include such items as number of clients, revenue, profitability, job satisfaction, and growth trends.

What Are the Components/Characteristics of My Proposed Practice?

Different types of practices demand different setups, approaches, marketing, perhaps even technology support.

- *Litigation*—Depending on what type of litigation you want to practice, you may wish to add a *lawyer referral strategy* to your marketing plan. For example, if you want to specialize in administrative appeals, nurturing contacts with trial litigation firms can garner you a lot of business from firms that focus their efforts on courtroom trials but eschew administrative hearings. Another example: Patent law firms often will not also handle trademark prosecutions and appeals that emanate from their patent clients because these are not as cost-effective for them as their patent practices. Consequently, a trademark practice could benefit from referrals from patent firms.

- *Transactional*—Demands an *institutional strategy* as well as one directed at individuals. There are many varieties of transactions going on throughout society at all times, ranging from small-business entrepreneurs to the most sophisticated international acquisitions, mergers, strategic alliances, and other types of arrangements largely handled by major, multinational law firms. What that means for the solo practitioner is that there are many niche opportunities that sometimes fall between the cracks. These can include venture capital startup or mezzanine financings, local partnering arrangements between physicians and hospitals or HMOs, as well as more basic transactions, such as partnership between two individuals, supplier agreements, etc.

- *Regulatory*—Requires *identifying organizations and individuals fairly heavily regulated* by the federal, state, and/or local government. Managing regulatory relationships is by no means the exclusive province of major law firms. In many small communities, for example, local radio and television stations hire local attorneys to handle their regulatory filings with the Federal Communications Commission, while funeral parlors engage local lawyers to make sure that they are in compliance with the Federal Trade Commission's Funeral Rule.

Are My Contemplated Practice Areas Growing?

Determining whether a practice area is on the upswing, treading water, or in decline is not as difficult as it might seem at first glance. Check on such items as membership in specialized bar associations, the number of positions you see advertised on jobs Web sites for certain kinds of practice, the membership growth or decline in member organizations of similar practitioners, the number of seminars and webcasts on this topic, and other statistical indicators.

For example, membership in the National Employment Lawyers Association and the American Health Lawyers Association has grown substantially in the last decade, a reflection of the impressive growth of these two practice areas.

Is This Practice Area Subject to Positive or Adverse External Influences?

If you are contemplating that the majority of your legal business will be in practice areas that are highly sensitive to external factors over which you have no control, you will need to undertake in-depth research to determine if this is a good idea. At the same time, you should be aware of opportunity in adversity.

See Chapter 13, "The Career Impact of External Phenomena," for a discussion of possible external influences on your practice.

Where Should I Locate My Practice?

You will need to consider geography on several different levels:

- First, *where to locate your practice* (assuming you have some geographic flexibility). For example, say you want to practice elder law. You need to determine how many elder law attorneys there are in your area. The National Academy of Elder Law Attorneys Web site (*www.naela.org*) reveals, for example, that there are 22 Certified Elder Law Specialists in Phoenix and 22 more within 25 miles (see also *West Legal Directory* and/or *Martindale.com*), an increase of 400 percent over just one year. Then you need to know the demographics of Phoenix and the demographic trends, for which there are numerous Internet sources of information (4.5 million estimated population in the Phoenix metropolitan statistical area, of whom more than 400,000 are 65 and older; population growth is impressive—almost 29 percent in just seven years—with a disproportionate influx of individuals age 55 and older, largely a high-income group). Conclusion: Elder law could be a very fruitful practice area in Phoenix.

- Second, *client geographic considerations*—clients who outsource certain operations are likely to require additional legal services at the beginning of the outsourcing project but fewer such services as time goes on; you can't count on them to give you long-term work.

Are There Secondary Markets Where My Practice Area Expertise Could Be Applied?

This is a very important question. If the answer is yes, your chances of establishing a successful solo practice go way up.

Say, for example, that you want to practice plaintiff's workers' compensation law. There is a natural affinity between workers' comp and practices such as representation of Social Security Disability Income claimants, Medicare appellants, and veterans claiming benefits for service-connected disabilities. All of these practices are at the nexus of medicine and law and have fairly similar claims application and appeals processes.

Think of these synergies as you would when you put together an investment portfolio. Savvy investors hedge their bets by not putting all of their eggs in just one basket. If possible, you should strive to do the same thing when contemplating your solo law practice.

Are There Other Services That I Can Master and "Cross-Sell" to Clients?

Cross-selling is something that major law firms engage in constantly. There is no reason why solo practitioners cannot do the same. If you have a client that comes to you for advice and assistance in forming a company, it makes sense to promote your services as outside "general counsel" to the new venture. In addition, your client may need help with succession planning, as well as more personal matters such as wills, elder care issues for parents, and so on. It is always much easier to sell additional services to an existing (and presumably satisfied) client than to search for and acquire a new client.

What Resources Will I Require?

It is absolutely imperative to have a detailed budget that realistically projects startup costs and operating expenses for at least your first year. Key components include:

- Capital investment, i.e., equipment, technology, and related support services
- Rent
- Human capital
- Special equipment
- Overhead
- Marketing
- Other resources, e.g., library, subscription services
- Unanticipated contingencies

How Should I Allocate My Time?

You need to determine early in the analytical process how you will allocate your time among the many responsibilities that entrepreneurs find themselves saddled with when launching a solo practice. Failure to do this will only frustrate you and may jeopardize your success.

You will first need to itemize all of the demands on your time: client development, office administration, training/CLE, case management, etc. The next step is to "drill down" into each major category in order to define subcategories demanding your attention. Take client development, for example—subcategories might include speaking engagements, writing articles, Web site development and maintenance, advertising initiatives, and so forth. Then you have to *triage* your time commitments, determining what is most important to do and when it is most important to do it.

Who (and How Formidable) Is the Competition?

Just because there *is* competition does not mean that you should abandon your idea of launching a solo practice. Your answers here, however, should help you devise a strategy of differentiating your-self from the competition if you deem that to be necessary.

- Other solo practitioners?
- Boutique firms?
- Small firms?
- Midsize firms?
- Large firms?
- Non-lawyers, e.g., CPA firms, real estate firms, independent paralegals?

What Are My Strengths and Weaknesses, and How Can I Compensate?

Look at several of the key ingredients of your business and determine what you're good at and what needs work, then focus your initial efforts on the things you know you do well.

- *Practice areas/expertise*: A litigator may recognize his or her experience in administrative litigation as a strength, and lack of trial experience as a weakness. That may lead to a decision to begin a solo practice by taking administrative cases while gradually working to expand into trial litigation.
- *Marketing-related skills*: A lawyer may see his or her writing skills as a strength and public speaking skills as a weakness. Initially, he or she might emphasize written marketing materials, including writing articles for local publications, while developing better verbal presentation skills.
- *Clientele/markets served*: An attorney may see a strength in the number of health-care clients with whom he has worked, but a weakness in having failed to develop personal relationships with key managers at these client entities. Having identified such a weakness, the attorney needs to devise a plan to mitigate it. Sending periodic newsletters or developing a blog on health law developments and proffering solutions to potential problems resulting therefrom is one way to begin this particular kind of relationship building, for example.

- *Organizational/time management skills*: This is a serious weakness for any would-be solo practitioner and would require immediate attention. One of the best resources for improving these deficiencies is the state bar's law practice management section, which can provide free consulting advice.

Who or What Are the Primary Markets for This Practice?

Think creatively when doing this part of the exercise. Just because a potential client pool is scattered geographically does not mean that you cannot market to them or serve their needs in this era of instantaneous electronic communications.

Step one is to identify potential clients:

- List potential client markets.
- Where are they?
- What are their primary legal needs?
- What must be done to secure them?
- Triage the hottest prospects
- Why are they hot?

Step two is to define them more precisely:

- Where are they concentrated geographically?
- What are their demographics?
- Individuals?
- Corporations?
- Other institutions?

Once you've identified your primary markets, craft your *value proposition* and use it as your message to reach your market (see the following two sections).

What Is My "Value Proposition?"

What is it that makes you unique, different, the "go-to" attorney? Identify what differentiates you from the competition and make it a centerpiece of your marketing efforts. This could be more than only one characteristic of you or your practice, but don't go overboard and include traits of lesser significance. In addition, remember that your potential clients' attention spans for this sort of marketing effort are limited. Don't force them to have to absorb too much information. Keep it simple.

President Ronald Reagan did this better than almost anyone. His value proposition was:

- Win the Cold War
- Cut the size of government
- Lower taxes

Whether you agreed with him or not, he distilled his governing principles down to their bare essence and made them extremely easy for the voting public to understand and rally behind. You need to do the same for your potential clients. Use your *competitive advantage(s)* in both your strategic planning and marketing efforts.

How Do I Reach the Market?

These are, of course, not mutually exclusive:

- Yellow Pages advertising
- Broadcast media advertising
- Internet advertising
- Display ads in publications
- Referrals from other lawyers
- Referrals from non-lawyers
- Personal contacts
- Web site
- Direct mail
- E-mail
- Memberships in organizations
- Letter-writing/surveys
- Seminars
- Public speaking
- Writing for publication, particularly in local media
- Outsourcing opportunities, i.e., things that you can handle for clients more cost-effectively than they do in-house

- Current and potential strategic marketing partnerships/alliances

How Can I Strengthen My Client Pitch?

You can enhance your credentials and thereby bolster your client presentations by enrolling in the following educational programs:

- CLE programs
- State specialty certification programs
- LLM and related programs
- Graduate certificate programs

How Do I Price My Services?

You have to know what the customary fees are for the services you intend to offer in the city where you are practicing. Once you have that information, you need to determine where you fit into the competitive fee structure and what opportunities there might be to increase these fees. For example, getting certified in a specialty by a bar-approved certification agency and being able to promote that fact to potential clients can help raise your fees.

How Long Will It Take to Collect My Fees?

This is a tricky problem for solo practitioners, and is often the reason their practices do not succeed. If you want to avoid the problem of collections, consider examining practice areas where such problems are minimal, such as claimant representation in Social Security administrative appeals, where the U.S. government acts as your bill collector. With respect to other practice areas, your options for timely collection are fairly limited. You can establish a relationship with a collection agency and/or request a retainer upfront where such a methodology is permitted by professional conduct rules.

What Happens if My Business Fails?

Most of us do not have a wealthy and willing relative to come to the rescue and bail us out when our businesses fail. In addition to planning for success, you also need a contingency plan: You need to consider whether what you contemplate doing as a solo practitioner would be marketable if you gave up your practice and sought employment elsewhere.

In considering your "safety net," do not focus only on the practice areas in which you will gain expertise; also assess the transferable skills you will develop that might be attractive to a prospective employer. As you now have experience running a business, you are likely to have become somewhat skilled at such areas as procurement, project management, human resources, reading and understanding business financial documents, legal marketing, coming up rapidly on the learning curve with respect to areas of law, etc. One or all of these skill sets, combined with your legal experience, might enhance your attractiveness to prospective employers. As you develop these additional skills, it would be a good idea to document them in some detail as you go along in the event you need to invoke them later.

Solo Practice Business and Marketing Plan

Now that you have answered the questions above and want to proceed to launch a solo practice, your next step should be to develop a *detailed* business and marketing plan. Such a plan is both a great learning experience that will serve you very well once your practice is a going proposition, and a business model that, if constructed properly, can go a long way toward assuring your success.

Why You Need a Business and Marketing Plan
- To provide a strategy for success
- To get a loan
- To measure your progress
- To keep you focused on what is important
- Discipline

Elements of a Good Business and Marketing Plan
These components of a business plan provide an overview of the existing opportunity for your business and market research to support it.

1. Executive Summary
- A succinct synopsis of the entire plan; keep it brief, no more than 2–4 pages.
- Highlight the key points of your plan; communicate—
  - the size and scope of the market opportunity
  - the practice's business and profitability model
  - how your resources/skills/strategic positioning make you qualified to execute the plan.
- Make it compelling and easy-to-read.

2. Firm Analysis
- Strategic overview of the firm
- How the firm will be organized
- What services the firm will offer
- Further detail on your qualifications to serve your target markets

3. Competitive Analysis
- Evaluate the overall playing field and your direct competition (other solo practitioners and law firms).
- Answer key market research questions, such as—
  - the size of each of your target market segments
  - trends for the legal industry as a whole
  - other industries that compete with you (indirect competition).
- Assess your competitors' strengths and weaknesses.
- Delineate your firm's competitive advantages.

4. Client Analysis
- Assess your potential client markets.
- Convey the legal needs of your target clients.
- Show how your services will satisfy these needs to the extent that clients will pay for them.

5. The Marketing Plan
This section should outline your strategy for penetrating the target markets.

   Key components:
- Description of your firm's desired strategic positioning.
- Detailed descriptions of your firm's service offerings and potential service extensions.

- Descriptions of your firm's desired image and branding strategy.
- Descriptions of your proposed promotional strategies, e.g.,
  - contacts
  - Web site
  - blogs
  - referral services
  - specialty certification
  - memberships
  - letter-writing/surveys
  - seminars
  - direct mail
  - teaching CLE
  - space ads
  - writing for publication
  - outsourcing opportunities
  - social media networks
  - prepaid legal service plans
  - current and potential strategic marketing partnerships/alliances
- Your pricing strategies

6. *Financial Plan*

This section involves the development of your firm's revenue and profitability model—how you plan to "monetize" the practice.

- Explain in detail the key assumptions you used in building this model.
- Analyze key revenue and cost variables.
- Describe comparable valuations for existing practices with similar business models. *Note: This may be difficult to do—ask the Law Practice Management Section of the state bar.*
- Assess the amount of capital the firm needs.
- Explain how you propose to use these funds.
- Expected future earnings
  - Include a summary of Projected Income Statements, Balance Sheets, and Cash Flow Statements, broken out quarterly for the first two years and annually for years 1–5.

Note: Financial Plan assumptions and projections must flow from and be supported by descriptions and explanations in other sections of the Business and Marketing Plan.

Appendix
- A full set of financial projections
- Any technical drawings—office space
- Step-by-step checklist of how you will execute the plan
- Time line for executing plan components

> Finally, it should be stated that it is much easier to launch a solo practice today than ever before—both the barriers to and costs of entry and are much lower than they've ever been. You do not have to purchase an expensive law library or even locate your office in a high-rent area near a bar or court library. You do not need a secretary. Both of these prior essentials have been eliminated by technology.

Part III

Documents

Chapter 16
Intelligent Preparation Before You Launch 155

Chapter 17
Vulnerability Management: Mitigating Your Weaknesses ...169

Chapter 18
How an Employer Reads a Résumé 177

Chapter 19
How to Read and Respond to a Job Ad 183

Chapter 20
Identifying Your "Hidden" Skill Sets . . . and Matching
Them with Opportunities 189

Chapter 21
Talking the Employer's Talk . . . Not Yours 201

Chapter 22
Getting Lost in the Ether . . . and Getting Found 205

Chapter 23
The Critical Importance of Storytelling 209

Chapter 24
Identifying Winning Writing Sample(s) 217

Chapter 25
Overcoming "Ageism" 223

Chapter 26
Coping with Disability 229

Chapter 27
Legal Job Hunting Out of Town 243

Chapter 16

Intelligent Preparation Before You Launch

Searching for a new job is serious business. It is worthy of being a full-time job itself. Consequently, it requires your best attention to planning, organization, and detail.

Job hunting is, for most of us, a very humbling experience. There are likely to be more bad days than good days while you are pounding the figurative pavement in search of employment. Psychological preparation for the down days is important; just as important is making sure that you establish a disciplined structural framework within which to perform your job quest properly so that even if it's not yielding the results you would like, you feel good about your efforts.

This chapter discusses the various components of a proper job search and describes a set of self-crafted tools that you can employ to ease the process and keep you focused.

Time Management

Job hunting requires the same good time management that you would be expected to utilize in a paying job. This means that you need to develop a "doable" schedule and a checklist of activities that keeps you disciplined and focused. It also means that you need to be able to multi-task and effectively perform several job-search functions simultaneously.

At work, you do not customarily work on only one major project or assignment all the way through to completion before turning to the next one on your list. The contemporary workplace does not lend itself to that kind of linear approach. Moreover, focusing exclusively on one project tends to dull and desensitize a person and can result in an inferior work product. It is much more interesting, stimulating, and enjoyable to switch from project to project at reasonable intervals.

These principles also hold true for job hunting. You will feel more energized if you schedule more than one job-hunting activity per day if you are currently unemployed, or several per week if you are employed and your time is limited to evenings and weekends. For example, you might intersperse developing additional résumés targeted to particular industries or types of employers with honing your interview skills by thinking through responses to the questions likely to give you the most difficulty.

Organization

Organizational skills are paramount in any job, including the job of job hunting. The use of printed or electronic calendars upon which you can plan and schedule your time and activities is central to an orderly, efficient, and effective job search.

View your scheduling calendars as fluid rather than rigid. You may discover that résumé preparation and later adjustment or revision in order to target specific jobs takes longer than expected or, once you get the hang of it, less time than you have scheduled. The best way to keep your schedule current and flexible is to review your calendars at regular intervals, even daily, incorporating what you have experienced and adjusting them as necessary.

You organize a job search for additional reasons, too. Organizing does not just mean preparing ticklers about what you do and when you do it. It is also a way to manage your "information flow." Automate the receipt of as much good job opportunity information as possible, so that you do not have to spend too much time engaged in online searches. Many job databases provide you with the opportunity to set up job search agents that will alert you when an opportunity in an area that you have targeted comes up.

Job Search Documents

To conduct an effective legal job search or legal career transition, you may need to prepare some or all of the following documents: contacts road map, résumé(s), résumé addendum, representative matters list, deal sheet, résumé "substitutes," e-mail résumé(s), video résumé(s), transferable skills list, KSA (knowledge, skills, and abilities) statements, cover letter, transmittal e-mail, transcript(s), writing sample(s), writing sample cover sheet(s), reference list, networking contacts form, networking contacts record, dissecting legal job ad form, letters of recommendation, annual reviews, performance appraisals, and conflicts check.

Every open position will not, of course, require every one of these documents. Moreover, not all of these documents will be for public consumption: Some are useful tools intended for your eyes only.

Internal Documents (for your own reference)

Transferable Skills List

This document is for your own internal job-search planning purposes. See Chapter 20, "Identifying Your Hidden Skill Sets . . . and Matching Them with Opportunities," which addresses the techniques involved in recognizing and evaluating your transferable skills—a valuable exercise in both knowing what kind of job suits you and uncovering your strengths to include in your documents and in interviews.

Dissecting Legal Job Ad Form

This form is designed to provide you with a framework for taking apart a job ad or vacancy announcement, separating it into its component parts, and analyzing your qualifications with respect to each component. The purpose of this form is to help you determine if you should apply for the position, and craft your application so that you will be better able to compete for the job. See Chapter 19, "How to Read and Respond to a Job Ad."

Networking Contacts Form

A basic chart with two columns (see Appendix B, Maximizing Your Contacts):

- Column One—Your networking contacts
- Column Two—Your networking contacts' possible contacts

Networking Contacts Record

A chart enabling you to document the networking contacts you have invoked and the results of your networking. Use this form to keep track of the networking contacts you have made, as well as what you learned from them. Without an organized contacts record-keeping system, it is very easy to become forgetful and/or confused. Also, always make sure to follow up contacts with a thank-you letter or phone call, and to keep your contacts informed of your progress. You can set this up any way that is appropriate for you. An example of a typical setup is included in Appendix I.

External Documents (for your contacts, references, and prospective employers)

Contacts Road Map

This is a document I developed as one of my standard legal career counseling tools. This document can help you pull together information for your networking contacts and your references to inspire them to advocate for you and to provide them with direction on the types of jobs you will be applying for, your applicable skills, and some talking points about your career achievements. You can provide the Contacts Road Map to your networking contacts and references so that they can better serve you in (1) identifying where you could work, given your background and aspirations, and (2) responding quickly to your request for advice and assistance. The Contacts Road Map helps your contacts easily pinpoint businesses and firms where you might fit.

Key Road Map elements:

- Examples of specific positions that interest you
- Examples of specific employers where such positions are found
- Why it is logical for you to be interested in such positions

Prepare your Contacts Road Map even before you put together your résumé(s). Building the Road Map will help you focus on where you really want to work and will influence what you include in your résumé(s). The Contacts Road Map can then serve as a platform upon which you construct your job or career campaign.

Don't think of your Contacts Road Map as locked in concrete once you construct it. Like your résumé(s) and cover letter(s), it should be a malleable document, one that can be adjusted as you proceed with your job search and learn more about both the legal and law-related job markets and yourself.

More detailed information about the Contacts Road Map can be found in Chapter 30, "Networking without Groveling," and Appendix F, "Contacts Road Map."

Résumé

The basic platform from which the job search proceeds.

Your résumé(s) has three purpose(s):

- To get you an *interview.*
- To provide details of your background to your *references* so that they will be knowledgeable and up-to-date about you when they are contacted by your prospective employer(s).
- To present to your *networking contacts* (along with your Contacts Road Map) so that they will have a clear picture of you when recommending you to others, and will also have copies to provide to their contacts.

Basic résumé considerations include:

- How many different résumés will you need? Once you have some professional work experience, it is unlikely that only one résumé will suffice. Options—not all of which are mutually exclusive—include:

- Traditional (reverse-chronological)—the most common résumé.
- Skills or Functional—substitutes substantive law and/or technical legal skills categories for the reverse chronology of employers.
- Hybrid—a combination of the traditional and the skills/functional résumé.
- Federal Format—a résumé that contains additional information required for some U.S. government jobs.
- Building a Résumé Online—via a template provided by the employer.

This is an important decision. Certain résumés work much better than others for certain attorneys. For example, if you have great experience derived from a job that you held years ago, you might want to present that experience in a skills/functional or hybrid format so that the prospective employer will see it earlier in the document. Résumés are obviously extremely important to a successful job search; they will be covered thoroughly in the following chapters.

Résumé Addendum

Create a Résumé Addendum if you wish to elaborate on your achievements in a narrative (two pages maximum). You can title this addendum many different ways. The most common titles are:

- Significant Highlights
- Significant Litigation
- Significant Transactions

See Appendix D for an example of a Résumé Addendum.

Representative Matters List

This is an attachment to your résumé in which you document examples of the matters you have handled. If they were reported cases, include *Bluebook* citations. The list differs from a résumé addendum in that (1) you do not elaborate extensively on these matters, and (2) you would include many more such items. Your list could contain litigation, transactional, regulatory, or any other matters on which you worked, or a combination thereof. You would typically only present a Representative Matters List if it is requested by an employer.

The following excerpts from a representative matters list are typical of the kinds of short entries you might include:

- Advised financial services client with respect to the changes to the 2007 SEC executive compensation and disclosure rules and assisted client in preparing its Compensation Disclosure and Analysis and accompanying tables under tight time constraints; managed and trained other associates. Accomplished this complex, new-to-the-firm project with only minimal partner oversight and produced a work product that was highly praised by the client.
- Developed long-term relationship counseling an emerging technology company by assisting it in a variety of corporate activities, including drafting and negotiating documents to raise private funding, stock grant agreements, non-disclosure agreements, employment agreements, and other employee issues. Also advised board of directors with respect to issues, including fiduciary duties, Delaware corporate law issues, and security issues; regularly participated in board meetings; and negotiated settlements of outstanding debts with creditors.

Deal Sheet

A Deal Sheet is an attachment to your résumé where you document examples of the transactions in which you participated. The Deal Sheet differs from a Résumé Addendum in the same way as does a Representative Matters List. Deal sheet entries go into more detail than those in a Representative Matters List. Like the latter, you do not need to prepare and submit one unless requested by the employer.

Résumé Substitutes

Résumé substitutes come in many different forms, generally at the discretion of the potential employer. They include:

- Special application forms
  - Certain U.S. government positions
  - Certain state and local government positions
  - Certain college and university positions
  - Certain private-sector organization positions
  - International agency and multilateral development agency positions
- Online application forms
  - Most major corporation positions
  - Many federal, state, and local government positions
  - Many law firm positions
  - Certain nonprofit positions

E-mailed Résumés

If an e-mail résumé is requested, or if you elect to deliver your unsolicited résumé via e-mail, be sure that you send it as an attachment using a word processing format that the employer uses, e.g., Word, WordPerfect, PDF. If you are uncertain, call or e-mail in advance and ask what format you should use.

Video Résumés

Video résumés are the "new kid on the block" and are only rarely requested by legal employers. However, if you receive such a request, make sure that you submit a highly professional video résumé that presents you most effectively. Do not submit a video résumé if one is not requested.

KSA (Knowledge, Skills, and Abilities) Statements

These are often required for U.S. government job applications. This government term of art is synonymous with or closely related to the following government vacancy announcement terms:

- Ranking Factors
- Rating Factors
- Technical Qualifications
- Selective Factors
- Specialized Experience
- Executive Core Qualifications

KSAs, et al. are posed in the form of questions. A typical KSA and candidate response might look something like this:

> A. Ability to analyze problems
>
> My ability to analyze and resolve problems is demonstrated by my experience in EPA's Office of General Counsel and in private law practice. With regard to EPA, this ability is evidenced by, among other things: 1) the sound legal, scientific, and policy written and oral analysis and advice I provided to EPA management, Regional Offices, and OGC on important and highly sensitive pesticide control and clean air program matters; 2) my effective legal analysis, development of winning strategies, and successful execution of those strategies in complex administrative and judicial litigation and related negotiations; and 3) my development of innovative approaches in providing sound legal support for complex regulations on controversial matters.
>
> With regard to my private law practice experience, I have demonstrated the ability to analyze and resolve problems by the following: my contributions to the successful defense of major clients of the firm in enforcement actions; my substantial contribution to the successful defense in federal district and appellate courts of environmental assessments for major federally approved infrastructure projects; my effective participation in other administrative and judicial proceedings; my sound counseling to clients' compliance with environmental and consumer protection laws; my advice to clients on performing environmental due diligence and audits; and my legal analyses to develop options for my clients and provide guidance on environmental planning.

Examples:
- EPA: Prepared many high-quality legal memoranda analyzing controversial and ambiguous provisions of FIFRA, in-

cluding recent amendments, and the Clean Act for immediate and high-level OGC supervisors (i.e., Assistant and Associate General Counsels and the General Counsel), the Deputy Assistant Administrator for Pesticide Programs, Directors of key Air Program offices, and Regional counsels. Certain of these memoranda were released to the public for guidance and/or incorporated into guidance documents.

- Private Practice: Negotiated on behalf of the Idaho Water Association, a complete reversal of State decision to hold a member water company responsible for substantial hazardous waste investigation costs, resulting in issuance of a favorable revision of State Superfund policy.

Cover Letter (or Transmittal E-mail)

A cover letter generally accompanies the résumé and provides an opportunity to:

- elaborate on your qualifications;
- highlight your key selling points; and
- mitigate certain résumé weaknesses. See Chapter 17, "Vulnerability Management: Mitigating Your Weaknesses."

Think of your cover letter or transmittal e-mail as the first writing sample that an employer will see. Try to limit it to one page and three components, as follows:

- Paragraph 1: The position for which you are applying and how you learned of the position.
- Paragraphs 2 and 3 (if necessary): The most compelling reasons why you are a strong candidate for the position, plus any explanations that might be necessary concerning your career.
- Paragraph 3: Your availability for an interview at the employer's convenience.

For example:

Dear Human Resources Director:

I am applying for the Attorney Director position with the Office of the Inspector General identified in vacancy announcement 10-01.

As you will see from my résumé (enclosed), my qualifications fit the position requirements very well. I have been responsible for investigations and legal audits of a variety of federal programs during my tenure at the Department of Energy, as well as in my position as a Senior Investigative Attorney with the U.S. Senate Special Committee on Investigations. In private practice, I was often the lead attorney in responding to Department of Justice and Federal Trade Committee investigations of my firm's clients. I have performed with distinction in my prior positions in both the public and private sectors.

I am available for an interview at your convenience. Should you have any questions, or require further information, please do not hesitate to contact me. Your assistance is greatly appreciated and I look forward to hearing from you soon.

Sincerely,

XXXXXXXXXXXX

Enclosure (1)

Transcript(s)

Employers may want transcripts from your law school and sometimes college. Unofficial transcripts are often accepted.

Writing Sample

A potential employer may want to gain insight into your writing and reasoning skills, and also assess your knowledge of legal writing and citation rules. Typical variations include:

- Unedited writing sample
- Writing sample draft pre-editing
- Excerpt from a lengthy writing sample
- Collaborative effort where your contribution was substantial

The writing sample may need to include a Writing Sample Cover Sheet to explain the context of the writing sample and/or your role in preparing it if it's not 100 percent your own work. See Chapter 24, "Identifying Winning Writing Sample(s)."

Reference List

Your reference list identifies your "endorsers" and authorizes prospective employers to contact them. Key elements:

- Name, phone number, and e-mail address of reference
- Preferred method of communication
- Relationship of reference to you
- Specific successful or interesting task you performed either jointly with or under the supervision of the reference.

See Chapter 28, "Managing Your References and Controlling the Conversation" and Appendix G, "Reference List."

Letters of Recommendation

Letters from references are typically only accepted if you cannot identify suitable references whom the employer can contact; consequently, letters are not as valued by employers.

Annual Reviews and Performance Appraisals

An annual review is the once-a-year evaluation of an associate by an employer; a performance appraisal is the government equivalent. Performance appraisals are generally more "formulaic" than private sector annual reviews, and employers sometimes discount them because of a perception that everyone receives a great appraisal regardless of merit. Varieties of reviews and appraisals:

- Oral evaluation
- Written evaluation
- Written evaluation with opportunity for written rebuttal or comments by you

Conflicts Check

Typically, part of the law firm examination of a prospective employee is determining if there might be any client conflicts of interest that would either preclude the hire or require recusal of the employee from certain matters. Conflicts checks should not be submitted unless requested by the employer, and need only indicate previous or current clients and the nature of your representation of them.

Lining Up References

It is a good idea to identify possible references and communicate with them before activating your job search. Take the time and make the effort to follow good reference protocol, which means:

- Contacting references directly, by phone or visit, to request that they serve on your behalf.
- Asking them how and when they would like to be contacted by prospective employers.
- Briefing them on your activities and career aspirations.
- Giving them an idea of where you will be applying, and your supporting rationale.
- Providing them with a résumé and Contacts Road Map.
- Indicating that you will keep them current on your progress, but promise not to be a pest.

See the more extensive treatment of references in Chapter 28, "Managing Your References and Controlling the Conversation."

Invoking Your Contacts

Galvanizing your network is something that you should begin early in the job-hunting process, ideally around the time you are putting together your job search documents. Presumably, you will have been building your network before it becomes necessary to invoke it.

The protocol that governs relations with your references applies equally to your contacts. However, you need to provide your contacts with additional information, principally a Contacts Road Map that does their thinking for them about where you could be gainfully and happily employed. See Chapter 30, "Networking without Groveling."

Record-keeping

You should establish a record-keeping system for your job search early in the process. The system should be simple, easy to access, and able to generate documents that you have prepared and submitted, interviews scheduled and completed, ticklers for application and interview follow-ups, communications with references and contacts, and background research on employers.

Your system of records should enable you to call up relevant information when necessary, such as when you receive a phone call from a prospective employer inviting you to interview. If the employer has questions for you about what was contained in your résumé, cover letter or transmittal e-mail, you want to have those documents in front of you when responding. A sound job-search record-keeping system will contain information about employers to whom you have applied, dates of applications, and application documents submitted.

A job search constructed around an organizing principle does four very valuable things for you:
(1) It enforces a disciplined, forward-moving job search campaign;
(2) It "routinizes" the job-hunting process;
(3) It permits you to continually assess your progress and make sound adjustments when necessary; and
(4) It has a positive psychological impact that can counter the more dispiriting elements of job hunting.

Vulnerability Management: Mitigating Your Weaknesses

The road to rejection is littered with résumés that clearly and unequivocally shout out to the prospective employer that there is a problem with this application. Unfortunately, many such Achilles' heels are unavoidable and cannot be easily hidden. Nevertheless, too many legal job candidates merely hope that whoever reads their résumé will overlook a weakness or discount it in light of the wonders to be found in the rest of the document.

In the unlikely event you are that fortunate, do not conclude that you are home free. Your résumé's weak point(s) are virtually certain to be raised during your job interview. In that case, you must be prepared to respond effectively.

This chapter discusses the most common résumé weaknesses and how to handle them when crafting your résumé and preparing for your interview.

A Red Flag for Employers

Without exception, employers zero in on what they perceive as the weak points in your résumé. This can happen at two critical decision points in the hiring process: initially, when résumés are evaluated, and subsequently, when job interviews are conducted. You need to be prepared to counter these through (1) extenuation and mitigation; and (2) employing certain résumé techniques that tend to deemphasize weak points or make them more difficult to pinpoint (without, of course, ever engaging in any cover-up).

You can address some weaknesses directly in the body of the résumé, others in your cover letter, and most in a job interview, provided that your résumé weaknesses do not foreclose that opportunity. When preparing for a job interview, it is absolutely essential that you prepare more thoroughly for these "weakness" questions than for the "home run" questions that you know you can easily knock out of the park. Unfortunately, most job seekers do just the opposite, honing their responses to the questions that they know will make them feel good and ignoring the ones that will make them squirm because they know how difficult and discomfiting these are. Try to avoid the natural human tendency to stay within your comfort zone.

The Most Common Résumé Weaknesses

The most common résumé weaknesses are:

- Less-than-stellar academic performance
- Gaps in employment
- Current unemployment
- History of job-hopping
- Checkered work history and/or unremarkable career progression
- Undistinguished job titles
- Too much "seasoning"—i.e., age
- Lack of a life outside of work

Employer Reactions to Résumé Weaknesses

Weaknesses reflected in your résumé often consume the attention of prospective employers. Employer reactions to résumé weaknesses typically take at least one—and usually more than one—of the following forms:

- Outright rejection of your candidacy upon reading the résumé.
- Obsession with the perceived résumé weakness, to the exclusion of the positive selling points and "gems" about you.
- Seeking an explanation from you in your cover letter.
- Seeking an explanation from you during your job interview.

Antidotes

You can temper certain résumé weaknesses within the résumé itself or in an accompanying cover letter or transmittal e-mail. Others only lend themselves to moderation or explanation should you be invited to interview.

Weakness: Less-Than-Stellar Academic Performance

This becomes a résumé issue only if (1) you are asked to provide transcripts of your grades as part of your application, (2) the job ad to which you are responding asks you to include your GPA and/or class rank, or (3) unasked, you nevertheless include your lackluster GPA and/or class rank anyway.

Antidote: If you cannot avoid including your academic performance, then make sure that you can also include a legitimate and honest reason why you did not excel academically, assuming that such a reason exists. One that applies to many candidates is something like the following: "I worked my way through school in order to support myself/my family." Left unstated is the very valid point that you were consequently unable to devote as much time to study as your more fortunate, well-heeled colleagues.

You can make this point in one of several places on your résumé:

- In a Profile or Summary of Qualifications at the top of the document, e.g.:

"Attended law school while working full-time," or words to that effect. Including such a statement in your Profile guarantees that it will be seen by a reader because it is close to the top of the résumé.

- As a bullet item beneath your law school, e.g.:

    J.D., Trixie Norton School of Law, Kramden University, New York, NY 2009

    - Worked full-time while attending law school.

If your Education section is close to the top of the document, as it likely would be if you are a recent law school graduate, this location probably would suffice because it is still likely to be seen and appropriately processed by the reader. If Education comes later in the document, you run the risk that the reader may never get to it, or that he or she will no longer be paying close attention, having already discounted you for the position.

- In the Work Experience section of your résumé, e.g.:

    Grill Man, The Burgers of Calais, New York, NY 2006–2009

The same positioning analysis applies here as with Education. However, there is an additional reason why this location is not prime. In a rapid read of your résumé, the employer may fail to connect that you were attending law school and working at the same time.

If your GPA is not great, leave it off. There is no line in the sand as to what constitutes a GPA worthy of inclusion on a résumé. My counseling experience has been that candidates make dangerous and thus self-defeating assumptions about where to draw the line. My very rough rule of thumb, gleaned from numerous discussions with employers, is that anything below a 3.5 GPA should be omitted.

However, if your law school or undergraduate institution grades low and your class rank looks better than your GPA, by all means include your class rank. Again, there is no hard and fast dividing line between a good and a less than stellar class rank. In fact, it is more difficult to state definitively what you should do here, for this reason. Some schools are deemed better than other schools. Finishing in the top half of the class at Yale Law School is considered pretty good by most employers. Finishing in the top quarter of the class at Trixie Norton School of Law may not be perceived as much of an achievement.

Weakness: Gaps in Employment

Antidote: If your employment gap(s) occurred during the same calendar year, you can avoid questions about an uncomfortable subject if you do not include months on your résumé. For example:

Employment History
Instead of:
    Associate, *Hamilton, Jefferson & Madison*, Philadelphia, PA, December 2007 – Present
    Associate, *Franklin, Adams & Washington*, Valley Forge, PA, February 2007 – March 2007
Use the following:
    Associate, *Hamilton, Jefferson & Madison*, Philadelphia, PA, 2007 – Present
    Associate, *Franklin, Adams & Washington*, Philadelphia, PA, 2007

If you had a very valid reason for taking time off from work, such as caring for a sick relative, raising children, taking a sabbatical to travel around the world, working in a political campaign, or relocating for family reasons, your best strategy might be to say so in your cover letter or transmittal email.

Weakness: Current Unemployment

While the Great Recession means that you are certainly not alone, savvy employers understand or suspect that economics are not the sole reason why attorneys are laid off. After all, unless your firm or law office disappeared completely, some of your colleagues *were not* laid off. Consequently, your prospective employer will likely probe to determine why you were among the ones who were terminated.

Antidote: If you were laid off, one of the following rationales, or something similar, may apply to you:

- The firm went out of business.
- My practice area dried up due to the economy.
- All of the younger associates were let go.
- The firm decided to close its Oshkosh office.
- My company was taken over by Global Amalgamated and our legal staff was eliminated.
- The firm applied a "last-in, first-out" policy to its lay-offs.

If you were fired, make sure that what you tell the interviewer will be consistent with what he or she might hear from your prior employer. You may want to discuss this with your prior employer and agree on what will be said. While such a conversation might be difficult, it is likely to be absolutely necessary.

If you have been unemployed for a long period of time, your résumé will look much better if you fill in the gap with something, such as a volunteer activity.

Weakness: A History of Job-Hopping

Fifteen years ago, there were very few excuses for an attorney bouncing around from one job to another, with only short stays in each position. Today that is no longer the case. Job-hopping is fairly common, often through no fault of the "hopper." I had a client several years ago who had four jobs in six years because his first three employers—two law firms and one corporation—all went out of business.

Antidote: Consider leaving very-short-term jobs off your résumé. State your dates of employment in years only, not months and years, so that periods of unemployment will not appear as long (similar to the advice above concerning dealing with gaps in employment).

Before

> Associate, *Barracuda & Serpent*, Redding, CA, December 2006 – Present
>
> Associate, *Serendipity & Chance*, Eureka, CA, December 2004 – January 2005

After

> Associate, *Barracuda & Serpent*, Redding, CA, 2006 – Present
>
> Associate, *Serendipity & Chance*, Eureka, CA, 2004 – 2005

Weakness: Checkered Work History/Unremarkable Career Progression

Résumés that present like this (I call them "sine wave résumés") immediately attract attention—unfortunately, not the right kind of attention. Most of the time, it is impossible to camouflage an up-and-down career.

Antidote: If you can, redirect attention via your résumé, beginning with your work experience in specific areas set off from each other by a substantive experience or technical skills heading, and only then presenting your employment history. If it comes up during your interview, counter with the substantive expertise and skill sets that you developed along the way. See Appendix A, 'Before' and 'After' Résumés.

Note: This is the *only* circumstance where I recommend submerging your employment history far down in a résumé. Otherwise, don't do it. Employers who do not see your employment history pretty quickly may think you must have something to hide.

Weakness: Undistinguished Job Titles

For example, if you are an attorney but working in a paralegal position.

Antidote: Talk to your prior employers about what *else* you might label yourself with their approval, e.g., Janitor—Custodian or Building Engineer; Paralegal—Law Clerk or Legal Researcher or Legal Analyst; Alternative Dispute Resolution Specialist—Mediator or ADR Manager.

Weakness: Too Much "Seasoning"

This is just a nice way of saying you may be perceived as too old by prospective employers. "Too old" in the legal job market sometimes begins at a shockingly young age, often an age when even a professional athlete is still capable of competing at a high level. And yes, being rejected for a position because you are deemed an antique *is* age discrimination. We are all SHOCKED that such a thing could happen!

Antidote: Include your strenuous outside activities on your résumé, such as sports and other involvements; point out how your seasoning would benefit an employer, e.g., mentoring less experienced attorneys, and your extensive substantive knowledge. Don't waste your time applying to places where it is probable that age could be an issue, such as major law firms, certain consulting firms, and certain government agencies such as the Department of Justice or the Securities and Exchange Commission. Don't omit dates of education on your résumé, a sure sign that you are hiding your age; rather, put education at the end of the document.

Weakness: Lack of a Life Outside of Work

The need for client development, good relations between the legal staff and both internal and external clients, and a pleasant, social workplace means that it is not enough to be a drone and sit by yourself all day long before your computer or in the law library.

Antidote: Join something; volunteer; get some community activities to note on your résumé. Demonstrate to employers that there is more than one facet to your career personality.

> Addressing résumé weaknesses head-on will enhance your success at securing job interviews. Once you arrive at the interview, you can assume that the interviewer will probe any weaknesses that he or she has spotted in your application, often as the opening interview gambit.
>
> Again, when you prepare for an interview, do not waste much time on your strengths. Any questions about your strong points are going to be easy for you to answer. Not so your weaknesses.

Chapter 18

How an Employer Reads a Résumé

If you understand how employers approach résumés, you will be light years ahead of your competition.

Understanding how an employer reads a résumé is central to how you should go about preparing your résumés. Unfortunately, the overwhelming majority of legal job seekers craft their résumés in a vacuum, oblivious to this crucial factor. It is also important to know that employers in different employment sectors often approach résumés differently. This chapter describes these differences.

Private-Sector Employers

The first thing you need to know about employers and résumés is that no one saddled with this task looks forward to it with enthusiasm. Quite the contrary; reading résumés is almost universally considered a burden, a necessary but highly distasteful ordeal. Anything you do in your résumé that annoys or irritates the reader, or makes what they already perceive as a dismal chore even more miserable, will be to your detriment. Moreover, the employer will likely obsess about the annoyance or irritation to the exclusion of identifying the great things you have included about your experience and capabilities. You need to do whatever is necessary to make the employer's task as palatable as possible.

You also need to know that employers typically read each résumé the first time with elimination paramount in their minds. Law being almost always a buyer's (read: employer's) market, any open position usually generates a great many résumés. Consequently, employers tend to want to do whatever is necessary to reduce the number of résumés they receive down to a manageable few before giving them closer scrutiny. They do this by scanning each résumé in the pile in front of them quickly, according each one no more than 20 to 30 seconds of attention. In that brief time span, it is impossible to read an entire résumé. At best, they are likely to make it about halfway through page one. And in so doing, they're mostly keeping an eye out for anything they can find that justifies rejecting the candidate.

There are two lessons to be learned from this employer technique:

1. *Your first objective is "to live to fight another day."* You need to think "survival mode" when putting your résumé together. That means positioning the key information designed to impress the employer up front, where it cannot be missed. One very effective way to accomplish this is to lead off your résumé with a Profile or Qualifications Summary immediately following your identifying and contact information at the top of the document. That way, you can immediately bring up the skills that distinguish you from other candidates from where they might otherwise appear, perhaps to be overlooked during this initial scan. If you graduated from a top school, for example, don't wait until the Education section at the end of your résumé to reveal that distinguishing fact. If you are fluent in Mandarin Chinese, make sure the employer doing the cursory scan knows it. Say it right up front.

2. You need to be very careful *not to make any typographical, spelling, punctuation, or other grammatical mistakes.* That means performing a spell check and proofreading your résumé with great care, and preferably also having someone whose proofreading skills you trust do the same. Because writing ability is central to good lawyering, any such error the employer encounters in your résumé is a license to reject your candidacy.

Once employers identify the surviving résumés, they generally give the few that make it this far closer attention under less frenzied circumstances. I used to take the surviving résumés home with me, retire to my study with a cup of tea, put Mozart on the CD player, and read the finalist résumés in this relaxed venue.

This more careful scrutiny often still suffers from a common employer malady that afflicts almost everyone who has to read résumés through to the end: PADD, or Progressive Attention Deficit Disorder. This means that the farther along one reads, the less attention one pays.

What this means for you is, *don't save the best for last.* If your greatest hits were things you did in jobs prior to your current or most recent employments, consider taking a different approach to presenting résumé information than the traditional, reverse-chronological descriptions of your job history. Instead, consider presenting the information differentiated by *what you did* rather than *when you did them.* Instead of job title and employer headings, substitute task and/or content headings. A skills or functional résumé approach, where the dividers in the Professional Experience section of your résumé are substantive areas and/or technical legal skill sets rather than your present and past jobs, will serve you better and have a stronger impact. If you practice employment law and are seeking another employment law position, for example, your headings might be such items as:

- employment counseling
- employment litigation and dispute resolution
- legal drafting

- teaching and training
- presentations

Each heading would then be followed by a number of bulleted statements germane to the heading, such as:

Employment Counseling
- Served as outside employment counselor to a variety of high-tech small-business clients.
- Advised client companies on labor relations, employee grievances, and EEOC mediations.
- Recommended preventive employment law solutions that reduced the number of grievance filings by over 50 percent.

In addition to liberating your résumé from the temporal constraints of a job-by-job, reverse-chronological approach, this technique also permits you to establish an "information hierarchy" where the most important information for a specific job opportunity can be placed in a triage sequence from highest to lowest priority. Moreover, the use of highlighted headings (boldface type in this example) and bullets draws the reader's eyes to them. You want to make sure that the employer who reads the document with declining concentration sees the key information about you while they're still paying attention. See also Appendix A, 'Before' and 'After' Résumés.

Government Employers

The U.S. government has a unique process when it comes to consideration of legal résumés. While not a uniform approach, as a general rule each application for a federal legal position goes through a review process something like this:

Step 1. A non-attorney personnel clerk or specialist reviews the application to determine that the candidate meets the minimum threshold requirements for the position. As these requirements are laid out in both the published vacancy announcement and in an internal manual, the personnel clerk usually does this review by reference to a checklist of minimum qualification requirements.

What this means for you, the candidate, is that you need to make sure that:

1. *Your application is responsive to the vacancy announcement.* If the announcement requires that a candidate be able to "leap tall buildings at a single bound," it is not sufficient to pass muster with the personnel clerk to say that you "leap tall buildings with a running start and by bringing your foot down on the roof before leaping off."

2. *You use language that the personnel clerk can understand.* Using "legalese" when plain English would suffice, or relying on the impenetrable jargon of your current or recent workplace is dangerous. See Chapter 21, "Talking the Employer's Talk . . . Not Yours."

Step 2. The surviving applications are forwarded to a rating panel consisting of attorneys who will each review all of the remaining documents and rank the candidates hierarchically. This is the stage where your application is scrutinized most carefully for content, organization, and "fit."

Step 3. The ranked résumés are forwarded to the hiring official, who will determine who gets interviewed and, ultimately, who gets hired.

Certain state legal offices employ a similar approach. However, states and localities have their own ways of hiring attorneys, many of which are constrained by state civil service laws and regulations. U.S. government law offices, in contrast, are not bound by civil service laws and rules when hiring attorneys.

> One final point about how employers read résumés. This has to do with the employer's *expectations* upon picking up the document. Employers expect to see certain information included in a résumé, and also expect to see that information presented in a logical order. If they do not find

what they're seeking, that is a big strike against you. If the important information is in the résumé but is difficult to locate, that also does not help your campaign.

Once you understand how an employer reads a résumé, you can put yourself in the employer's shoes and craft a document that is reader-friendly—or, at the very least, easily accessible and tolerable to a reader with a giant pile of résumés.

Chapter 19

How to Read and Respond to a Job Ad

Both as an employer and a legal career counselor, I have always been baffled by résumés and cover letters that were unresponsive to the position advertised. "Didn't they read the job ad?" I would ask myself. Apparently not. It was often as if two ships were passing in the night.

Regardless of how otherwise impressive the candidate, I always felt that my company could not assume the risk of hiring someone who could not follow simple instructions. I have yet to encounter a legal employer who did not feel the same way. After all, one of the core traits of good lawyering is the ability to take apart a legal problem in order to analyze it and derive a solution. Someone who demonstrates that they cannot even do this with a one-page or shorter job ad is clearly announcing that this essential trait is lacking.

This chapter attempts to help you accomplish two very important job-hunting tasks:

1. To provide a template that you can use to dissect any job ad or vacancy announcement; and
2. To recommend strategies for effectively responding to either one of them.

Dissecting the Job Ad

To respond competitively to a job advertisement, you first have to take it apart, breaking it down into its constituent parts. This "dissection" accomplishes three things:

1. It helps you determine if you should apply for the position;
2. It enables you to analyze your qualifications with respect to each component; and
3. It helps you craft your application to be as responsive as possible.

If you apply for the position without going through this analysis, you are highly likely to submit an application that is less competitive than it could be. If this is a job you really want, then you might have carelessly, if inadvertently, opted out of the competition.

Here is an example of a typical legal job ad.

> ### Corporate Associate, Smith & Jones LLP, Los Angeles, Cal.
>
> We are seeking an associate with 3-5 years of experience with a strong corporate background including public M&A and private equity experience. Demonstrated experience in M&A transactions, private equity investments, 1934 Act reporting and Sarbanes-Oxley is essential. Candidates should have excellent writing, negotiating and research abilities, top academic credentials, a willingness to assume responsibility, demonstrated leadership qualities, and will be interested in sharing those talents through mentoring and training junior lawyers. Large law firm experience preferred.

The simple, filled-in template that follows is one that you can adopt—and adapt—to virtually any legal job ad or vacancy announcement. It is designed to break down the job ad into its various components.

Required Qualifications
1. 3–5 years of experience
2. Strong corporate background
   a. Public M&A transactions
   b. Private equity investments
   c. 1934 Act reporting
   d. Sarbanes-Oxley
3. Excellent writing ability
4. Excellent negotiating ability
5. Excellent research ability
6. Top academic credentials
7. Willingness to assume responsibility
8. Demonstrated leadership qualities
9. Interest in mentoring and training junior lawyers

Preferred or Desired Qualifications

---

10. Large law firm experience

Responding to the Job Ad

Numerous studies on learning techniques have concluded that writing about something is by far the best way to absorb and comprehend information. Legal educators quite rightly hammer us in law school with a continuing drumbeat about the critical importance of "issue identification." This template approach to dissecting a job ad is designed to merge both strategies.

What follows is the same template, but with the second column filled in:

Required Qualifications	My Qualifications
1. 3–5 years of experience	No—2.5 years of experience
2. Strong corporate background	Yes—work for corporate practice group in current firm
a. public M&A transactions	Yes—participated in several transactions $1.5–$40+ million
b. private equity investments	Yes—part of team structuring one deal
c. 1934 Act reporting	Yes, but only limited exposure
d. Sarbanes Oxley	Yes—advise clients' audit committees on filing requirements
3. Excellent writing ability	Yes—two annual firm evaluations cited me for my writing ability
4. Excellent negotiating ability	Yes—participated in five successful transactions
5. Excellent research ability	Yes—called upon by partners to research issues in preparation for presentations to clients and professional audiences
6. Top academic credentials	Yes—top 25% of law school graduating class
7. Willingness to assume responsibility	Yes—seek out new and diverse assignments
8. Demonstrated leadership qualities	Yes—chair of PTA Safety Committee; organized fundraiser for local charity
9. Interest in mentoring and training junior lawyers	Yes—as 3L, trained 2Ls in Legal Aid Clinic in intake procedures and trial techniques
Preferred or Desired Qualifications	**My Qualifications**
10. Large law firm experience	Currently work for a 30-attorney firm with a diverse, sophisticated corporate and litigation practice

After filling in the template, the candidate must decide whether to apply for the position. While not a perfect match to every required qualification, the candidate determines that she comes close enough to be a serious competitor.

Note: When examining a job ad and deciding whether or not to pursue the opportunity, it is important to keep in mind that *virtually* *all legal job ads are written with the perfect candidate in mind.* And every employer understands that the perfect candidate is probably not out there.

My last piece of advice when it comes to being as responsive as possible to what an employer is seeking: Every job ad is an announcement that the employer has a *problem*. When responding, you should think about how to demonstrate that you represent the *solution*.

> If you employ the methodology I describe in this chapter, you are assured of being one of the more responsive candidates for a position. That alone will earn you "subliminal" points with the employer. Being highly responsive tells an employer that you are careful, methodical, highly organized, and adept at following instructions.

Chapter 20

Identifying Your "Hidden" Skill Sets ... and Matching Them with Opportunities

I am often surprised at the lack of knowledge and/or misinformation that I see in, and hear from, attorneys in career crisis who seek my legal career counseling advice. A classic, recurring example is the litigator who is stressed out by the pressures of litigation, but cannot see where else she can practice:

> "All I have ever done is general commercial litigation, so I guess I will have to continue to do that even though I can't handle the pressure any longer."

Or the real estate lawyer who has no idea where to turn when the real estate market tanks:

> "Real estate transactions have dried up and there is no other place I can go. Help!"

Not true in either case.

The Burnt-Out Litigator

If the litigator stops, takes a deep breath, and examines her skills and experience, she would see that she has many options:

1. *Administrative litigation.* If the courtroom has become too stressful, she could ratchet down a notch and limit her practice to litigating before administrative bodies. There are several hundred agency adjudication entities at the federal level alone, with hearings for many agencies held all over the country, and hundreds more when you factor in state and local government. These forums have given rise to a large number (over 200) of diverse U.S. government law offices with administrative litigation practices. The counterweight to these numerous government practices is the many law firms and practitioners who represent private parties before these bodies.

Administrative litigation is a growth industry. Litigation inundating the courts has prompted government at all levels to attempt to ease the strain on the judicial system by creating new administrative forums to which cases can be diverted, heard, and hopefully resolved. The number of administrative hearing bodies has been growing rapidly now for a generation, with no end in sight. Pressing issues such as healthcare reform, climate change, prescription drugs, and homeland security will inevitably generate additional administrative hearing authorities and bodies.

What makes administrative litigation different—and much less stressful—than court litigation? Six very important features:

-   Relaxed rules of evidence.
-   Less rigorous procedural rules.
-   Rules of evidence and procedure that are often the same from one forum to the next. No fewer than 32 federal government agencies hold hearings governed by the Administrative Procedure Act, 5 U.S.C. §§ 551 *et seq.*
-   Administrative hearings are generally one-day affairs at most.

- Scheduling of administrative hearings is much more predictable than court trials.
- Some hearings are non-adversarial, meaning that there is no opposing counsel.

2. *Appellate litigation.* Arguing appeals is very different from presenting a case at trial. Appellate oral arguments are short, often lasting no more than 30 minutes. They are also scheduled enough in advance to give the appellate litigator ample time to prepare. Appeals are often decided on the basis of the briefs. In short, appeals work is appealing because it is far less stressful than courtroom litigation, where uncertainty, lack of adequate time to prepare, and sudden surprises are often the order of the day.

More disputes mean more court and administrative litigation, which in turn lead to more appeals, which means that appellate litigation is also a growth industry.

In addition to major law firm appellate practice groups, there are a number of boutique firms that focus their entire practice on appellate litigation. The U.S. government has more than 100 legal offices that have an appellate practice. Add to this every state attorney general and public defender office, plus the for-profit and non-profit corporations that conduct their own appellate litigation in-house, and the list of appellate practice opportunities becomes quite large.

3. *Litigation management.* A seasoned trial litigator is perfectly suited for litigation management positions in insurance companies, other corporations, and consulting firms. Litigation managers in insurance companies and other corporations manage the company's litigation, including selecting and managing outside counsel, budgeting for litigation, strategizing cases jointly with outside counsel, and managing litigation expenses. Litigation management consultants advise their clients on selecting, budgeting, and managing outside counsel.

Litigation management divisions and consulting firms are interested in attorney candidates who can itemize their relevant experience, hitting as many of the following items as possible:

- Selecting cost-effective outside counsel
- Working within a litigation budget
- Familiarity with corporate outside counsel retention agreements
- Negotiating discounted billing rates
- Negotiating the level of a professional to be used on a matter
- Negotiating fixed fees for particular matters
- Partnering with in-house counsel on cases
- Strategizing cases
- Familiarity with legal fee budgets
- Experience reviewing legal bills
- Optimizing legal expenditures
- Negotiating legal fee disputes

4. *Transactional law.* Every experienced litigator is also an experienced transactional lawyer. Litigators, as a rule, settle the overwhelming majority of their cases through negotiations with opposing parties. A settlement agreement is as much a transaction as a negotiated deal. The dynamics of the negotiation and documentation process differ very little.

I have yet to meet a litigator who realizes this. Almost every time I point this out, it is received as a stunning revelation.

The best places to look for transactional opportunities are law firms that focus on negotiating, documenting, and closing deals for their corporate clients, and corporate in-house counsel offices.

The Panicked Real Estate Attorney

Now let's turn to the real estate attorney. He needs to perform the same kind of analysis that the litigator undertook. When he does, he will be surprised at the variety of opportunities that exist for him, even in a deeply troubled real estate environment.

1. *Real estate distress law.* This is the perfect storm. When real estate development and sales wane, transactions surrounding distressed real estate will flourish. A real estate attorney with experience in the former practice is ideally situated to segue into the latter practice. He already understands the dynamics of the real estate market and of real estate transactions. Now he just needs to approach it from the other side—marshalling assets of failed and threatened institutions, valuing them, and attempting to find a market for them and get them off the holder's books.

    The organizations likely to have job—and contract— opportunities in a bad real estate market are real estate investment trusts, pension funds that hold a lot of real property, banks and other financial institutions that have had to foreclose on properties, and government regulators, primarily the Federal Deposit Insurance Corporation (FDIC), which takes over failed banks and disposes of their assets. When the FDIC had to assume this role during the savings and loan collapse (1989–1995), the agency hired more than 400 attorneys and contracted with hundreds of large, mid-size, and small law firms and solo practitioners to help it resolve bad assets and loans. The Great Recession put the agency in a similar position, more than 175 banks having failed since December 2007.

2. *Company/nonprofit real estate departments.* Positions like this exist in a number of different employment sectors. Hundreds of colleges and universities have real estate departments and staff them with attorneys and other professionals. Companies that deal with facility acquisitions, dispositions, and management, such as supermarket chains, bookstore chains, telecommunication firms, hospitality and recreation companies, insurance companies and pension plans with real estate portfolios (see *www.pionline.org*), and real estate investment trusts (see *www.nareit.org*), also have real estate departments that include attorneys.

3. *Energy company "landman" positions.* Oil and gas companies all retain "landmen" on their staffs. Landmen, who are often attorneys, negotiate with property owners in order to

buy or lease their land and/or mineral rights for energy development projects, among many other legal and law-related duties. These positions are located in areas where oil and gas deposits are concentrated, such as Texas, Oklahoma, Louisiana, and Arkansas. However, recent major natural gas discoveries have expanded the geographic possibilities to include New York, Pennsylvania, Maryland, and West Virginia.

Watch for more and more landman positions in the emerging "green" economy, particularly wind and solar energy companies and the companies that will be building the delivery infrastructure to bring electricity from wind farms and solar arrays to consumers.

4. *Government real estate practices.* Governments at every level (federal, state, local, and special-purpose districts) are heavily involved in real estate legal matters. The U.S. government has more than 100 legal offices that maintain a real estate practice. Many of the tens of thousands of special-purpose districts in the United States handle real property legal matters. Federal law offices with real estate practices can be identified in the Federal Careers for Attorneys database at *www.attorneyjobs.com*. This Web site also lists specific federal real estate job opportunities, as does *www.usajobs.gov*. State and local government and special-purpose district positions are listed on state job Web sites as well as agency and district Web sites.

5. *Real estate trade associations.* There are a large number of real estate trade associations in Washington, D.C., state capitals, and other cities. All of them have government relations departments often staffed by attorneys, and many of them have legal counsel offices. Some of the more prominent ones are:

- American Hotel and Lodging Association
- American Industrial Real Estate Association
- American Land Title Association
- American Society of Real Estate Counselors
- Association of University Real Estate Officials
- Building Owners and Managers Association

- Institute of Real Estate Management
- International Council of Shopping Centers
- International Real Estate Federation
- International Right of Way Association
- Mortgage Bankers Association of America
- Multifamily Housing Institute
- National Association of Corporate Real Estate Executives
- National Association of Home Builders
- National Association of Housing and Redevelopment Officials
- National Association of Realtors
- National Association of Industrial and Office Properties
- National Association of Real Estate Brokers
- National Association of Real Estate Investment Trusts
- Pension Real Estate Association
- Urban Land Institute

6. *Land trusts.* The 1,600-plus nonprofit land trusts in the United States (up from 450 in 1992) preserve and protect land from development. They do this through purchases of land, donations of land from landowners, and conservation easements encompassing land and/or endangered species on the land that they negotiate with municipalities.

    Thanks to a temporary tax incentive that became effective in 2007 and expired at the end of 2009, many land trusts doubled the pace of donated easements in just one year. Land trusts' top legislative priority right now is to make the temporary incentive a permanent part of the Internal Revenue Code. The proposed legislation has four times more co-sponsors than any previous land trust tax incentive bill. The Land Trust Alliance, the umbrella organization representing land trust interests in Washington, D.C., is developing a Conservation Defense Center to help ensure that conserved land remains protected for all time.

    Land trusts do not just operate in the wide open spaces. They also focus on blighted urban neighborhoods, historic homestead conservation, coastal access for fishermen, and the preservation of streams to ensure healthy drinking water.

Attorneys work for land trusts in a variety of capacities that require real estate law knowledge, including:

- legal counsel
- land trust management
- land protection
- stewardship
- conservation management
- development, planned and charitable giving

Specific real estate-related functions include:

- negotiating land protection transactions, including all stages of conservation easements, fee gifting, and management agreements.
- developing relationships with landowners and government-client elected officials and agency staff.
- collecting natural areas information and developing and implementing plans for appropriate stewardship, which includes: invasive species control, prescribed burning, native plant seed processing, species monitoring and research, and arranging and overseeing volunteer stewardship activities.
- writing grant proposals and reports.
- environmental advocacy.
- policy analysis.
- developing and implementing land conservation initiatives.
- producing baseline reports for land trust properties.
- building and maintaining positive associations with private landowners, public agencies, conservation organizations, and local governments.
- land-use planning.
- natural resources management.

Senior positions can pay up to the low six figures.

7. *Eminent domain practice.* Governments have a constitutional right under the last clause of the Fifth and Fourteenth Amendments to take a citizen's private property without the owner's

consent for a government or public purpose (including economic development), as long as the owner receives "just compensation" for the taking. The most common purposes for which eminent domain is invoked are for public utilities, highways, and railroads.

The American Recovery and Reinvestment Act of 2009, Pub. L. 111-5 (a.k.a. the Stimulus Package), invests heavily in public works, including such massive infrastructure projects as building wind energy transmission systems and retrofitting water and waste-disposal systems. The eminent domain power of the government is being extensively employed in order to effectuate the purposes of the law.

States also possess eminent domain powers (through the Fourteenth Amendment) and are also employing them to condemn property that will be transformed into public uses.

Real estate–savvy attorneys make good eminent domain lawyers, especially when it comes to negotiating a fair value purchase with the government, plus the aspects of condemnation that may involve a variety of different types of takings that raise complex questions of real estate law and valuation. These include:

- Complete taking, where all of the property in question is taken.
- Partial taking, where the owner should receive "dual compensation," first, for the piece of land taken to widen a road, for example; and second, for any effect the taking has on the value of the owner's remaining property.
- Temporary (time-limited) taking, under which the owner retains title, is compensated for any losses associated with the taking, and regains complete possession of the property once the property is no longer needed by the government.
- Easements and rights of way, where a condemnation action is initiated in order to obtain a more limited property right, such as a utility easement to install and maintain power lines.

8. *Bankruptcy.* When the economy turns south, bankruptcy practices thrive. Bankruptcies often involve real estate matters, and there is a long history of real estate lawyers reinventing themselves as bankruptcy lawyers during recessions, then returning to real estate law when the economy improves.

When bankruptcies increase, the government entities responsible for administering the bankruptcy program must also increase their staffs. The principal government employers are the U.S. Bankruptcy Court Staff Attorney Offices (94 nationwide) and the U.S. Department of Justice's Offices of the United States Trustee (95 nationwide).

In addition to Bankruptcy Courts, U.S. Trustee Offices and the many private practice attorneys who thrive in bankruptcy practice during economic downturns, there are a host of U.S. government law offices that also have a steady and ongoing bankruptcy practice (bankruptcy is, of course, largely a federal practice).

Every attorney, regardless of his or her practice specialty, has hidden skill sets that could match other practice opportunities. Virtually any practice area lends itself to this kind of analysis. Selected examples include:

- *Intellectual property:* IP asset management, technology licensing, international counterfeiting and piracy investigations, and enforcement
- *Securities law*: securitization, plus any other complex regulatory arena
- *Trusts and estates:* planned giving, trusts administration, land trust stewardship, nonprofit management, and elder law
- *Government contracts:* contract negotiator, contract administrator, procurement officer, grants and contracts compliance, technology transfer
- *Criminal law:* child support enforcement, healthcare fraud, civil penalties officer, asset forfeiture, civilian complaint reviewer, inspector general, FBI agent, drug enforcement agent, victims' compensation officer

- *Energy law:* mineral appeals specialist, carbon trade manager, energy regulatory affairs professional, public utilities specialist, landman

These two exercises in identifying attorneys' hidden skill sets and matching them with opportunities are representative of the analysis that every attorney should undertake. This technique can be applied to any lawyer who finds himself or herself mired in a practice area that is declining or has suffered a (hopefully) temporary economic downturn.

Chapter 21

Talking the Employer's Talk ... Not Yours

Becoming an attorney means joining a "priesthood"—to an outsider, the law is a rather mystical, near-Masonic guild with its own arcane language that no one else can understand. Once initiated into the priesthood, we discover that this exclusive organization contains within itself numerous smaller preserves with their own jargon, terms of art, and acronyms that cause even other attorneys to scratch their heads in incomprehension.

The world of banking and finance law has its "D'Oench Duhme Doctrines," CDOs, and CMOs; environmental law its "EIS's," "CITES," and "caps-and-trades"; securities law its "8(a)'s" and "10(k)'s"; not to mention the "Latinisms" co-opted as their own by estate planning attorneys with their "per stirpes"; courts with their "stare decises"; and so forth.

Once immersed in a particular practice area or venue where law is practiced, the peculiar language of our everyday environment becomes second nature. That is important for our practice or milieu, but can be a disaster if we venture outside when job hunting.

Translating Gobbledygook

The use of insider idioms in résumés is one of those quirks of the legal recruitment and job-hunting process that drives employers who have to slog through these documents up the wall. Consequently, this is something you should avoid, with one exception: If you are applying for a position with an employer who you know beyond any doubt will understand your vernacular, then go ahead and use it. Presumably that will be limited to employers who work within the confines of your practice or industry. Otherwise, you will need to translate your "priestly" language into plain English.

The following *Before* and *After* examples are taken directly from two versions of an experience section on a résumé in which the candidate initially used the most "inside" of insider language conceivable—a nightmarish experience for any employer forced to read such obscure gobbledygook and a virtual guarantee of rejection for any legal position, even one within the Department of Defense. This classic example of obscurantism comes from an actual résumé sent to me by a legal career counseling client immediately prior to our first meeting.

The second version is the actual "clean-up" performed on the first version, where I translated his jargon into English and universalized his experience in order to render it both comprehensible and palatable to prospective employers.

Before: Experience Portion of
Résumé Using "Insider" Jargon

"Drafted DOD rules and regs on DOA, DON, USAF, and USMC's (and USCG in time of war) DOPMA and ROPMA staffing requirements and obligations in the event of a 50 U.S.C. 447, as amended (Act of 14 June 1947, ch. 6, §17(a)91)(ii), 49 Stat. 1685) mobilization; liaised with HASC, SASC, DMDC, DMA, DNA, UUHS, JCS, and other DOD components, and with Unified and Specified Commands on pending legislation and regulatory proposals; advised ASD (ISA), PDASD (Antiterrorism), and DASD (RA) on personnel and national security law issues; and coordinated legislative development of legislative program for GC office."

After: Same Experience Expressed
in Universal Language

- Drafted comprehensive regulations governing personnel matters applicable to all of the military services.
- Coordinated and explained pending legislation and proposed regulations to congressional committees and Department of Defense components.
- Advised senior management on employment, international, counterterrorism, and national security law issues.
- Participated in the development and review of the annual departmental legislative program.

Do not think that because this is a very short chapter, it is not crucially important. It is short because it is able to rely on the stark contrast between two "pictures" in order to get the point across. As the eighteenth-century French polymath Blaise Pascal once wrote to a friend:

"I apologize for writing you a five-page letter. I did not have time to write you a one-page letter."

Chapter 22

Getting Lost in the Ether . . . and Getting Found

In the good old pre-Internet days, applying for a job was much easier. If that sounds counterintuitive or suspiciously Luddite, let me elaborate: All you had to do back in the "dark ages" was send a résumé to the appropriate recipient. You had at least the vague comfort of knowing that a marketing effort of your own devise was likely to be seen by someone in a position to make a decision about your future.

That is mostly gone now, replaced by online applications, résumé/application databases, and other technological innovations that establish barriers between job applicants and legal hiring managers.

The purpose of this chapter is to help you get your strong points across to the employer anyway, both via the new technologies that govern recruitment and job hunting and, if necessary, by circumventing them—and not getting demerits for so doing.

Getting Lost in the Ether

Three horror stories paint a troubling picture of what can happen to an online application.

1. The U.S. Office of Personnel Management (OPM) contracted with an outside organization to build a government-wide online job application system that every federal department and agency could use. Millions of dollars later, the system was discovered to have a lot of bugs that required ironing out, including completed applications that got lost in the ether and never made it to OPM; applications that arrived, but then disappeared from the database repository; applications that froze while being completed by job candidates and could not be unfrozen; and so forth.

    So the OPM spent additional millions on the same outside contractor that built the first system to fix what they had delivered. The second iteration also had too many problems to function smoothly. Now OPM has launched its third attempt at an online application system (talk about a "killer app!").

2. A second OPM online application process designed exclusively to receive federal Administrative Law Judge (ALJ) applications also worked poorly, suffering some of the same problems that afflicted the government-wide system. The ALJ application is a lengthy and complicated ordeal for candidates, and, like a bar examination, no one who has been through the process looks forward to having to do it all over again.

3. A very accomplished antitrust attorney worked for the Office of Competition Policy at a federal department. He wished to move into the private sector, preferably into a major law firm with a substantial antitrust practice. He applied for a position with a prestigious national law firm, "building" an online résumé per the firm's lateral application process. Throughout the résumé, he used the terms "competition" and "competitive" instead of antitrust. His résumé,

along with those of numerous other applicants for the antitrust as well as other positions, fed directly into a firm database.

When the firm's antitrust practice group head asked his secretary to retrieve the résumés that had come into the database seeking the antitrust position, she entered the key word "antitrust" and delivered a large number of résumés to her boss. My client's résumé was not retrieved because it lacked the word "antitrust." Despite his stellar qualifications, he was not considered for the position.

(I'd like to add here that this sad tale occurred *before* he became my client.)

. . . and Getting Found

What these horror stories of job-hunting futility mean for you is the following:

1. If you have to apply online for a position, follow up with the employer to make sure that your application is received.
2. Make sure that your online application contains every possible key word that might be used to retrieve your document from the database.
3. Always submit a résumé in addition to the online application. Transmit it to the hiring official or someone proximate to him or her using a cover letter or transmittal e-mail. State that you submitted the online application per instructions, but that you also want to make sure that the employer has an opportunity to see your résumé, which presents a better picture of who you are and what you bring to the table.

A final note: If the employer gives you the option of applying online or submitting a résumé directly, *always* choose the latter approach.

Applying for a legal job is not what it used to be. Technology has leveled the playing field in the sense that everyone's online application now looks the same. In other words, if you are restricted to completing an online template, you lose the opportunity to distinguish yourself by demonstrating your organizational and presentation skills or elaborating on your achievements in an addendum. That places the emphasis completely on pure, restricted content, while also divesting the employer of the opportunity to judge these other important factors.

Compounding the dilemma is the uncertainty that (1) your application arrived and arrived intact, (2) will be extracted from the database, and (3) will be considered by someone who can grasp the value you represent.

This combination of potentially harmful factors makes it all the more imperative that you have an outstanding, well-crafted résumé that you can use to supplement your online application.

Chapter 23

The Critical Importance of Storytelling

Two of the most important steps you can take in your quest for new legal employment or a change of careers are to:

1. differentiate yourself from your competitors, and
2. make yourself memorable to the key people who can move your career along.

You can accomplish both steps by becoming a storyteller. This may sound foolish or frivolous, but it is very serious and is a key to getting noticed by both your intermediaries (references and contacts) and by prospective employers.

Why a Story?

Telling a story to the key individuals on your path to new employment accomplishes two very important factors in advancing you toward your career goals:

- First, anecdotal information about you is much more interesting than your job description, duties, and responsibilities. When your applications and your interviews contain relevant, job-related anecdotal information about you, references, contacts, and potential employers perk up and read and listen more intently, with more focus and attention to what you are saying. Storytelling gives your references good, specific talking points that they can speak about with enthusiasm to an employer. Networking contacts become more energized and committed to acting as your advocate. And employers are much more likely to become interested in you.

- Second, a good story makes you more memorable to these individuals. This is particularly important with respect to employers who, after reviewing numerous applications and interviewing multiple candidates, have to decide whom to hire based on their impressions, which, with the passage of very little time, tend to become murky. The candidates they are likely to remember are the ones who imprinted themselves in the employer's mind. There is no better way to imprint yourself (positively) than by leaving the employer with a story that demonstrates your capabilities.

Who Needs to Hear Your Story?

Your story needs to be told to your references, to your networking contacts and intermediaries, and to prospective employers. Each of these three groups will read or hear it somewhat differently and be motivated in your favor for different reasons.

Your references and contacts will be able to employ your story in their conversations with potential employers who call them to get an insight into your performance and capabilities. Your good story can accomplish several very positive things for you vis-à-vis your references and contacts.

- It can stimulate them to be enthusiastic about you when speaking to a potential employer. Tone of voice is very important to an employer who telephones a reference. If the reference's tone is upbeat, that alone can make a difference.
- It can give them some "meat" to provide to the employer beyond the usual bland comments about what a good em-

ployee and solid citizen you are. Meat is memorable. Vacuous, abstract statements about your character and capabilities are not.

- It can give you the opportunity to have some control over the conversation between the employer and the reference, despite your absence from the dialogue. A good story focuses the reference's attention and often mitigates the risk inherent in a more open-ended, unscripted exchange.

- Your networking contacts will also be able and likely eager to impart your story to the prospective employers that they know.

- It can act as a motivator to a contact to actually do something positive for you, and to become more enthusiastic about, and more committed to boosting, your candidacy. It's more fun to tell a cool story than it is to list credentials.

- It gives a contact something concrete that he or she can use on your behalf.

- It establishes a comfort zone for contacts about going ahead and endorsing your candidacy to an employer because they can see that you are both accomplished and highly organized with respect to your job search.

- Since so very few job seekers actually take the time and trouble to craft something like this, you will stand out, impressing your references and contacts with your uniquely compelling approach.

Finally, potential employers, the most important group of all those who populate your career path, are much more likely to react favorably to a candidate who tells them a good story than to those who rely exclusively on the information usually found in resumes and derived during interviews.

- A good story gives an employer a talking point when communicating with references.

- It makes it easy for an employer to distinguish the storyteller from other applicants for the position.

- It gives an employer a deeper insight into how you might perform on the job.

- It gives the employer an idea of how you might "fit" into the organization and, conversely, gives you an opportunity to demonstrate your fit.

What Constitutes a Good Story?

Elaborating on one or more specific accomplishments—work-related projects or tasks that you undertook that had positive outcomes for your organization or your client—makes for an exceptional story. These could be things like an innovation you proposed, a problem you solved, an initiative you advanced, an argument you crafted that prevailed, or a cost-saving measure you recommended or implemented successfully. In other words, anything that you did on the job that positions you in a positive light in the eyes of an employer.

If you cannot come up with anything along these lines, then a decent fallback is a story that shows how you tackled a particular issue or problem. This can be effective even if you do not have a triumph to tout. The benefit of this fallback approach is that it demonstrates to the employer how your mind works, i.e., how you go about considering and dealing with a matter that is given to you to handle.

An effective story has to be easy for the reader or listener to follow. It should be lively, concise, and, if possible, entertaining. It should not be so complicated that the recipient will lose interest halfway through it. It should also not be so esoteric that it would be difficult for an outsider to comprehend. It should, of course, be in plain English with a minimum of insider jargon.

Here is an example of a good—and very successful—story.

The Boffo Gelato Transaction

I played the lead legal role in a unique multi-step transaction that allowed Amalgamated to achieve its strategic objective to become the world's largest gelato company.

I had to assemble and lead a team of lawyers (outside antitrust counsel, outside benefits counsel, outside transaction counsel, and in-house experts) to represent Amalgamated in negotiating a complex set of agreements with Boffo Gelato, including the merger agreement, employment agreements with key personnel, and the key terms of a revised long-term incentive plan.

Once these agreements were executed and the deal was publicly announced, I coordinated the work of Amalgamated's counsel, Boffo's counsel, benefits consultants, investment bankers, economists, and M&A personnel to lead the various SEC and antitrust filings. Due to the unique nature of the transaction—whereby Amalgamated contributed its ice cream subsidiary to a public company—the SEC required that we provide Boffo's shareholders with financial information regarding Amalgamated's ice cream business that had not been maintained by Amalgamated in the ordinary course of business. Thus, I led the effort to create the necessary GAAP financial statements for the joint Amalgamated/Boffo SEC filing. In doing so, I had to motivate Boffo's finance personnel whose positions would be eliminated as a result of the transaction.

Finally, I led the effort to collect all the relevant materials that Amalgamated needed to produce for the FTC. This encompassed virtually all electronic and written materials maintained by both Amalgamated's and Boffo's ice cream businesses.

The transaction presented numerous challenges. From the beginning, Boffo's management and counsel had a hard time coming to grips with the fact that they had agreed to sell their business to Amalgamated (albeit in a multi-step transaction that allowed them to remain public and in control notwithstanding Amalgamated's 67 percent ownership of the company). This created complex antitrust issues with respect to the FTC, which authorized its staff to sue to block the merger. Consequently, Boffo's management finally agreed to offer to divest certain assets. I brought in new antitrust counsel in an effort to improve the dynamics of the situation. I briefed the global Amalgamated CEO and CFO on our strategy and the issues, gained their support, and was able to get everyone aligned and to turn the situation around.

A divestiture acceptable to all parties was negotiated and the transaction closed in June 2005, one year after the signing of the merger agreement. In early 2006, I had the foresight to urge Boffo to commence work with Amalgamated on the joint tender offer and going-private transaction filing required by the SEC in order to allow the shareholders to put their shares to Boffo at the previously negotiated $88 per-share price within the previously negotiated time-table. As I anticipated, the process was more complex and unique than Boffo's management or counsel had recognized, and it was only due to the early start that SEC approval was obtained in time to allow for a seamless completion of the transaction at year-end. Consequently, in January 2007, Boffo became a wholly owned subsidiary of Amalgamated, allowing Amalgamated to achieve one of its key strategic objectives.

How to Tell Your Story

The storytelling component of your legal job or career campaign lends itself to a good deal of efficiency and synergy. The key document you will want to create to record your story is, generically speaking, a resume addendum. A resume addendum is a very valuable addition to your resume. You could entitle it "Significant Highlights" or "Significant Transactions" or "Significant Litigation" or something along those lines. It should not be longer than two pages (one is ideal). You should reference it in the body of your resume so that the reader will be compelled to turn to it. Something along the following lines is recommended:

- Played key role in General Motors' emergence from Chapter 11 bankruptcy (*see Significant Highlights, attached*).

I know of no employer who has reacted negatively to a resume addendum, despite the fact that the inclusion of an addendum generally means that the resume is longer than the typical two-page maximum that constitutes the very rough rule of thumb concerning resume length. On the contrary, employer feedback is invariably positive, often enthusiastic, since the narrative elaboration of a bulleted accomplishment often provides a deep insight into what makes the candidate tick, something impossible to glean from a by-the-book resume alone.

Each player in the job-hunting process should receive a copy of both your resume and resume addendum. In addition, it is highly likely that your story will come up during your interview with the employer. If the employer fails to reference it, you can always bring it up by incorporating it into one or more of your responses to a question from the interviewer. When you do, be sure to indicate that you have documented it in your resume addendum.

Finally, you are, of course, not limited to developing only one good story that illustrates your exemplary work-related qualities and talents. If you have more than one in your stable, experiment with multiple stories. This will give you the flexibility to select from among them the one that is most appropriate for a particular employer.

> A good story keeps the listener's or reader's interest, compensating for the otherwise dreary task of having to read resumes and job applications and interview prospective candidates—exercises that most employers are not enthusiastic about. It also distinguishes you from the vast majority of applicants who follow the customary resume and interview routine of providing their job descriptions and not much else, and remains imprinted in the memories of the hiring decision makers.

Chapter 24

Identifying Winning Writing Sample(s)

As an attorney, you earn your living largely by writing. Consequently, the importance of being able to write well and compellingly is central to both the lawyer's— and the prospective employer's—livelihood, not to mention the employer's decision whether to hire you. The hiring decision often depends, to some extent, on the employer's assessment of your writing sample(s). Perhaps a better way to state this is to say that a great writing sample will not always get you the job, but a poor one will almost always get you rejected.

Legal employers are becoming much more particular when it comes to writing samples, on two levels: First, they tend to scrutinize them more carefully than they have previously; and second, they sometimes will request specific types of writing samples, such as a transactional writing sample or a litigation writing sample.

The 17 writing sample evaluation factors below, derived from conversations with hundreds of legal employers, are designed to permit you to make good decisions about what writing sample(s) you should submit when requested by an employer. They are not in order of importance because what might be critically important to one employer might be less important to another.

It is highly unlikely that any writing sample could satisfy all 17 criteria; nor does it have to. The criteria are designed as a guideline to help you to choose among the documents that might qualify as suitable writing samples.

Writing Sample Evaluation Factors

1. How current is your writing sample? Employers are more likely to be impressed with a recent writing sample than one that is dated. Moreover, a dated writing sample implies that you have not done any serious legal writing for a long time. A very rough rule of thumb would be to try to submit a writing sample that you prepared within the past two years.

2. Is your topic interesting? Keeping the reader's interest is important regardless of what you write. You are far more likely to "imprint" your writing prowess on an employer and have him or her remember your writing sample if it is interesting. Lively facts and/or a timely topic are the best way to satisfy this evaluation criterion. A murder case beats the daylights out of an analysis of the nuances of drafting a qualified pension plan document any day.

3. Is your writing sample "quickly absorbing"? Does it capture the reader's interest quickly? Just like a resume with a "grabber" at the top of the document, an ideal writing sample will open strongly and rivet the reader's attention quickly.

4. How complex is your topic? This could be a double-edged sword. Complicated issues that require—and clearly manifest—the application of your analytical and reasoning skills can be a significant plus. At the same time, they can cause the reader to become confused or dazed and lose interest. This is something you will have to determine, ideally with the assistance of a significant other, a friend, or a colleague whose judgment you respect.

5. Is it a legal writing sample? Naturally, if you are seeking an attorney position, a legal writing sample is more appropriate than something else. However, if you do not have a legal writing sample, make sure that the document you select satisfies as many of the other criteria as possible.

6. Is it related to the position for which you are competing? This is the best of all possible worlds. If you are applying for a litigation position, for example, a pleading, a brief, an argument in support of a motion, etc., are ideal submissions. If it is a transactional job you seek, then a properly redacted transactional document would be best. If a regulatory position, then either a regulation you drafted or a paper commenting on a proposed or final regulation is ideal.

7. Is it related to the employer's industry? If, for example, you are applying for a position as a trademark attorney for a cosmetics company, then a writing sample concerning a cosmetics industry trademark issue cannot be topped.

8. Is it related to an issue of significance to the employer? While you may not be able to submit a writing sample that speaks to either the position or the employer's industry, one that discusses a timely issue applicable to the employer would also be a strong submission. For example, the impact of the results of the Copenhagen climate change conference would be very interesting to an energy industry or environmental employer, regardless of the employer's specific industry niche.

9. Is it confusing? If your analyses and/or arguments are difficult to follow, you will lose the employer's interest and lose points. This criterion calls for you to have someone you trust read your writing sample and provide you with feedback prior to submission to the employer.

10. Is your argument/analysis persuasive? The bottom line of all lawyering is persuasion. If the logic of your argument or analysis is convincing and compelling to the reader, you will receive credit for your persuasive ability and be well on your way to winning the writing sample component of the job competition.

11. What was the impact of your writing sample (if any)? Did your argument or analysis prevail? Was this a winning document? Did it contribute to a positive outcome for your client? Did it change something? **Note:** This is not quite the same as submitting a persuasive writing sample. A document can be persuasive, but still not a winning one for many reasons.

12. Is it readable? Does it read easily and flow smoothly? Your writing style should demonstrate that you have a strong command of English spelling, grammar, syntax, usage, etc., and that you are a good editor. Reading it should be an enjoyable—or at least a tolerable—experience for the employer, not an excruciating ordeal.

13. Is it concise? Remember what Blaise Pascal wrote to a friend: "I apologize for writing a five-page letter. . . . I did not have time to write a one-page letter." Something stated in fewer words virtually always beats something said verbosely. An economy of words is to be prized in a writing sample or any other document.

14. How much of it is your own work? Every legal employer understands that lawyering is often a team effort. Consequently, it is generally not a rule that you must only submit a writing sample that is 100 percent your own work. At the other extreme, you want to avoid submitting a document that has been heavily revised or edited by someone else. The closer you can get to a document that is entirely your own work, the better. If you cannot, then indicate on the cover sheet accompanying your writing sample that: (1) the document is "_____ percent my own work," and (2) how and where it reflects someone else's contribution. **Note:** Some legal employers specifically request that a job applicant who submits a writing sample that was revised or edited by someone else submit a document that tracks the changes.

15. Are you a capable "*Bluebook*er"? Ideally, there should be a sufficient number and variety of legal citations to enable the employer to judge whether you understand *Bluebook*ing. Of course, your citations need to be both correct and consistent.

16. Was your writing sample published or cited? A document published by a third party or cited in a court opinion or other writing gains considerable credibility because someone with some "heft" has, by virtue of publication or citation, vetted your writing and/or persuasive ability.

17. Does the cover sheet accompanying it put the document in context? Every writing sample needs a cover sheet explaining what the document is about, when it was prepared, why and for whom you prepared it, how it was used, whether it is complete or excerpted, how much of it is your work, etc. A cover sheet provides context, is very reader-friendly, and sends a positive message about your organizational skills and forethought.

Note: You should redact your writing sample sufficiently to preserve client confidentiality, if necessary.

Like references, writing samples have a history of not being considered very important by legal job candidates. That is a big mistake. Employers may not read your entire writing sample, but they will read some of it—just enough to get an idea of how you might represent them in writing. Therefore, you need to accord your writing sample(s) the same attention that the employer does, and be very careful that what you submit is your best work and the example most appropriate for the job you are seeking.

Chapter 25

Overcoming "Ageism"

"Ageism" as an obstacle to legal employment has never been a more important factor. The Great Recession has put tens of millions of retirees and employees whose retirement was supposed to be imminent into a difficult position. Thousands of retired attorneys are seeking employment because their 401k's have become 201k's (OK, maybe 301k's), leaving them in a financial bind. Thousands of other baby-boomer attorneys who planned to retire soon must continue working—assuming they don't get laid off—in order to make ends meet.

Ageism can begin very early in life for attorneys. You have only to look at legal employment recruiting advertisements to see that, unless you are lightly "seasoned," you are probably not going to find a new position easily. This occurs most often in large law firms and major, publicly traded corporations, as well as in certain government agencies, such as the Justice Department and the Securities and Exchange Commission. Age discrimination will almost never be blatant or overt. Employers are usually too smart for that. Rather, it is likely to take subtle forms and be tacit rather than obvious.

One tactic available to an older job seeker is to determine which employers are most likely to let age get in the way of considering competence and capability and avoid applying to them. Another strategy is to make sure their résumés reflect their energy and vigor.

Résumés

Opening Gambits

If, as I invariably suggest, you begin your résumé presentation with a Summary of Qualifications or Profile, *don't* lead with something like this:

"Over 25 years of experience . . . ."

This kind of opening immediately focuses the employer on how old you are. It is much better to impress them with your accomplishments first.

Handling Dates

If you started your career during Warren G. Harding's presidency, consider leaving your first few jobs—and the dates of your employment—out of the résumé, unless what you did back then might still resonate very strongly with the employer.

However, don't—as so many job seekers do—omit your dates of graduation from college or law school. Such omissions stand out like a sore thumb, and everyone—especially savvy employers—knows exactly why you left out the dates and will assume, perhaps incorrectly, that you are quite a bit older. Since, in most experienced attorney résumés, education is at or near the end of the document, an employer will have read through everything that preceded it by then and will already be favorably or unfavorably disposed toward your candidacy.

Activities

At a minimum, the fact that you are involved in volunteer or community activities outside of work sends a subliminal message that you are an active, vigorous person. If you are not engaged in such activities, now that you are job-hunting might be a good time to find one or two outside pursuits that interest you.

Volunteer and community activity aside, I don't generally recommend including your interests and hobbies on your résumé. The reason is that most individuals share the same or similar leisure-time interests— running, reading, gardening, music, etc. There are, however, exceptions:

- When a job candidate discovers that the individual who will review the résumé shares a common interest ("Oh, I see you also play the zither!");
- When a candidate has a truly unusual hobby ("So you competed in the Sahara Ultramarathon?"); and
- For purposes of this discussion, when a seasoned job candidate wants to demonstrate youthful energy ("It must have been extremely difficult to climb Everest without oxygen!")

Cover Letters and Transmittal E-mails

Mystery writers use the following techniques when describing a dramatic "action" scene:

- Sharp action verbs to heighten the suspense
- Short sentences to increase the tempo
- Short paragraphs to concentrate the reader's attention
- Dots and dashes to keep a fast pace

While I am not suggesting that you clone or channel Mickey Spillane, the studied use of these techniques can work just as well in your cover letter or transmittal e-mail, again sending a subliminal message that you are someone with energy and dynamism. See Appendix J, Sample Cover Letter/Transmittal E-mail, for an example of some of these techniques.

Interviews

- Dress and groom "young." Don't come into the interview wearing plaids and white bucks and pants belted above your navel, with an airline ticket to Boca Raton hanging out of your pocket. The best interview dress is always going to be a conservative business suit and matching accessories (shoes, socks, tie) in a mainstream, contemporary style. Grooming "young" does not mean piercings, tattoos, multi-colored hair, etc. Use common sense and don't go to an extreme.
- Get your "vigor" across.
  - The way you shake hands
  - The way you walk
  - The way you talk
  - The way you sit and comport yourself
  - Through hobbies and interests that might come up in the conversation
- Manifest personal flexibility in your responses to any question.
- Manifest a "whatever it takes" attitude.
- Don't be condescending to younger interviewers.
- Emphasize your experience.
- Emphasize your mentoring ability.
- Emphasize your reliability.
- Avoid saying anything that could be deemed negative and thus be attributed to you being "set in your ways."

Age discrimination in America is soon going to become a very big issue. The "aging up" of 78 million baby-boomers will see to that. Exacerbating the age issue is the fact that the Great Recession has caused many would-be retirees to defer their retirement dreams and, among recent retirees, to return to work.

Attorneys are by no means exempt from what the Great Recession has wrought. And since age discrimination against lawyers begins much earlier than their seventh decade of life, attorneys must be more sensitive to its possibility when planning and executing their job campaigns.

Chapter 26

Coping with Disability

No one likes job hunting, and with good reason: It is intimidating, stressful, anxiety-ridden, and has an uncertain outcome. Each of these negatives are magnified several-fold if you also have to contend with a disability.

Disability discrimination is quite likely the most rampant form of discrimination extant today. This is underscored by U.S. Bureau of the Census's tabulations of disability and its impact on employment:

- The unemployment rate of disabled Americans of working age is 50 percent.
- The unemployment rate of the severely disabled is 67 percent.
- The unemployment rates of individuals with a visible disability are as follows:

    - Wheelchair: 78 percent
    - Cane, crutches, or walker: 75 percent
    - Severe visual impairment: 70 percent
    - Severe hearing impairment: 52 percent
    - Severe speech impairment: 76 percent
    - Severe ambulatory impairment: 77 percent

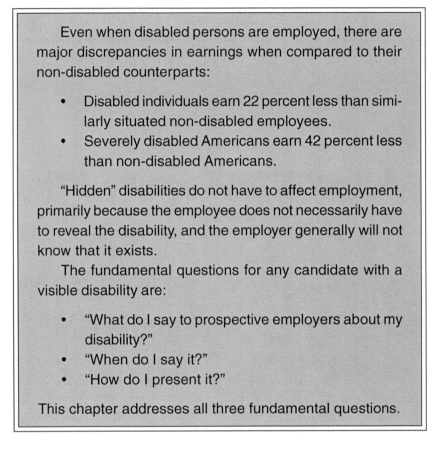

Even when disabled persons are employed, there are major discrepancies in earnings when compared to their non-disabled counterparts:

- Disabled individuals earn 22 percent less than similarly situated non-disabled employees.
- Severely disabled Americans earn 42 percent less than non-disabled Americans.

"Hidden" disabilities do not have to affect employment, primarily because the employee does not necessarily have to reveal the disability, and the employer generally will not know that it exists.

The fundamental questions for any candidate with a visible disability are:

- "What do I say to prospective employers about my disability?"
- "When do I say it?"
- "How do I present it?"

This chapter addresses all three fundamental questions.

Tilt the Odds in Your Favor

Before addressing these key questions, there is one very important thing you can do to improve your odds: Try to identify employers who are more likely to be favorably disposed toward candidates with disabilities.

Here are the best ways to target such employers:

- Talk to fellow members of your disability support group (if you're in a support group; if not, think about finding and joining one) about their job-hunting experiences.
- Pick the brains of both career service officials and disability program managers at the schools you attended. Virtually every U.S. college and university now has staff profession-

als responsible for advising and assisting disabled students with accessibility and accommodation matters. These experts often also know a great deal about disabled employment issues.

- Identify employers with good track records of recruiting candidates with disabilities, which you can do by consulting:
  - the U.S. Department of Labor's Office of Disability Employment Policy (*www.dol.gov/odep*);
  - other advocacy organizations; and
  - publications such as *Careers and the Disabled* (*www.eop.com*).
- Pinpoint government organizations that sponsor disability hiring programs, such as the U.S. government's *Selective Placement Program for Individuals with Disabilities* (*www.opm.gov*).
- Research state government disabled employment programs.

What Do You Say to a Prospective Employer . . . and When Do You Say It?

Initially, when you first communicate with an employer, you will be best served if you say nothing. Let your paper credentials (résumé and cover letter) speak for themselves and get you in front of the interviewer. Your résumé and cover letter should focus only on your qualifications for the position, not on any factors that may, in the employer's mind, disqualify you before you have had a chance to impress.

The track record of job candidates who reveal their disabilities early in the job-hunting process is not encouraging. Employers are typically flooded with job applications. As discussed, rather than looking for positive reasons to interview candidates, their initial aim is to pare down the pile of applications to a manageable few. The easiest way to do this is to take a "rejectionist" approach and look for a reason to eliminate candidates. You do not want to present an employer with a convenient reason to reject you before having an opportunity to learn about your skills and capabilities.

If you are concerned that your disability might emerge during a telephone or personal interview, be prepared to take the initiative and discuss it frankly with your interviewer up front, *but only after* you are invited to interview. In that case, it is better for you to raise it than for the interviewer to bring it up upon observing or listening to you. The interviewer is prohibited from doing so by both the Americans with Disabilities Act (see *www.eeoc.gov/policy/ada.html* and *www.usdoj.gov/crt/ada/adahom1.htm*) and the Equal Employment Opportunity Commission's *Interviewing Guidelines* (see *www.smallbusinessnotes.com/operating/hr/hiring/ada.html*), but these constraints do not necessarily affect employer conduct in the real world. If the interviewer comments about it first, depending on what is said, you may want to reconsider working for his or her organization.

If you think you can make it through the interview but your disability might be noticeable during the workday (if you get the job), you have a difficult decision to make. Should you discuss it now or wait and let the chips fall where they may? The answer to this question is not easy and is highly individual, depending on the nature of the job for which you are applying as well as many other factors, including your rapport with the interviewer, your boss, and your colleagues. Employers do not like to be surprised, so if, how, and when you reveal your disability while keeping your qualifications foremost needs to be carefully considered.

How Do You Present It?

If you have to say something about your disability, present it as accurately as possible, and make sure to state if it would have little or no impact on your performance on the job (with or without accommodation). If this is accurate, note that you are largely able to control it with medication and that the medication does not affect your ability to work.

To that end, the most important thing you can do is to rehearse for the moment when you might have to talk about your disability. Do this in front of a mirror as well as in front of a spouse, significant other, relative, or friend with whom you can role-play the interview. However, remember that you do not want to come across as too rehearsed, but certainly prepared.

Prepare as You Would for Any Interview

Learn as much as you can about the employer's operation, products, and services. Also, find out as much as you can about the interviewer if you have advance notice of who that will be. Plan ahead to make a great first impression. Exude confidence. Look sharp. Dress appropriately (that means "to the nines," regardless of what you know of the employer's dress code). Be upbeat. Be friendly. Be honest. Be on time. State how you can add value to the employer's business. And anticipate the unexpected.

Employer Concerns about Hiring and Working with Disabled Employees

To give yourself the best opportunity to make a positive impression on the employer, you first have to understand the employer's concerns about disabled employees, chief among which are the following:

- Ability to do the job and any limitations due to your disability
- Potential for absences for medical reasons
- Costs of accommodating your disability
- Additional cost of supervision, if any
- Additional cost of training, if any
- Potential workplace grievances or lawsuits
- Attitudinal barriers

Once you understand what employers worry about when it comes to hiring an employee with a disability, you will be able to institute "countermeasures."

Countermeasures

Some of the countermeasures you can use to neutralize negative impressions or reactions to a disability are the same as or similar to those that you might employ to counter ageism (see Chapter 25, "Overcoming 'Ageism'").

Résumés

Just like with ageism, you can counteract concerns about a disability by including your volunteer, pro bono, or community activities outside of work in your résumé. This sends employers a positive message about your energy level and "can-do" spirit. If you are not so engaged, now would be a good time to get active.

If you have hobbies or outside interests that also demonstrate vigor, include them too. They underscore the point that your disability does not slow you down.

Cover Letters

You do not have to reveal anything about your disability at the cover letter stage of the recruitment process. Again, all applicants should give employers the opportunity to be initially impressed with their abilities.

Draft your cover letter with the idea in mind that you want to bolster what your résumé says about your active and dynamic life. You can do this by using the following stylistic techniques:

- Sharp action verbs
- Short sentences
- Short paragraphs
- Dots and dashes for faster pacing

Interviews

The interview stage is where the strategies utilized by older candidates and disabled candidates diverge. If you have an observable disability, such as a visual, hearing, speech, or mobility impairment, you may want to alert the employer before you appear for your interview (but after you have been invited, of course) that you may need an interview accommodation. For example, if you are hearing-impaired, you may want to request a signing interpreter. If you are wheelchair-bound, you may want to inquire as to the employer's building and office accessibility.

Employers cannot ask you any questions likely to elicit information about a disability, or related questions about whether you can perform major life activities. However, they can ask you about your ability to perform specific job functions, including asking you to describe or demonstrate how you would perform such functions. If you have a visible disability, or if you voluntarily disclose a disability, an employer can also ask whether you will need a reasonable accommodation.

You can also use strategies similar to those you incorporated in your résumé and cover letter in order to sway the odds in your direction, namely:

- Emphasizing your energy and enthusiasm
- Dressing well
- Shaking hands firmly
- Speaking confidently
- Demonstrating both flexibility and a "can-do" attitude
- Emphasizing your reliability

Accommodations

If you are going to need a reasonable accommodation to do the job effectively, consider the following possibilities as part of your preparation for the interview, so that you are ready with suggestions.

- Restructuring the job
- Flextime
- Telework
- Structural adjustments, e.g., restrooms, doors, hallways, etc.
- Flexible application of personnel policies
- Modified work environment, e.g., orthopedic or ergonomic chair, lower desk, better lighting, etc.
- New or modified equipment or devices, e.g., Kurzweil Reading Machine, larger computer screen, etc.
- Parking or transportation accommodations
- Readers or interpreters
- Written job instructions
- Modified training materials

Note that these accommodations are not necessarily mutually exclusive.

If your prospective employer has little or no experience with accommodating a disabled employee, you might recommend the following resources:

- The Job Accommodation Network (*www.jan.wvu.edu*), a free consulting service that provides individualized workplace accommodation solutions.
- Regional   ADA   Technical   Assistance   Center (*www.dbtac.vcu.edu*), a nationwide resource on the Americans with Disabilities Act and accessible information technology.
- The United States Access Board (*www.access-board.gov*), a federal government agency that serves as a leading source of information on accessible design.
- The local office of your state vocational rehabilitation agency.
- A local independent living center.
- The labor union, if any, that represents your prospective employer's employees. **Note:** While 36 percent of public-sector employees are covered by collective-bargaining agreements, unions represent only 7.4 percent of private-sector employees.

As further reassurance, you might also point out to your interviewer that:

- 75 percent of employers surveyed by the Cornell School of Industrial and Labor Relations reported that no workplace changes at all were needed when they hired a disabled employee;
- When an accommodation is necessary, the average cost is under $500 total; and
- A national study spearheaded by Du Pont found that disabled workers had equal or higher performance ratings, better retention rates, and less absenteeism.
- Note the special skills and abilities that come with being disabled, e.g.:

- *Problem solving*—long history of developing alternative plans on short notice because of unanticipated obstacles.
- *Time management*—having to schedule rides on alternative transit systems.
- *Flexibility and adaptability*—developing coping mechanisms to deal with the expected and unexpected problems that inevitably confront disabled people.

- An employer tax credit or deduction for hiring and/or accommodating a disabled individual may be available in his or her jurisdiction (check to determine if such a credit is available in your jurisdiction *before* arriving at the interview). Also, the U.S. Internal Revenue Code contains three tax incentive provisions designed to encourage employers to hire disabled persons. The Internal Revenue Service (IRS) says that few employers are aware of these tax incentives, as only a handful take advantage of them. These provisions are summarized below.

  - *Title 26, Internal Revenue Code, section 51* provides a targeted job tax credit to employers of up to 40 percent of the first $6,000 of first-year wages of a new employee with a disability who is referred by state or local vocational rehabilitation agencies, a State Commission on the Blind, or the U.S. Department of Veterans Affairs, and certified by a state employment service. There is no credit after the first year of employment. For an employer to qualify for the credit, a worker must have been employed for at least 90 days or have completed at least 120 hours of work for the employer.

  - *Title 26, Internal Revenue Code, section 44* provides a tax credit to eligible small businesses ($1 million or less in gross revenues or 30 or fewer employees) in the amount of 50 percent of eligible access expenditures between $250 and $10,250 per taxable year. Such expenditures include:

    - removal of architectural, communication, physical, or transportation barriers that prevent a business from being accessible to, or usable by, individuals with disabilities;

- providing qualified readers, taped texts, and other effective methods of making materials accessible to people with visual impairments;
- providing qualified interpreters or other effective methods of making orally delivered materials available to individuals with hearing impairments;
- acquiring or modifying equipment or devices for individuals with disabilities; or
- providing other similar services, modifications, materials, or equipment.

- *Title 26, Internal Revenue Code, section 190* allows an employer a tax deduction up to $15,000 per year for "qualified architectural and transportation barrier removal expenses." Expenditures to make a facility or public transportation vehicle owned or leased in connection with a trade or business more accessible to, and usable by, individuals who are handicapped or elderly are eligible for the deduction.

Special Hiring Programs

Very few private-sector employers have any kind of special emphasis program for hiring disabled workers. This is largely the preserve of government (which does a poor job of it).

Federal Selective Placement Program for the Hiring of Individuals with Disabilities

U.S. government hiring officials are authorized to use special hiring authorities when considering certain people with disabilities (those who have a severe physical, cognitive, or emotional disability, or a history of having such disabilities, or are perceived as having such disabilities). These authorities provide a unique opportunity to demonstrate the potential to perform successfully the essential duties of a position, with and without reasonable accommodation in the workplace. The program provides for temporary appointments to Federal jobs, at the conclusion of which the positions can be converted into permanent jobs.

Although this program is mandated by law as an affirmative action program (Rehabilitation Act of 1973, as amended, Pub. L. 93-112, section 501), it has historically been severely underutilized by federal agencies. However, the rules governing this program were recently liberalized in an effort to recruit more disabled employees.

Each U.S. government agency has a Selective Placement Coordinator (sometimes called a Disability Coordinator) whose job is to assist you with the hiring process. A searchable directory of Selective Placement Coordinators is available at http://apps.opm.gov/sppc_directory/.

Success invoking the Selective Placement Program depends on two factors out of your control:

- First, the interest level and capability of the Selective Placement Coordinator. My long experience with coordinators leads me to conclude that very few are both interested and able.
- Second, the agency head's commitment to the program. A proactive agency head is essential to program success.

Disabled Veterans' Employment Program

Federal government agencies have the authority, by law, to give noncompetitive appointments to any veteran who has a service-connected disability of 30 percent or more. Unlike the Selective Placement Program, this authority is discretionary with each agency. To be eligible, you must be a disabled veteran who has a compensable service-connected disability of 30 percent or more, and the disability must be officially documented by the U.S. Department of Defense or the U.S. Department of Veterans Affairs. You must serve initially under a temporary appointment not limited to 60 days or less. After successfully performing in such a temporary appointment, the federal agency may convert you to a permanent position.

You should contact the federal agency personnel office where you are interested in working to find out about opportunities. Agencies recruit candidates and make appointments directly. As a part of your application package, you will need a copy of a letter dated within the last 12 months from the Department of Veterans Affairs or the Department of Defense certifying receipt of compensation for a service-connected disability of 30 percent or more.

Executive Order 13518, "Employment of Veterans in the Federal Government"

This November 2009 executive order is designed to "enhance recruitment of and promote employment opportunities for veterans" within 24 agencies in the executive branch. Each agency must develop an agency-specific operational plan, establish a Veterans Employment Program Office by March 2010, develop and implement training programs for disabled veterans, and promote the development and application of technology designed to assist veterans with disabilities.

Having observed a spate of prior laws and executive orders issued by five presidential predecessors that are supposed to accomplish the same or similar goals, it remains to be seen if this one will play out any differently in terms of positive results for disabled veterans' employment. Don't bet the mortgage.

Ten-Point Veterans' Preference

Certain disabled Armed Forces veterans are given preference in competing for federal government jobs. However, the veterans' preference laws do not guarantee the veteran a job, nor do they give veterans preference in internal agency actions such as promotion, transfer, reassignment, and reinstatement.

Veterans entitled to Veterans' Preference have five or 10 extra points added to their passing score on a civil service examination ("examination" does not necessarily mean a written test; it can be merely an evaluation of your qualifications). Five-Point Veterans' Preference is awarded to honorably discharged veterans whose military service meets certain statutory criteria. Ten-Point Veterans' Preference is reserved for:

- honorably separated veterans who (1) qualify as disabled veterans because they have served on active duty in the Armed Forces at any time and have a present service-connected disability or are receiving compensation, disability retirement benefits, or pension from the military or the Department of Veterans Affairs; or (2) are Purple Heart recipients;

- the spouse of a veteran unable to work because of a service-connected disability;
- the unmarried widow of certain deceased veterans; and
- the mother of a veteran who died in service or who is permanently and totally disabled.

Comparable State Government Disabled Employment Programs

Many states have programs similar to the U.S. government programs discussed above. The federal government's Office of Disability Employment Policy maintains links to its state counterparts at *www.dol.gov/odep/state/state.htm*. State programs vary; consult your state's disability commission or comparable body to determine (1) the scope of its programs, and (2) whether you meet the eligibility criteria. You may also be able to obtain information about these programs from your nearest state vocational rehabilitation office.

Private-Sector Programs

Careers and the Disabled Magazine (*www.eop.com*) maintains lists of employers that actively recruit professionals with disabilities, and of the top 50 employers of disabled individuals. Another useful resource is EnableAmerica (*www.enableamerica.org*).

> Let's not kid ourselves: It is monumentally more difficult for disabled attorneys to secure employment than for almost any other category of job-seekers.
>
> A case in point: One of my legal career counseling clients was a blind attorney who was underemployed in a position with a government agency. He earned his B.A. in astronomy with a minor in mathematics from an Ivy League school, followed by a Master's degree in aerospace engineering from a second Ivy League institution. He then earned a J.D. and passed the Patent Bar examination.

Whenever he mentioned his disability in his cover letter or transmittal e-mail (not recommended), he never got asked to interview. If he said nothing about his disability in his cover letter or transmittal e-mail, he almost always got invited to interview. However, he did not receive a job offer after two years of looking for new, meaningful employment.

Disabled attorneys who are fortunate enough to get hired usually have exceptional performance records. All they need is an opportunity to prove themselves.

Chapter 27

Legal Job Hunting Out of Town

There are special problems faced by attorneys who wish to relocate. The vast majority of relocating attorneys do not understand the additional, distinctive issues they must confront and overcome in order to conduct a successful job-hunting campaign without actually being there. Consequently, many find their efforts frustrating and give up, or wind up in the "wrong" position, or even feel compelled to take the drastic step of quitting their current job in order to move to the new location and then resuming their job search.

None of this has to happen if you understand the underlying concerns of employers when contemplating an out-of-town hire, and prepare yourself to allay those concerns.

Employers, especially in a "buyer's market" such as law, invariably raise a number of concerns when considering out-of-the-area job applicants. While, depending on the predilections of the particular employer or hiring official, any one of these concerns may prevent an applicant from being considered, that is less and less the case as lawyer mobility from job to job and place to place increases. Moreover, intelligent planning and forethought on your part can disabuse the distant employer of some, if not all, of these concerns.

Economic Concerns

The bottom line for any employer is always the "bottom line." Employers are naturally focused on costs and assume that out-of-town candidates cost more to recruit and hire. It is vitally important to know about that assumption, to understand the underlying reasons for it, and to be prepared to nip it in the bud early in your job-hunting process. Economic concerns generally break down into two fundamental issues: paying for travel to interviews and paying relocation expenses.

Paying for Travel to Interviews

Fewer and fewer legal or other employers offer to pay for travel to interviews. Employers are very sensitive to the costs involved in interviewing, and have experimented over the years with a variety of mechanisms for keeping those costs down. One of the simplest and surest ways of accomplishing this is not to spend any money on flying in, boarding, and feeding out-of-town candidates.

Don't be misled by the largess showered on two unique categories of attorney candidates:

(1)   Certain law students, typically those from top law schools and/or who have outstanding academic credentials (law review, Order of the Coif, multiple CALI awards); and

(2)   Candidates presented by headhunters, typically those who:
  • are one to five years out of law school, currently with prestigious law firms, with top academic credentials;
  • have expertise in an area in great demand, such as patent law; or
  • partnership-level attorneys with substantial, verifiable portable business.

These categories of individuals are the rare exceptions (they are usually in demand, even in a buyer's market), and a different set of rules applies to them than to the rest of the attorney community in many situations.

The vast majority of long-distance attorney job seekers, however, must be cognizant of employer concerns about interview costs (which can be considerable) and must take steps to assure the employer that these costs are not an issue. The ideal way to accomplish this is to alert the employer in your cover letter or transmittal e-mail accompanying your résumé or job application that you understand that you will incur any interview travel costs yourself.

However, before you automatically conclude that an employer will not pay interview expenses, you should try to confirm that fact. A few general principles typically apply in performing this investigation:

- The smaller the organization, the less likely it is that interview expenses will be paid by the employer. Conversely, the larger the organization, the more likely it is that such expenses will be paid by the employer.
- Private-sector employers, such as law firms and corporations, are more likely to pay interview expenses than public-sector, public-interest, or nonprofit organizations. There are, however, public-sector exceptions, particularly at the federal level. A handful of government agencies will pay for interview travel, typically when the candidate is a graduating law student and the interview is the result of the agency's formal fall on-campus recruitment efforts. However, even this is rare and inconsistent from agency to agency and recruitment season to recruitment season. Government agencies almost never pay for the interview travel of lateral candidates.
- If the position is being advertised nationally, not just locally, it is more likely that the employer will pay your interview expenses.

A little research before jumping to the conclusion that such expenses customarily are—or are not—paid by the employer is always recommended. For example, contacting trade or professional association(s) of which the employer is a member may elicit this information. Similarly, communicating with someone who recently worked for the employer may enable you to obtain good intelligence about the employer's policies. Law school career placement officials (particularly in law schools in the employer's community) may also be valuable sources of this information.

However, if your research come up empty, it is safer to assume that interview expenses will not be paid. In that case, you will want to alert the employer in your initial communication that you plan to foot the bill for any interview costs incurred.

Paying Your Relocation Expenses

The current job market militates against this benefit, although there are still quite a few employers who will pay this much larger expense, either as a blanket policy or in selected, negotiable circumstances. Organizational relocation expense policies are much more difficult to pinpoint than interview expense policies. This is, at first glance, odd, since relocation costs are enormous compared to interview costs. However, as relocation is not an issue until an employment relationship has been forged, you can understand why employers might more readily pay for relocation than for interviews.

The same three general principles applicable to interview cost policies also apply to relocation expenses, with one possible exception: Government is less likely to pay relocation expenses than interview travel costs.

Given the substantial costs of relocation ($25,000 for a family to relocate is not unusual), it is in your interest to find out as much information as you can about a particular employer's policy. Again, if you are uncertain about the employer's relocation policies after diligent research, and this is a position of interest to you, you should allay the employer's anxieties about who pays in your initial cover letter or transmittal e-mail.

Liability Exposure if the New Job Does Not Work Out

The saga of relocating attorneys is littered with lawyers who uprooted themselves and moved elsewhere, only to discover that, for various reasons, the new arrangement did not work, and are forced to leave. While few of these lawyers sue their new employers, the risk of such a lawsuit is always there.

For example, an environmental partner in a New England firm was enticed by a headhunter to move to Washington, D.C. to become an environmental partner in a much larger firm at considerably higher compensation. He sold his New England home, moved his family, bought a home in a Washington suburb, and began his new job at the moment environmental work began to wane, thanks to a change of political administration. The firm let him go within weeks. His employment agreement did not specifically cover his termination, and he filed a lawsuit against the firm for breach of contract. A settlement was eventually negotiated.

Another attorney left his East Coast job with a law firm for one with a West Coast corporation's in-house counsel office. Once he arrived and began working, he realized that the position was far different from what he believed had been advertised and described for him during his job interviews. He left after a short stay and sued the company for misrepresentation.

While this second example could have happened regardless of relocation, it and cases like it send a warning shot across the bow of any employer considering an out-of-town hire.

Other Employer Concerns

The "Inconvenience" of Conducting an Out-of-Town Search

In a buyer's market (which law usually is), why take on all of the risks and potential difficulties of conducting a long-distance recruitment when there might be many qualified local candidates? It is much easier to schedule interviews and follow-ups if all of the candidates are local.

There is a certain ebb and flow to this, depending on the tightness of the legal job market and particular practice areas. When the economy and the legal economy are booming (they are not always in lockstep with each other), searches tend to extend a bit wider, geographically, than in bad times. Hard-to-find practice area expertise, such as lawyers with life sciences experience, for example, prompt more national searches, despite employer concerns about inconvenience and anything else. If you are looking to relocate, you may want to try developing a rare specialty via either education or practice.

Candidate Commitment to Relocating

Announcing in your communications to the out-of-town employer that you are "considering" jobs in that location, or are "considering" a move, is virtually always a kiss of death. An employer tends to read statements like this as bespeaking a fishing expedition. What it says to the employer is that you are not sure about relocating. Why would they bother considering you at all if you are not serious?

You can put this employer concern to rest with an unambiguous assertion of your intention to move to the new location. "I will be moving to Wynot, Nebraska this summer." You cannot make a more forthright statement than that. You have told the employer that you are dead serious about relocating.

Bar Admission Issues

This is a threshold issue for most out-of-town employers. It even comes up if the position advertised consists only of a federal practice. Employers often raise these issues upfront with out-of-state attorney applicants. The important thing for you is to beat the employer to the punch and dispel all bar admission concerns right away.

If you are not licensed to practice in the new location, advise the employer immediately how and when you intend to become a member of the local bar. Better yet, indicate the steps you have already taken to get admitted in the employer's jurisdiction.

You also need to be cognizant and up-to-date on the bar admission requirements in the employer's state. For example, if you can get admitted under one of the exceptions to a requirement to take the state bar examination, such as a limited admission for corporate in-house counsel, you don't want to misstate your intentions or manifest your ignorance of the nuances of that state's bar admission requirements. It is essential that, before you take pen (or keyboard) in hand to write your cover letter or transmittal e-mail, you check the state bar admission agency Web site for the latest requirements.

Be aware that some employers of attorneys in law-related positions are often misinformed about how necessary and/or easy it is to become admitted to practice in their state. For example, if you go to work for a CPA firm as a consultant to in-house counsel offices and law firms about litigation management matters, you do not have to be admitted to practice in order to perform this work in most states.

You should also note that if you want to move to a new state to work as an attorney for the U.S. government, the only bar requirement for 99 percent of federal attorney positions is that you be admitted in one U.S. jurisdiction, not necessarily the one in which you will be working. In other words, you can work as a federal attorney in California even though you are only admitted in Pennsylvania.

Potential Employer Guilt if the New Job Does Not Work Out

Employers do not like to buy into trouble, and they will feel fewer qualms about being forced by circumstances to let someone go who is locally based rather than newly arrived from out of town. They often prefer to avoid the latter situation altogether. The best way to overcome this potential hurdle is to state, unequivocally in your earliest communication, that you intend to relocate to the employer's locality, period.

Additional Distance Job-Hunting Tips

In addition to the advice above, here are a few additional suggestions, several of which address more than one employer concern:

Get the Jump on the Employer

This is crucial, and it bears repeating: If you want to relocate and be seriously considered for a position, you need to address these employer concerns as early as possible in the hiring process, preferably during your initial communication with the employer.

Interview Strategies

- *The "coincidental" trip.* If you are able to travel to the new location, advise the employer that you plan to be in his or her area on specific dates and would be able to interview at that time.
- *Long-distance interviewing.* If a trip to the employer's area is not feasible, consider suggesting one of the following interview alternatives:
    - *Videoconference option.* If there is an available videoconference provider, suggest doing a long-distance interview using this medium.
    - *Local office option.* If the employer has a local office near you, you could propose that you meet with someone there.
    - *Telephone option.* Telephone interviews are becoming increasingly popular. Some government employers rely exclusively on telephone interviews.

Relocation Expense Strategies

- *The "negotiation" approach.* There are circumstances where relocation decisions are deferred, or not even raised, until a job offer has been made. Then, it might be possible to negotiate for such expenses as part of the broader negotiations surrounding your employment contract.
- *The "half-a-loaf" approach.* Once an offer is presented to you, you could attempt to probe the possibilities of getting a portion of your relocation expenses paid for by the employer.

Do's and Don'ts

- Do comfort the employer by emphasizing your ties to the area:
    - "I grew up in Death Valley and have wanted to return to your lovely area ever since I moved away."
    - "We've visited Aunt Mabel in Boring every summer for years."

- "I have been to Walnut Bottom on business on many occasions and fell in love with the town."
- "I went to school at Serendipity State and spent four happy years there."

- Do not assume that the employer will also take on the responsibility of finding a new job for your spouse or partner in the new location. Not only is this an inappropriate assumption, it also weighs down your candidacy for the position with a lot of additional cost and concern, as well as putting a cloud over the quality of your judgment. Today, very few employers will offer to find your spouse a new job; don't expect such a fringe benefit, and don't ask for it.

- Few legal employers will buy your current residence as part of a relocation package. This kind of benefit is usually associated with a handful of *Fortune* 500 corporations. One of my counseling clients actually turned down a position at a major law firm because the firm refused to purchase his home as one of his relocation benefits.

- Research the new location. Living costs can vary widely from one place to another. You should have some knowledge of these variations before you launch your out-of-town job search. If you move, for example, from Manhattan, Kansas, to Manhattan, New York, you will need to make considerably more money to maintain your standard of living. Conversely, if you move in the other direction, you may be able to reduce your compensation requirements considerably (unless you were fortunate enough to live in a rent-controlled apartment in New York City).

There is a lot of good information available on the Internet on living costs and on how to compare living costs from one location to another. Just Google "cost of living" and you will find everything you need to help you assess your move in terms of cost of living as well as quality of life and amenities. Some of the best sites are maintained by local real estate agencies and chambers of commerce. An excellent site for comparing cost-of-living and compensation scales is *www.homefair.com*.

- Pay special attention to your presentation documents. Out-of-town candidates need better résumés and cover letters than their local competitors in order to overcome the employer attitude of "all-other-things-being-equal, I'd-rather-hire-the-local-candidate." You want to do what is necessary to make sure that *all other things are not equal*.
- If you arrive in the new city for an interview, make sure you conduct a "trial run" prior to the interview date and time. Candidates who don't do this are often surprised by local transportation and other "quirks" and wind up late and embarrassed, at best.

> Candidates seeking a job in another city can do a great deal to mitigate the obstacles they are likely to face. Some forethought, research, and "sweat equity" invested in your communications with prospective employers and application documents can go a long way toward putting you on a par with local candidates.

Part IV

Contacts

Chapter 28
Managing Your References and Controlling the
Conversation 255

Chapter 29
What Headhunters Do . . . and Don't Do 271

Chapter 30
Networking without Groveling 279

Managing Your References and Controlling the Conversation

One of the biggest mistakes job-hunting attorneys make is to consider references an afterthought rather than an important early component of the process. All too often, when an interviewer asks a candidate for his or her reference list, the response is a long pause, followed by something like, "Ah, I don't have a list, per se. Let me think for a minute."

Reference management does not begin and end with identifying your references. There is protocol that should be followed, communications between you and your references, and reference lists to be prepared in order to have something suitable to hand to a potential employer. These steps are important because (1) legal employers tend to take more time and make more effort to elicit key information about candidates from their references than ever before (for reasons that will be elaborated on below), and (2) it has become increasingly difficult for attorney job candidates to identify and enlist suitable references.

Timing: When to Find References

An impressive young attorney who interviewed with me for a position in my office was one of those disappointing candidates who failed to come in prepared with a reference list. She visibly blanched when I asked her for one. After hemming and hawing for a few seconds, she asked me for a sheet of paper and a pen and wrote down two names, only one accompanied by a telephone number. She said she wasn't sure the phone number was current, and that I should look up the home number for the second reference, since she did not remember it.

"But," I said, "your résumé says that 'References are available upon request.' I am requesting them."

Not only were her references unavailable upon request, it was also apparent that she had given no thought at all to them. She obviously did not communicate with them, and thus never determined whether they would agree to serve as her references and give her a positive endorsement, or what exactly they might say about her. Assuming I had taken the next step and called them, the fact that she had cited them as references would have come as a complete surprise to them.

That was the end of that, as far as I was concerned. I could not countenance someone so unprepared and disorganized working for me and representing our company. An otherwise impressive candidate lost out because of how she mishandled reference management.

This applicant is hardly unique. Reference mismanagement is a common occurrence. Inattention to reference management occurs because job seekers tend to focus most of their attention on other important aspects of the job search—résumés, cover letters, interviewing, researching employers—rather than on what they perceive as a mere formality. They assume that references are the last step in the hiring process—confirmation that the job is theirs and that the employer's conversation with the reference is just a rubber stamp, since references only say good and positive things about candidates.

That reasoning might have been fairly sound at one time. Not anymore. Employers have learned that close scrutiny of references pays dividends; that appearance and reality often diverge. Job offers get both made and not made due to references checks. Moreover, in an increasingly competitive legal job market, sometimes the only competitive advantage of one qualified candidate over another is the quality of the references, their enthusiasm when discussing the candidate, the strength of their endorsement, and so on.

Employers are also aware that applicants may say things on their résumés and in interviews that are not always accurate. Studies reveal that outright lying on résumés is on the increase. Reference checks are one way employers confirm résumé and interview information.

References make a major contribution to the due diligence that an employer needs to perform with respect to job candidates. A wrong hiring decision can be very expensive. In addition to law firms, financial services companies, technology employers, and companies in highly regulated industries perform a lot of candidate due diligence. Their efforts may include contacting your schools to verify attendance, degrees, and transcripts, as well as professional licensing authorities to corroborate licenses to practice the profession and assertions of good standing.

Most job seekers tend to postpone the reference piece of the job-search puzzle for as long as they can. However, instead of being the last step in your job campaign, it should be one of your first steps.

Early attention to references is even more important if you anticipate reference problems for any reason. Such problems most often occur if you leave a position under adverse circumstances, such as having been fired, being laid off for economic reasons, having resigned under pressure, because of personality conflicts with a supervisor, or worse.

Should you find yourself in this situation, you are likely to experience some difficulty identifying and enlisting the customary references. You may have to structure your reference list, and even your entire job campaign, to allow you to place such an event in its most advantageous perspective. It is probably going to take you a longer time and greater exertion to put together a passable list of references.

Another frequent reference challenge is the clandestine nature of many job searches. If you are not in a position to reveal your job search to your current employer, or to individuals outside the workplace whom you would like to use as references but cannot for fear they might let it slip that you are seeking new employment, you may also be shut out from using the usual references.

Attention to references is not only an issue for experienced attorneys; it should be taken just as seriously by law students and recent graduates. Employers are no less concerned about making good hiring decisions with respect to entry-level employees as they are about lateral hires. Often, they are even more concerned about newly minted lawyers. At least with regard to a lateral hire, an employer has a track record to evaluate. Unless you have served as a summer associate or intern for the employing organization, your lack of an extensive employment history could mean even greater scrutiny of your references.

How Many References Do You Need?

A rough rule of thumb is that legal job candidates should have three or four references. However, I recommend that you try to build a stable of at least five or six "core group" references. Given the intensely competitive legal job market, you are likely to find yourself applying for multiple positions, and you don't want to have to return to your same references over and over again. As enthusiastic as your core references may be, they might begin to feel less so the more times they are contacted by prospective employers. If you want your references to remain as enthusiastic as they were when you enlisted them, you should do whatever you can to ensure that they will be imposed upon as infrequently as possible. Moreover, after they have been contacted multiple times and see that you do not yet have a new job, even your most dedicated references might begin to have doubts about you, a feeling that is not conducive to continued enthusiasm.

Another reason for going modestly overboard on the number of references is because of something that an increasing number of employers do when checking references, best illustrated by what happened to one of my clients: He relocated to a new city and provided the names of three partners for whom he had done work at his prior law firm to a very interested employer. The potential employer called each of the three references and, at the end of each conversation, asked each of them if they could provide him with the names of three other individuals in the firm whom he could contact for information about the candidate. By providing more than the customary number of references, you may be able to obviate an employer's propensity to do something like this. It gives you more control over the reference check.

Selecting Your References

A good starting point for identifying potential references is to create a master list of likely candidates. This should include all the people even remotely under consideration. Less experienced attorneys and new graduates will, of course, wind up with fewer names than their more seasoned counterparts. Think expansively and consider the following, at a minimum:

- *Supervisors.* Your current and former supervisors comprise the A-list of possible references. Current supervisors will obviously not make your list if you are conducting a clandestine job search. Former supervisors are both the most frequently utilized references and the ones most sought after by potential employers. Your most recent former supervisors are preferred. If you rely only on your favorite bosses from many years past, your potential employer will wonder why you had to go so far back to uncover suitable references.

    The problem is a boss who, for various reasons, would not give you a favorable reference. If you were fired or quit your job because of a personality conflict, office politics, or other difficulty, you have a particular problem in this area. You may be compelled to use this supervisor despite the circumstances surrounding your departure. If that becomes necessary, you need to talk to this person and determine in advance what he or she might say or is willing to say to a potential employer. That discussion itself will serve to put your supervisor on notice that you are concerned about what will be said and help to restrain or temper any negative comments. It will also put both you and your ex-boss on the same page, both telling consistent stories concerning the circumstances of your departure from that job.

- *Law professors.* Academic references are more appropriate for a law student or recent law graduate. Employers are quite comfortable with students and recent graduates including professors on their list of references. Professors are not, however, the best references for more experienced job-seekers; employers usually prefer references who can address your work experience.

- *Professional co-workers.* These are not as good as supervisors. However, there may be circumstances in which, for a variety of reasons, no supervisors are available to you. While avoidance of supervisors as references raises at least a partial red flag, employers will generally accept your colleagues as references if they are able to discuss your professional competence, demeanor, accomplishments, etc., as well as your personal integrity. Other attorneys working at a higher level than you are preferred, followed by co-workers at your same level, which are better than no reference from an important past employment at all.

- *Subordinates.* The use of subordinates as references is a growing area of interest for employers because they might come forth with insights that an employer cannot get from anyone else. They can be important for jobs that include supervisory responsibilities, for which your new boss wants assurance that you are not a despot or an incompetent supervisor.

- *Clients.* External or internal clients could turn out to be your most supportive and enthusiastic references. No one is better positioned to judge your work product, competence, integrity, and communication skills than someone whom you represented.

- *Opposing counsel.* If you have earned the respect and regard of your adversaries, they can be terrific references.

- *Adjudicators.* Judges, administrative law judges, and hearing officers before whom you have appeared can also be highly effective references.

- *VIPs and politicians.* Such individuals can be impressive and effective references in certain rare situations. They can also be risky. Such individuals are almost always difficult to contact because of their busy schedules. You might risk coming across as a name-dropper, particularly if your "celebrity" reference is only a casual acquaintance. If they do not have direct, personal knowledge of you, your background, etc., you probably should not use them at all.

Identify Enthusiasts

Enthusiasm, as long as it is genuine and not "over the top," is infectious and usually elicits warm and fuzzy feelings about you, the candidate, from prospective employers. If the reference experiences an adrenaline rush when discussing you, it will be difficult for the prospective employer to remain impassive. That almost always results in a positive hiring decision.

The best reference is someone who will act as both your advocate and publicist. Anyone with these capabilities and level of enthusiasm is a big plus. Such an individual should be high on your list. I have occasionally been so impressed with what the very first reference had to say, and the manner in which he or she said it, that I decided then and there to offer the job to the candidate without checking any additional references.

Dual-Use References

Putting together a list of potential references at the beginning, rather than the end, of your job search provides an added bonus: It serves a dual use in that you are simultaneously identifying individuals who could serve as useful job search contacts who might be aware of possible employment opportunities in which you would be interested, and/or who have good contacts of their own to whom you could be referred or introduced.

This networking opportunity is another reason not to limit the number of people on your master reference list. You have every reason to be overinclusive.

Who to Avoid

- *Personal acquaintances.* That means family and friends. Exceptions are (1) if your personal acquaintance also qualifies as a professional reference, or (2) if personal references are specifically requested by your prospective employer.
- *Religious officials.* That means imams, rabbis, cantors, priests, ministers, mullahs, shamans, or any other cleric. These are personal, not professional, references. If they are your confessors in any formal or informal context, they may also feel themselves constrained by their private, personal, protected relationship with you. An exception to this recommendation might be if you were seeking a position with a religious organization. Another exception is if the cleric or his or her organization was one of your clients.
- *Anyone who might give you a poor reference.* Although this may seem obvious, I've encountered many instances where the reference for an applicant for a job with my company gave less than a ringing endorsement or "damned with faint praise."
- *Anyone who does not know that they are your reference.* It is both disrespectful and foolish to use a "cold" reference. You risk getting a surprised, indifferent, or lukewarm reference, if not an outright negative one. You may have precluded future use of someone who, if asked, would have been an enthusiastic reference, had you taken the time to request permission and had occasion to refresh his or her recollection of your many accomplishments.
- *Pregnant pausers.* I once called a reference on an applicant for a job with my company and asked, "How did he get along with his co-workers?" A pregnant pause of approximately five seconds was followed by, "Oh, fine." After that, I decided not to hire the candidate. Employers are able to read between the lines. Words of praise, when separated by several seconds of dead silence, convey reservations.

It may not be very easy to determine if a chosen reference is a pregnant pauser. Hopefully, your face-to-face or telephone conversation during your initial contact with the reference will help you make that determination.

Why Not a Letter of Recommendation?

Letters of recommendation are poor substitutes for references. With few exceptions, they are all likely to read the same—"Sally is one of the best employees and finest individuals it has been my privilege to know"—and consequently do not carry much weight with employers. There is no substitute for direct contact with a reference.

There are, however, circumstances when a letter of recommendation may be unavoidable. It may be the best endorsement you can get if you leave an employer in poor standing. This is not necessarily the end of the inquiry, however, if the reference checker decides to pick up the phone and call the employer despite the letter. Moreover, in this suspicious age, signatures on letters of recommendation are usually difficult to verify.

The only other time a letter of recommendation might be of some value is if the writer states that a prospective employer should feel free to contact him or her for additional information about you.

The Unselected Reference

Your interview was a smashing success and a job offer is imminent. The interviewer asks for references and says:

> I am offering you the position, assuming your references check out, and . . . contingent on being able to speak to your current supervisor. OK?

What should you do? You want the job but, for whatever reason, you have valid concerns about agreeing to let your potential employer talk to your current boss.

This is not an easy question to answer, particularly if your current employer does not know that you have been looking. You may be quite properly worried that he or she may not give you the ringing endorsement you want, whether for valid reasons or simply to keep you where you are. And worse, in the event the job falls through, you will be in the uncomfortable position of continuing to work for your current employer when they know you've been job searching. If your relationship with your current boss is not the best, these concerns become magnified.

Nine times out of 10, you have no choice but to agree and hope that the conversation between the two will go well. However, you need to be prepared in the event you are among the roughly 10 percent for whom the exchange might be toxic.

The best alternatives all carry some risk, but probably not as much as agreeing to the communication with your direct-line supervisor. You might suggest that the interviewer speak to another senior person in the organization because then there will be less risk of going public with your job search, or that the interviewer speak with a former supervisor who is no longer with the organization. Another possibility is that you race back to your office and tell your boss that he or she is going to receive a phone call from your prospective employer, and attempt to mitigate the situation before it happens. If you decide on this approach, consider requesting that no contact be made until you have been able to communicate the fact of your job search to your boss so it won't come from a third party and be as much of a shock. You might then approach your boss and say something like the following:

> Boss, the general counsel of Hermann Amalgamated has talked with me about a wonderful offer to join her company. While you know how much I enjoy my work and relationships here, I think it would be a disservice to myself and my family not to take this offer. She may be contacting you about me. I would very much appreciate it if you would inform her of my positive relationships here and my contributions to Findum & Forgetum.

You need to decide for yourself what to do under these circumstances. Everyone's situation is different and has many nuances, and there are different degrees of risk you might be willing to accept. Fortunately, most employers understand the personal ramifications inherent in such requests and don't push back.

Initial Contact with Your References

Once you have determined the individuals you want on your list of references, the first thing you must do is contact them and request their permission to be listed. Second, you will need to assure yourself that the reference is not reluctant, but eager to serve as your reference. Just because you have asked someone to be a reference does not mean that you must list that person if you have any hesitation after discussing the matter.

The conversation should bring them up to date on your career history, strengths, and accomplishments. Advise them that you will send them a current résumé and a "Contacts Road Map" detailing what you want to do, where it could be done, and the logic of doing it (see Appendix F). If you feel confident about your references' enthusiasm for you, consider also sending them a list of talking points to use when contacted by a prospective employer. Vary the talking points for each reference so that the employer does not hear exactly the same thing from each one. As with your résumé, specific examples are superior to subjective statements about how wonderful you are. Talking points might include the following:

- How long the reference has known you, and in what capacity
- Reminders of projects you worked on together or under the reference's supervision
- The quality of your work
- Your admirable personal characteristics
- Your professionalism
- Your ability to work independently and as part of a team
- Your flexibility, initiative, and ability to learn and apply new knowledge
- Your personal integrity

All of these points should be accompanied by examples, if possible.

Keep any negatives out of the conversation. Whining or complaining about your current job or the travails of job searching will get you nowhere. Instead, infect your references with your enthusiasm and excitement about the opportunity your job search or career change represents. People like and gravitate to optimists.

Finally, ask your references how they might respond to questions about you.

Keeping Your References Informed

Good reference management etiquette means that you keep your references up-to-date on your job search, and their potential participation in it, without becoming a pest.

You do not have to notify your references each time you give out their names to a prospective employer. However, if you know or believe that they might be contacted by a potential employer, you need to alert them beforehand. Make sure that you take that opportunity to provide information about the name and position of the person likely to contact them, the organization to which you have applied, the fact that you are very interested in the position, why you think the employer is interested in you, and a précis of the position and why you fit well with it. This kind of briefing will also serve to refresh the reference's recollection of your initial discussion and energize him or her to advocate on your behalf.

Reference Lists

Think about the order in which you list your references on the employment application or résumé. Employers are almost always going to contact the reference at the top of the list first, then work their way down. Don't save the best reference for last; lead with your best shot. In some cases, the caller will be so impressed with the first reference that he or she will not bother to contact the others.

You need not confine yourself to only one reference list. Certain names may do you more good for some employers than for others. You should strive to tailor your reference lists to specific positions, employers, industries, and employment sectors.

A good—and compelling—reference list should contain the following elements in brief: (1) your relationship to the reference/why this person is your reference; (2) ideally, something that you did vis-a-vis the reference that shows you in a positive light; and (3) contact information (where, when, and how). This kind of reference list can give your candidacy a big boost because it underscores for the employer both your thoroughness and your organizational skills, as well as your superb anticipation of just what an employer needs to know. In addition, if you are able to include something that you did with or for the reference, you also gain an opportunity to have some positive control over the conference between the employer and your reference. This approach aims the employer, and the reference, in the direction you want them to go.

"Aiming" can also mitigate an unavoidable reference who is likely to be lukewarm or worse. If you cannot avoid including someone like this, such as the name of a supervisor who terminated you from employment, one way to ease your apprehension about what he or she will say (even if you were promised a "fair" reference) is to include an accomplishment or other positive event during that employment on your reference list. For example:

> I reported to Mr. Bloodsucker during my tenure with Evil, Vicious & Mean. He named me chief negotiator in more than 20 major commercial finance transactions the firm successfully completed.

Proofread your reference lists carefully. The path to a great job is littered with the detritus of candidates who supplied incorrect addresses, phone numbers, or e-mail addresses for their references. Once they make your list, keep current as to your references' contact information and what they know and love about you. (See Appendix G, Reference List.)

When to Provide References

You need to provide your references when you are asked for them. In a minority of instances, they will be requested with your initial application. However, most of the time the request does not come until you are interviewed, if it comes at all; some employers do not request references, or request some in a follow-up communication after they've narrowed the candidates during interviews. A good rule of thumb: If an interviewer does not ask you for references before the conclusion of the interview, consider offering the refer-ence list before you walk out of the door, provided you sense that the interview went reasonably well and that you are still a con-tender for the position.

Employers That Do Not Provide References

References are not only a problem for potential employers and can-didates; they have also increasingly become a vexation for current and former employers. Candidates have sued their former employ-ers for alleged bad references. New employers have sued former employers for glowing references that allegedly were not true.

The consequence has been the institution of a "no reference" policy by many employers, legal employers being in the forefront of this trend. The standard mantra is something like this:

> It is our policy not to provide references, but only to con-firm dates of employment.

It is incumbent upon you to determine your current and former employers' reference policies before you begin job hunting. If your potential employer is unaware of such a policy before contacting your current supervisor, you may suffer the consequences.

Of course, such a policy may benefit you if your relationship with your current or former supervisor leaves something to be de-sired. This means that you would need to provide another name for your potential employer to call, giving you some control over the selection and subsequent conversation.

A final note about such policies. In the real world, they are often ignored by individuals within your current organization who might be your colleagues or friends.

Legal job campaigns sometimes fail because of problems with references. Selecting and managing references has become much more difficult for legal job seekers, thanks to disputes between present and prior employers over reference accuracy, as well as employer policies disfavoring references altogether. This often overlooked job campaign component merits the same careful attention that you put into developing a strong résumé.

Chapter 29

What Headhunters Do...
and Don't Do

"Headhunting" is one of the most misunderstood components of legal job hunting. Law students and attorneys often erroneously assume that they know what headhunters do and how they do it. This leads to them wasting large amounts of their time and effort that could have been better spent on other job-hunting and career transition avenues. Worse, it leads to complacency—less urgency about job hunting because they believe that a third party is searching on their behalf when the reality is quite different.

This chapter is designed to clarify this greatly misunderstood topic.

Headhunting Defined

Before proceeding further, examine the label "headhunter." It is a very accurate description of how the legal search process works. The legal search consultant, a.k.a. the headhunter, hunts for stellar attorneys that he or she can place with a new employer and thus earn a handsome fee for the placement. The attorney looking for a new job, in most instances, is not the hunter but the hunted.

Legal headhunters find attorneys to fill positions with employers. They act as intermediaries between attorneys and prospective employers, performing some, most, or all of the recruiting functions that might otherwise be tasked to the employer's human resources department. Occasionally, a superb unsolicited résumé will come to the headhunter via mail, fax, or e-mail. This is, however, a rare occurrence.

Headhunters Are Not for Everyone

Headhunters use the term "placeable candidate" to describe an attorney who is likely to be attractive to their client. Remember that the client (almost always a major law firm) is paying the headhunter handsomely to identify its ideal candidate and persuade that person to come to work for them. Clients establish rigorous criteria that the candidate must satisfy. A placeable candidate is one who meets those criteria.

Typical criteria for assocaties may include:

*   Graduation from a *top* law school, *and*
*   Law review (preferably via grades/class rank as opposed to a writing competition), *and*
*   Class rank in the top 20–25 percent of the law school class, *and*
*   At least one year of experience, preferably two years, *and*
*   No more than five years of experience, *and*
*   Experience with a prestigious law firm.

Legal headhunters are *not interested in law students or recent law graduates* without experience. *Period.*

For partners, there is usually only one criterion:

*   Significant, *provable* portable business. In major cities such as New York, Washington, D.C., Chicago, San Francisco, or Los Angeles, that could mean $2 million to $3 million per year.

Only a handful of attorneys can meet these stringent requirements. Virtually all of those who can already have good jobs, and the vast majority are hesitant to leave something familiar that is well-compensated to take a leap of faith to a new employer. A good deal of headhunter time is spent persuading such candidates to make the leap.

Most placements result from the headhunter's initiative, not the candidate's. Headhunters are subject to a constant barrage of résumés, almost all of which come from non-placeable candidates. Unfortunately, most such candidates believe that upon receiving the résumé, the headhunter is actively engaged in attempting to place them. That is an unwarranted and very dangerous assumption, particularly if the candidate thinks that submitting a résumé to a headhunter means that he or she is moving forward in the job search. Most unsolicited résumés that headhunters receive wind up in the waste basket.

There are, however, a few rare exceptions to the otherwise strict criteria laid down by headhunter clients:

- Proximity sometimes breeds a less-than-objective perspective on rankings. Local law schools sometimes achieve a higher rank in the eyes of local employers than their national ranking would warrant. In such cases, the local law school might be included in the definition of a top law school, and candidates from that school would be deemed to meet this criterion.
- The "top 10 law schools" criterion is sufficiently fluid that there are, at any given time, probably 15 to 17 law schools might be deemed by the client and/or the headhunter to be in the top 10.
- Someone at the very top of the class at a lower-ranking law school might be considered worth a gamble.
- Someone with experience in a very hot practice area might satisfy the client criteria despite not meeting academic or prior work history standards. Patent attorneys are the most frequent exceptions.

Legal Headhunting Demographics

While precise statistics do not exist, it is likely that fewer than 1 percent of U.S. attorneys change jobs via headhunters. The other 99 percent are on their own when it comes to finding new employment. The overwhelming majority (and that term is an understatement) of attorneys who change jobs via headhunters go from one major law firm to another. Law firm placements constitute virtually the entire market for legal headhunting. Corporations will, on rare occasions, engage legal headhunters. Government counsel offices, nonprofit law offices, and all other legal employers simply do not.

What Are the Law Firms Actually Paying For?

Law firms that utilize the services of legal headhunters would much rather hire directly from either solicited or unsolicited résumés that come across their transoms. That way, they save a great deal of money on legal search fees. Consequently, unless the candidate search is a retained search, the law firm may simultaneously engage one or more headhunters while also advertising the same position online and/or in print.

The typical circumstance that prompts a law firm to employ a headhunter is the difficulty of finding the highly qualified candidate that it seeks. In addition, firms are willing to pay for the prescreening that the headhunter provides.

The Legal Search Process

The legal search process typically proceeds as follows:

- An employer provides a "job order" to one or more headhunters and requests that the headhunter find candidates that fit the employer's specified criteria.
- The engagement is often documented by a written agreement or memorandum of understanding, covering:
    - *Fees and conditions governing payment.* Headhunters are paid by the employer for a "successful placement" (i.e., where the attorney remains with the employing organization for a specified time period, usually 12

months). Fees range widely and are often negotiated ad hoc. Fees depend to some extent on the state of both the national and the legal employment economy. When the economy is doing well, fees typically range from 20–30 percent of the placed candidate's first-year salary or overall compensation. During bad times, fees are usually lower.

The candidate pays the headhunter nothing. The placement fee is entirely borne by the organization seeking the attorney. If you are told otherwise by a headhunter or an individual or organization purporting to be a legal employment agency, you need to refrain from doing business with them.

- *Headhunter obligations.* If the attorney does not remain with the employer for the specified time period, the headhunter is often obligated to find a replacement in order to retain the full fee for the original placement. There will usually be no additional charge to the employer for the replacement.
- The headhunter researches potential candidates who fit the client's criteria, talks to them about the opportunity, and presents qualified candidates' résumés to the employer.
- The headhunter might conduct screening interviews and résumé and/or reference checks of candidates, and report on the results to the employer.
- The headhunter usually schedules employer interviews of candidates and prepares candidates for interviews.
- If any issues arise that require clarification, the headhunter might assist the employer in resolving them.

Headhunters operate under conditions of strict confidentiality. They should not reveal any information about an attorney candidate to anyone without the candidate's prior approval.

Contingency v. Retained Searches

The vast majority of legal headhunting is on a contingency basis. The headhunter earns the fee only if (1) the search results in a successful placement, and (2) the headhunter is the first legal search organization to present the candidate's résumé to the employer. In other words, only the headhunter who found the successful candidate and presented him or her first earns the fee.

In retained searches, the employer has entered into an exclusive engagement for the recruitment with only one headhunter, and that the headhunter gets a fee regardless of the success of the recruitment. Very few legal headhunter recruitments are retained searches.

A Three-Way Relationship

Three parties are involved in every legal talent search conducted by a headhunter: the employer, the candidate, and the headhunter.

Too many candidates contact headhunters believing that they are the headhunter's client. That is not the case. The employer is the headhunter's client. Unfortunately, this error leads to candidates who behave inappropriately toward headhunters, coming on strong and arrogant. It also leads to less aggressive and proactive job searches because the candidate is under the misimpression that the headhunter is assiduously working to find him or her a job.

Think of this tripartite relationship as analogous to a real estate transaction. The seller (i.e., the employer) "hires" the real estate agent (i.e., the headhunter) to find a buyer (i.e., the candidate). The agent's client is the seller, not the buyer. It is the seller's proceeds of the sale that funds the agent's fee.

Note: Unlike some real estate transactions, there is no equivalent role to that of a buyer's agent, a real estate phenomenon that is not replicated in any way in a legal search or other legal employment transaction.

The Potential Value of Non-legal Headhunters

Remember the saga of Sam Searcher in Chapter 20? Despite his age and job-hopping, both of which would likely have precluded him from serious consideration by a legal headhunter, I concluded that Sam's combination background— attorney, civil engineer, tax expert—might be attractive to certain (non-legal) construction industry headhunters, and suggested that he include this direction in his job search campaign.

Virtually every industry is served by a number of executive search firms. When it comes to attorneys with education or experience that is useful to their industry focus, client companies generally impose less strict criteria on their executive searches than those imposed by law firms on legal headhunters.

For More Information

The National Association of Legal Search Consultants (NALSC) (www.nalsc.org), is a professional association of legal headhunters who have pledged to operate under a Code of Ethics. Any legal search consultant may join NALSC. The organization's Web site has a searchable member directory.

Legal headhunters often advertise in legal trade publications and their online manifestations.

Bureau of National Affairs subsidiary Kennedy Information publishes the *Directory of Executive & Professional Recruiters* in both print and online editions (www.recruiterredbook.com/index.php).

Legal headhunters are not for everyone. A successful legal placement most often results from a headhunter identifying a happily employed candidate with top law school academic and professional credentials and experience, then persuading that person to leave his or her "sure thing" for an unknown destination. If you do not fit these criteria, you are probably better off job searching on your own and, if you have additional education or experience, possibly testing generic professional search firms to see if they might be interested in your "law-plus" background.

Chapter 30

Networking without Groveling

Network, network, network. I'm sure you've heard that a million times, particularly in the context of legal job hunting. While networking is not the only important job-hunting tactic that you should have in your arsenal, it is very important.

Networking is intimidating, but it does not have to be something to fear and thus to avoid, downplay, or postpone. This chapter will show you how to network fearlessly, with gusto, confidence, and positive results.

If you want to maximize the value of your networking contacts, you need to provide them with enough information about you so that they will (1) be motivated to perform for you, and (2) channel their thinking to be in line with *your* job-hunting agenda. In other words, you need to both energize your contacts and shape their idea of who you are and where you want to go. The more good information you can supply them, the more effective they will be on your behalf, the more self-confidence about networking you will develop, and the easier your path to a new legal job or career will be.

Why Bother with Networking?

Most attorneys find networking both distasteful and intimidating. Nevertheless, it is a must if you do not want to shortchange your job search and want to give yourself the best opportunity to wind up where you want to be. For example, the U.S. Department of Justice's Office of Attorney Recruitment and Management (OARM) advertises hundreds of attorney positions on its Web site every year. However, that number is far less than the actual number of positions available in the department. Some Justice Department offices do not send their job vacancies to OARM for posting. Others do not publish vacancy announcements at all (federal attorney positions are not required to be advertised). The only way to find out about these jobs is to have a good contact within the department who can tell you about them. Depending on how good your contact is, the best way to be considered for them is if your contact hand-carries your résumé to the hiring official.

Networking also confers additional benefits. It expands your circle of acquaintances, which can lead to early intelligence about career and business opportunities. It provides you with a platform for future career moves and growth. And it can serve to build your confidence by prompting you to interact with professional colleagues and others.

When to Communicate with Your Contacts

Ideally, you should make the effort *before* you need to invoke their assistance (see Chapter 28, "Managing Your References and Controlling the Conversation"). However, most attorneys don't bother to nurture a network of possible contacts before they need them. Consequently, they have to scramble to put a set of contacts together at the eleventh hour. I define the eleventh hour, by the way, as the moment you decide to launch your job search.

Once you have established your contacts, you need to keep them informed of your progress, any changes in your job campaign strategy, and any positive developments along the way. Once you have landed in your new position or career, you need to thank your contacts for their advice and assistance.

Whom to Contact

Virtually anyone you know or have met qualifies as a possible direct networking contact. This includes relatives, friends, professors (law school, graduate school, undergraduate school), fellow alumni, current and former supervisors and co-workers who know about your job search, workplace alumni, membership organization colleagues, clergy, professional associates, politicians, clients, vendors, etc. The possible community of contacts is vast and open-ended. You should include everyone who might be in a position to serve as an information resource, help you directly or indirectly (through their own contacts who are strangers to you), act as intermediaries in getting your résumé to potential employers, etc. That would even include your hair stylist, postal carrier, dog trainer, physicians, CPA, and anyone else with whom you come in contact.

It is critically important to expand your network beyond the people who occupy the same professional or social "space" that you do. People outside of your circle are the ones most likely to be of assistance because they operate in different spaces.

Building a Network from Scratch

Even if you are introverted, you can still create a network out of whole cloth. There are three actions you can take to accomplish this:

1. *Fellow alumni* from your undergraduate institution, law school, and other academic experiences can be valuable resources. This is particularly true the more miles there are between you and your school. The greater the distance, the more fervent the "old school tie" tends to be. You can find out who the alumni are and where they work by contacting your school's career services office, alumni office, and alumni association in the city where you want to work.

2. You can join various *relevant membership organizations* that exist, in part, to provide a business development or job search network for their members. I urged one of my clients, an out-of-work attorney with a degree in construction engineer-

ing, to contact Fellows of the American College of Construction Lawyers, a very prestigious and highly selective membership organization, in order to develop a network of contacts who could advise and assist him in combining his two degrees. It took him several months to obtain membership, but once he did, the College proved such a valuable networking medium that he was able to select from several job offers in a very short time. A selection of legal networking organizations can be found in Appendix E.

3. *Social networking Web sites*, such as Facebook, LinkedIn, Twitter, and others are tools that you can use to establish a job-hunting network without having to "perform" face-to-face or feel like you are begging.

A telling statistic: A May 2009 survey by Jobvite found that 80 percent of companies use or intend to use social networking sites to recruit candidates. In addition, two-thirds of the companies surveyed that already used social networking sites to recruit had successfully hired a candidate.

Social networking sites have three big advantages for employers.

1. They enable them to check the recommendations of persons who have worked with the candidate;

2. They can get an idea of the potential hire's written communication skills, especially if the site links to a blog; and

3. They can dig up "dirt" on a candidate, if there is any dirt to be found. A Careerbuilder survey found that more than one-third of recruiters eliminated a candidate from consideration after viewing information on the candidate's personal page. An informal survey of law firm recruiters conducted by the author found that each of the responding law firms had rejected a candidate due to information they found on a social networking site.

This third employer advantage is, of course, a big disadvantage to the candidate. Not only do you need to be extremely careful about what you post about yourself or others, you also cannot control what others may say about you. Thus, you need to think very carefully before relying on a social networking Web site.

Without getting into a detailed description of social networking site features and functionality (you can read all about them on the sites themselves), the following points should be observed when contemplating their use:

- *Linkedin* is probably the number-one social networking site for professional networking. The Jobvite survey found that Linkedin is the site favored by employers. You can use it to locate industry experts and participate in groups of like-minded or similarly-situated individuals. It provides a good way to gain insights about companies, including applying for jobs, interviewing, evaluating a job offer, and performing due diligence on the employer. LinkedIn's attorney job boards are decent.
- *Facebook* ranks second, in my estimation. Keep your Professional Profile separate from your Personal Profile. It is advisable to avoid Facebook Quizzes, which might provide prospective employers with too much personal information about you.
- *Twitter* permits you to be a "microblogger," thanks to its 140-character limit. Twitter depends upon the principle of "followers," people who choose to follow another Twitter user.

If you already have a Twitter Personal Profile, create a separate Professional Profile and keep your personal information and tweets separate from your professional ones. This is important because, even though Twitter's value as a professional networking medium is growing, it is still primarily a medium for what one market research firm labels "pointless babble." You don't want to be barraged with tweets from the multitude about what they are having for lunch and other uninteresting and time-consuming drivel. Establish a professional sounding e-mail address, which will make it easier to sort tweets coming to you.

The way in which companies are using Twitter is instructive for job seekers and career changers. Companies that are trying to sell products or services target potential buyers based on their tweet history. Sometimes, they even quote from tweets in their own tweets to buyers.

Caveat No. 1: Twitter is, for many users, a "here today, gone tomorrow" phenomenon. The user retention rate is quite low.

Caveat No. 2: People have been known to set up fake Twitter accounts in the names of people they wanted to harm and then send out messages purportedly from them.

What Your Contacts Need to Know About You

You need to provide your contacts with enough information to be able to represent you capably with prospective employers or with their own contacts. This means that they need to have a current copy of your résumé(s) as well as your "Contacts Road Map" (see Appendix F), an essential job-search document that accomplishes three things: (1) providing detailed information about your career and career aspirations; (2) energizing and enthusing your contacts; and (3) easing your anxiety and possible embarrassment about asking for help.

Your résumé alone is not sufficient. Supplementing it with a Contacts Road Map provides a clear path for your contacts to follow. Instead of having to devise a plan for conversations with your potential employers themselves—which is a burden and a reason why so many contacts are unproductive—the Road Map does their thinking and planning for them. Moreover, they're certain to be impressed with your sophisticated approach to networking and legal job hunting, so much so that they'll exert themselves enthusiastically on your behalf once provided with a Road Map. In addition, by sending your contacts down the proper path, they are unlikely to misconstrue who you are professionally and go off in a wrong direction.

The Contacts Road Map provides the clarity and direction that your network needs in order to advise and assist you effectively in your career transition. It removes the ambiguity and confusion that often negates their ability to serve as good conduits to both a wider circle of good contacts and actual job opportunities. I have yet to encounter a contact who was not impressed by the Contacts Road Map.

For Future Reference

Keep up your contacts once you have made them. This means communicating with them even after you have secured the job of your dreams. The legal economy grows more volatile every year, a trend that is likely to continue. You never know when you might have to invoke your network again. Make sure it is there when that time comes.

> I never met an attorney who looked forward eagerly to networking. No one likes to be perceived as a supplicant, someone who is begging for help.
>
> While that attitude may not be able to be completely avoided, it can certainly be tempered by approaching networking as suggested in this chapter, especially the crafting and submitting of a Contacts Road Map—arguably the most important job-search document, and one that also confers two very important collateral benefits: boosting your self-confidence and reducing your trepidation about networking.

Part V

Interviewing

Chapter 31
Understanding What You Will Confront 289

Chapter 32
What You Need to Accomplish 297

Chapter 33
Handling the Tough Questions 301

Chapter 34
Bridging the Power Chasm 313

Chapter 35
When to Explain a Termination 319

Understanding What You Will Confront

Two "Tales of the Weird" make the point that legal job interviews are unpredictable, and the related point that you need to be prepared to be surprised.

Roads Not Taken
During my 3L year, I interviewed with a New York state government general counsel office in Albany, New York. I boarded a train for Albany and had to stand in the aisle the entire two-and-a-half hour trip due to overbooking by Amtrak. By the time I arrived at the interview, I was tired and irritable. The receptionist ushered me into the general counsel's office and closed the door behind her. The room was pitch dark, with blackout curtains on the high windows. The only illumination came from small lights mounted below a series of paintings covering all four walls. Each painting was of exactly the same scene: a two-lane highway receding into the distance and disappearing at the "vanishing point." The only difference among them was that each was a different color. Suddenly, a disjointed voice

proclaimed: "So what do you think of the artwork?" Up until this point, I thought I was alone in the office. I strained my eyes and saw a shape behind the desk. It was the general counsel. "Interesting," I replied. "They are all the same, aren't they?" A long, painful pause. "No, they are not. My daughter did them. Too bad you can't see the differences." The perfunctory interview lasted only 10 minutes, after which I was hustled out. I never heard from the interviewer or the department again.

Company without Walls

I also interviewed three times with a large manufacturing company (yes, back in the day, some corporate in-house counsel offices actually hired new law grads without any experience). The final interview was with the general counsel. I was escorted into a huge room the size of an airplane hangar. The general counsel's "area" of the room was demarcated only by a set of potted plants arranged in a square. All of the other areas in the room were offset from each other the same way. A low but very audible unceasing hum that sounded like the background instruments in a Japanese "Noh" (aptly labeled) drama pervaded the room. After greeting me, the general counsel explained the unusual office layout. "We run an open company here, with no secrets from each other. We arranged our senior management offices this way so that no one, the CEO, the CFO, me, or the other senior managers would ever feel that we were putting up barriers to open, uninhibited communication. We love it so much we're going to roll the concept out into the rest of the company." OK, I thought. So you can't even pick your nose or scratch yourself without being observed. George Orwell would have loved this arrangement. I didn't get an offer, and two years later the company was absorbed into the maw of a much larger one, and the entire legal staff, potted plants, low hum et al., was let go.

Categorizing Interviews

Interviews do not come neatly packaged. Rather, there are many varieties, and these are not necessarily mutually exclusive. You can categorize interviews in several ways, and I do that in this chapter. I also suggest tips for dealing with certain kinds of interviews that merit a closer look. The more you know about what you will be facing, the better you will be able to prepare, and fare.

Who Will Interview You?

Single interviewer. Try to find out as much information as you can about the interviewer beforehand; Google his or her name, search a legal research database for articles he or she might have written. Talk to your contacts who might know something about the interviewer.

Panel or group. Give "equal time" to eye contact with each panel member, despite which one asks the question or dominates the questioning and interaction. Be alert to "one-upmanship" among panel members trying to impress or compete with one another. Try to determine who is the *first-among-equals* (if it is not obvious) so that you can address your follow-up thank-you note/e-mail to that person.

Serial interviews (i.e., one interview on the heels of another). Get the names of all of the interviewers so that you can (1) address thank-you notes/e-mails to the appropriate parties, and (2) communicate afterward with the appropriate contact about the status of the recruitment.

What Medium Is Used?

Face-to-face. Make sure your dress* and grooming are impeccable, your handshake firm but not crushing, your eye contact appropriate, and your mannerisms suppressed.

Telephone. Have your résumé or a copy of your application form or online application, as well as your cover letter and any other documents that the interviewer also received (e.g., reference list, writing sample), in front of you on your desk for ready refer-

---

* Studies show that, all other things being equal, the best-dressed candidate gets the nod.

ence. Have your watch in front of you so that you don't ramble. Don't speak in a monotone.

Videoconference. Dress as you would for a face-to-face interview. Address yourself to the camera, not to the video screen or technician. Be alert to possible transmission delays. Speak slowly and distinctly. Do not "trail off" at the end of your sentences. Make sure that the videoconference connection is completely switched off before commenting about the interview.

How Many Interviews?

Single. This is your one chance to dazzle, so leave nothing in reserve.

Multiple (same day). Get a very good night's rest. If the interviews are in more than one building, make a test run prior to the day of the interviews to ascertain how much time you will require to traverse the distance between buildings.

Sequential (different days). Summarize in writing what ensued at each interview immediately thereafter so that you can refresh your memory before the next interview.

What Type of Interview?

Screening interview. Prepare as if it were a final interview. Be alert; if the interviewer is a human resources professional, not an attorney, you may have to resort exclusively or often to "plain English."

"Traditional" interview. Be prepared for the tough questions about your background, as well as the questions you will want to pose to the interviewer.

Scripted interview. The same questions are asked of each candidate, often in the same sequence. The interview is often scored by the interviewer(s) using a score sheet (see Appendix H, Interview Rating Scale).

"Good cop–bad cop" interview. Also known as the "Mutt and Jeff" interview, with one friendly, empathetic interviewer counterbalanced by one cold, unfriendly interviewer. Don't get sucked into thinking that the good cop is your buddy.

"Gotcha" interview. This is the best example of the point that all interviews are, at least in part, gamesmanship. The interviewer is trying to determine how you handle adversity, confrontation, or stress, as well as your ability to think on your feet. One technique is rapid-fire questions that you do not have sufficient time to answer. Another is long periods of silence on the part of the interviewer, who is waiting for whatever you might blurt out. A third technique is bizarre questions from the interviewer. The substance of your responses is often less important than how you come across in handling the stress.

Case study interview. This is popular with consulting firms that hire attorneys for law-related consulting assignments. The interviewer presents you with a hypothetical fact situation in order to evaluate your analytical and problem-solving skills.

Presentation interview. This is increasingly popular with corporate in-house counsel offices. The candidate makes a 20- to 30-minute presentation to a panel on a legal topic and then fields questions from the panel about the presentation. Variations in this method are: (1) the employer chooses the topic; (2) the candidate chooses the topic; (3) the candidate chooses the topic from among several offered by the employer; or (4) the candidate chooses the topic within a topical area selected by the employer. As this is probably the most high-pressure interview type, below are some suggestions for getting through it successfully.

Here are some things you should definitely do:

- Prepare, Prepare, PREPARE.
- Role-play until you get it right (smooth delivery; no distracting habits; self-confidence).
- Assume that the audience is ignorant of your topic.
- Practice speaking in complete sentences.
- Speak with enthusiasm.
- Be conscious of your body language.
- Insinuate your key strengths.
- Pepper your presentation with good, simple, and lively examples.
- Incorporate visuals, e.g., PowerPoint, unless you are instructed otherwise.

- Pose questions to yourself that the audience is likely to pose to you.
- Make eye contact equally with everyone in your audience.

Here are some things you should definitely avoid:

- Eliminate "fillers" and verbal crutches.
  - "You know?"
  - "Like"
  - "Ahh," "err," and "umm"
  - "Right?"
  - "Are you with me?"
  - "Do you know what I'm saying?"
  - Avoid inappropriate smiles.
- Restrain your hand gestures.
- Steer clear of weird body language, e.g., fidgeting, constant moving around, etc.

Mealtime interview. Be mindful that this will likely last longer than a normal interview or a normal meal. Prepare as you would for a standard interview. Table manners are very important, e.g.,

- Be polite to the server.
- Don't be a glutton.
- Keep your elbows off the table.
- Speak with your mouth empty.
- Chew with your mouth closed.

Choose something in the same price range as your interviewer. Don't order an appetizer unless the host(s) does. Don't drink alcohol, except if you are asked to select the wine. If so, avoid *Chateau Lafitte Rothschild 1947*—keep the price at or under mid-range. Don't order soup. Don't complain about the food. The interviewer will pick up the tab. Thank your host for the meal.

Behavioral interview. The interviewer asks questions that probe specific behavioral characteristics consistent with a successful employee. He or she is testing (1) how you bring your experience and knowledge to bear on a problem, (2) your reaction speed, and (3) how you think on your feet. Give detailed responses. Look for analogies between your current or past positions and the one for which you are applying. Itemize the skills needed in the new job. Document for yourself specifically when and how you used the same or comparable skills in your present or past positions, and practice a way to work them into your interview. Script a few success stories you can relate to the interviewer that underline those skills.

What Is the Employer Thinking During the Interview?

It is essential that you go into a legal job interview sensitive to what is going through the interviewer's mind while he or she is interviewing you. Here are the core thoughts that legal employers consistently cite when this question is posed to them:

1. What will it be like having this person around at least eight hours a day?
2. Can I trust this person to represent me capably?
   a. Is he articulate?
   b. Can she think and speak at the same time?
   c. Will he embarrass me with internal and external clients, adjudicators, opposing counsel, etc.?
3. Will this person get along with everyone else in the office?
4. Can this person do the job?
5. Will hiring this person advance my career?

> Understanding what you are likely to face in a job interview is the first step in plotting what you need to do to prevail at the interview. Moreover, the more you know about the interview setting, participants, and type, the more self-confidence you will feel when you walk in the door.

Chapter 32

What You Need to Accomplish

A legal job interview is not an open-ended, agenda-less affair. We know that, certainly, from the perspective of the interviewer, who will use the interview to zero in on the best candidate for the position offered.

But what does the candidate need to accomplish? Getting a job offer, of course. But the intermediate interview steps toward that goal are often unclear. Consequently, many job applicants "blow" the interview.

This chapter outlines these steps toward the ultimate goal of the job offer, and suggests strategies and techniques designed to help you ascend them successfully.

The following are the most important goals a candidate has to achieve or impart at a job interview.

Why You Are the Best Candidate for the Position

You convey this by getting across to the interviewer the *key points about yourself*—which means you have to decide beforehand what these are. They will not necessarily be exactly the same for each opportunity you are pursuing. However, you likely cannot go wrong if the following are included in your preparation:

Tangibles
- Your ability to do the job
- Your intelligence
- Your verbal ability
- Your listening skills
- Your significant professional accomplishments
- Your persuasive ability
- Your other strengths

Intangibles
- Your self confidence
- Your "normalcy"
- Your leadership qualities
- Your problem-solving skills
- Your commitment to being a team player
- Your initiative
- Your organizational skills
- Your temperament

Your Energy Level and Enthusiasm

You achieve this with both your words and your body language during the interview. Liveliness, unless overdone, is infectious and interviewers respond positively to it in a candidate. We all like to feel that what we are describing is enticing, and the best way to demonstrate you are enticed is to show it.

Your "Fit" with the Employer's Organization

"Fit" consists of two elements—your alignment with the organization and your alignment with the interviewer(s). The best way to manifest your fit is to know as much about the organization and the interviewer(s) as you can possibly learn prior to appearing at the interview. That knowledge will provide you with markers on how to behave.

Your Likeability

Employers do not hire people they do not like. As we proceed through life and gain experience in professional and social settings, we learn what people like and what they don't like. You may be the most qualified, credentialed, and brilliant legal job candidate on the planet, but if the interviewer does not warm to you, you are not likely to wind up with a job offer.

You achieve likeability by affecting the interviewer with your mood and emotions. If it is apparent that you are in a great mood, the interviewer will react in two ways: (1) He or she will think that her description of the job opportunity has put you in a great mood; and (2) his or her own spirits will be picked up by being around someone in a great mood.

What Will Be the Next Step in the Recruiting Process?

Never leave an interview without attempting to get an answer to this question. My experience has been that only 10 percent of legal job candidates ever bother to find this out. There is no point in operating in limbo following the interview. So ask. A side benefit is that interviewers are impressed with candidates who have the foresight and presence of mind to ask what comes next.

Leave the Interviewer(s) Wanting More

In addition to infecting the interviewer(s) with your energy and enthusiasm, you can seal this part of the deal if you ask great questions (see Chapter 34, "Bridging the Power Chasm"). Since questions from you, the candidate, usually come toward the end of the interview, view them as your "closing argument," what you want the jury to remember when they retire to consider their verdict. This is what will be remembered after you walk out of the door. Making yourself memorable—for all the right reasons—will go a long way toward getting you the job offer.

Do You Really Want to Work There?

This is a critical question that the interview will help you answer. The signals—both overt and subliminal—that you receive from the interviewer(s), the support staff, and the overall office environment will go a long way toward answering this question.

> This brief chapter is designed to break down the customary candidate interview goals into their component parts. It provides a template—a checklist—for you to use when you prepare for an interview.

Chapter 33

Handling the Tough Questions

Interviews are not supposed to be easy. A good interviewer will want to test the "cut of your jib." Being prepared for this grilling means focusing more attention on the difficult and discomfiting questions you might be asked than on the "home run" questions that you know you can knock out of the park. In preparing, go back over Chapter 17, "Vulnerability Management: Mitigating Your Weaknesses." As stated in that chapter, interviewers almost always zero in on what they perceive to be your weaknesses.

Next, think about the worst question(s) that could be directed your way in an interview—the ones that could cause your pulse to escalate wildly and your respiration rate to go off the charts. Practice answering them. "Role-play" a mock interview with a spouse, significant other, or friend, and ask them for an unvarnished critique. You simply have to be prepared for these questions. If you can answer them calmly and with confidence, the rest will be easy.

The Mother of All Tough Interview Questions

This question may be posed in several different ways, depending on your circumstances and the penchant of the interviewer for making you squirm:

> Q: *Why do you want to leave your current job?*
>   OR, if you are currently out of work:
> Q: *Why did you leave your last job?*
>   OR
> Q: *Why are you unemployed?*

For many attorneys, this will be the most difficult question of all. Much less stigma is attached to job loss today than 10 years ago, but there is still a lingering taint. Many attorneys have been affected by reorganizations, mergers, downsizings, and layoffs, especially in the dark economic times brought on by the great recession. As a result, potential employers today tend to be more sympathetic and receptive to candidates who have experienced these career disruptions. Nevertheless, it is easier to find a new job if you are currently employed than if you are unemployed.

The fact that you are being interviewed at all is a positive sign. One of the most important variables in successfully addressing either a resignation or a termination is your demeanor when responding to this question. If you come across as nervous or discomfited by the question, your response may not strike the interviewer as credible, which will likely mean the end of any chance of getting a job offer. Similarly, if you manifest anger about a job loss, or a "doom-and-gloom" attitude, you can likely kiss the job goodbye. Negativity is easy to spot. Nobody likes being around a negative person. Interviewers and employers do not customarily empathize, so don't go looking for sympathy from them. In other words, move on.

One of the most important things to remember when you are tempted to seek sympathy for your plight from a prospective employer is that you are speaking to an *employer* who is more likely to identify with your former *employer* than with you, the *candidate*. Consequently, don't waste your time seeking understanding.

If you are voluntarily leaving—or have already left—your job, this question will not pose a problem for you. You can respond with something on the order of:

I have gone as far as I can at _____ and am now seeking new challenges.

OR

I advanced as far as I could at _____ and now wish to pursue an opportunity where I can grow with an organization.

If your departure is—or was—compelled by economic circumstances beyond your control, your response might be any of the following:

The company was acquired and the acquiring company already has its own legal staff, thus is eliminating my company's legal staff.

The company has decided to outsource a significant portion of its legal work and several positions are being eliminated.

The firm lost a large client and has to cut back on personnel.

The firm lost its private equity practice group to another firm and was forced to eliminate positions.

The firm went out of business.

If you were fired for cause, or in retaliation for blowing the whistle on someone or on some questionable conduct, or due to a personality conflict with a colleague or supervisor, or for some other reason (you may not even know the reason), the answer becomes more difficult. You have to decide how much you are going to reveal, mindful that the reasons behind your termination may be revealed in the event the prospective employer contacts your prior employer, and that the story that the latter tells will definitely be from his or her slant.

The bottom line is: Your response will be controlled by what your former employer would say about you if contacted by your prospective employer. Thus, the most important piece of business you can conduct and conclude before, during, or even after a firing is to determine what your employer would say about your reasons for leaving the organization. Ideally, you would get your former employer to agree to say something positive that will not diminish your opportunity for new employment.

Law firms and many corporations are especially anxious about keeping a lid on employee terminations and often enter into written settlement or release agreements with their employees. If you find yourself in this position, make sure that the agreement contains specific language covering this point. If it does not, then you need to speak to your employer and attempt to get him or her to agree on what you will both say about your departure. Both you and your former employer have to be on the same page.

I realize that approaching someone who terminated your employment is uncomfortable for most people. Nevertheless, it is supremely important to make sure that your former employer does not undercut your job opportunities. My counseling clients found that, more often than not, their former employers were willing to agree about what to say about a termination that did not kill off any hope of future employment (if for no other reason than to avoid any liability exposure should the former employee seek redress for a bad reference).

An important collateral point to remember is that law firms are especially sensitive when it comes to admitting that they have cut back on attorney personnel due to economic circumstances. A recent example (2008) is the Wall Street firm that abruptly terminated a large number of attorneys, then insisted to the media that the economy had nothing to do with the job cuts. Sure.

A fallback position, in the event your former employer balks at saying anything other than that you were fired, is to attempt to persuade him or her to say that *it is the organization's policy not to provide references, but only to confirm the term of employment.* This is increasingly common, particularly in the legal industry, since attorneys are so sensitive about potential litigation arising out of either a negative or even a (false) positive endorsement. Consequently, many legal employers have decided to say nothing at all other than that, "yes, he or she worked here from _____ until _____."

Whatever your reason for leaving, craft a succinct statement of the circumstances of your departure and practice saying it aloud and making it sound as unpracticed as you can. This will help organize your thoughts about an often very emotional and uncomfortable situation and assist you in presenting yourself in the best possible light.

Other Tough Questions and Suggested Response Strategies

Most such questions may seem meaningless and sometimes stupid, but keep in mind that the interviewer is not always asking them because of a real interest in the *content* of your response, but rather in *how* you respond. Please note that although sample answers are given for most of the questions below, some of the questions are not followed by suggested responses because the "right" answers very much depend on your individual circumstances. Also, keep in mind that the suggested answers are often examples that may not be applicable to your particular situation. Nevertheless, they are designed to stimulate your thinking about responses that might apply.

Q: *Where could your greatest improvement be as an attorney?*
Answer with something that you have never done before. Do *not* respond with something that you perceive as a weakness in your current practice or position, e.g., "I keep missing deadlines."
Sample A: *Appellate work. I hope to have the opportunity to become involved in appeals.*

Q: *What is your greatest strength?*
When talking about your greatest strength, make sure you *relate* it to the position for which you are applying. That is a great way to imprint your talents in the interviewer's mind. Also, respond with specifics.
Sample A: *I firmly believe that preparation wins cases, so I always prepare as thoroughly as I possibly can. My preparation skills should fit nicely into a firm such as your's, which handles so many complex commercial disputes.*

Q: *What is your greatest weakness?*
This is a particularly difficult question for most interviewees. Don't say that you cannot think of any weaknesses, *and* don't ad-

mit to a "real" weakness that might remove you from consideration for the position (e.g., "I can't handle a lot of pressure"). Rather, turn the negative into a positive.

You can do this in two ways: First, by labeling something a weakness that is really a strength when viewed from the employer's perspective, such as:

I'm a workaholic.
OR
Sometimes I get impatient with colleagues who aren't 100 percent committed to getting the job done.

The problem with this, though, could be that the employer is "on" to what you are attempting, since this tactic has become rather commonplace. Your second option is to admit to a modest weakness and talk about what you employ as a coping mechanism, e.g.:

I'm not as organized as I would like to be, so I always answer my e-mails and phone calls right away. I'm aware of the problem and I have adopted this disciplined strategy to deal with it.

Q: *Why didn't you do better in law school?*

This is another question designed to make you sweat. If you do not have a good reason for your less-than-exceptional performance, this will be difficult to answer. However, you should have an answer prepared, e.g.:

My grades were a reflection of my having to work 25 hours per week in order to finance my education.
OR
I became heavily involved in practice-oriented jobs and clerkships while attending law school because I wanted to learn how to practice law in the real world in addition to the theoretical one of the classroom.
OR
I was not the best student, but I buckled down once I joined the workforce and, as you can see from my résumé, have become a very capable attorney.

Q: *Tell me about yourself.*

This is an open-ended request, your response to which runs the risk of droning on ad infinitum. The interviewer is not asking you this question because of a deep interest in your detailed biography. Rather, the question is designed to test two important skills: (1) your ability to speak eloquently at some—but not too much—length and (2) your ability to prioritize what is truly important. Consequently, you can leave out where you were conceived, the course of your mother's pregnancy, what you customarily ate for dinner, your high school cheerleading career, where you went on spring break, and all other such details. Rather, *focus on your academics and experience.* Ask yourself the following question: "What are the top four or five things I want this person to know about me?" Keep your response to 90 seconds or less.

I was born and raised in Nebraska and was always fascinated by the workings of the national government, so I majored in political science and then headed directly for Washington, D.C. for law school in order to take advantage of the many internships and clerkships available there. Then, as you can see from my résumé, I used these experiences as a platform to launch my legal career.

Q: *Where do you see yourself in five years?*

Your answer should assume that you will still be with the employer with whom you are interviewing, and that you will have been promoted. Do not say that you will be holding the job the interviewer currently holds, or a job higher up on the food chain than the interviewer's current position.

I would like to advance within the company as I acquire more skills, knowledge and experience, and be able to assume more responsibility and make a larger contribution to the organization.

Q: *Are you a team player?*

Of course you are! However, that four-word response is insufficient. Tie your "yes" response into something that you successfully collaborated on in your current or prior positions.

Yes, I am. For example, in my position as an associate at Serendipity and Serpent, it was essential to run every transaction that I participated in by our Tax and Regulatory Practice Groups. This had always been done rather haphazardly and informally. I saw real advantages for the firm in having the Tax and Regulatory Groups engaged much earlier in the transaction process, and proposed that a more formal mechanism be established so that those groups received advance notice of every potential transaction in which the firm was—or would soon be—engaged. This proposal was endorsed by the Management Committee, and I was asked to supervise the implementation, which entailed developing strong relationships with the group chairs and their deputies. These relationships then translated into a very harmonious working environment for our negotiating teams, not only for team members, but also for our clients."

Q: *What would you do if. . . .?*

This kind of hypothetical question is designed to assess your ability to think on your feet and your judgment. The actual answer is less important than the analytical process you describe going through to arrive at it. Try to relate your response to an analogous situation you confronted in a prior employment.

Q: *What experience related to this position have you had?*

Your answer will be easy if you have had directly related experience. However, if you have not, you need to do one of two things— itemize your transferable skills that would be valuable in the new position, or, if you have no transferable skills, recite how, specifically, your accumulated knowledge, past experience, and/or abilities would be valuable in the new position.

I am a very quick study. For example, when Sarbanes-Oxley was enacted, I had no experience with corporate governance and had to come up the learning curve very rapidly. I was able to do that, as evidenced by my company's perfect record vis-à-vis SEC filings since then.

Q: *Give an example of something you did that was "above and beyond" the normal call of duty.*

Your response should demonstrate that you (1) have leadership skills; (2) organized or initiated successful projects; (3) chaired a committee or group; and/or (4) manifested a willingness to go the extra mile in classroom work, clinical work, research projects, or other activities. These skills can be exhibited in an extracurricular setting as well as in a work or academic setting.

Q: *What do you know about our organization?*

This is where your interview preparation comes in. It is an opportunity to demonstrate both your knowledge of the employer and your efforts to prepare for the interview. Make sure you reply with enthusiasm when speaking of the organization. However, do not go overboard and tread into realms where the adage: "A little knowledge is a dangerous thing" might apply. One candidate for a position with my company had gained access to our Dow Jones research report and questioned me about our financial performance during the initial job interview. Stick to fundamentals.

Q: *What can you do for us that someone else cannot?*

Your response should relate past experiences that show that you succeeded in solving problem(s) that may be similar to those facing your prospective employer.

I had to manage the delicate and very contentious relations with the union when _____ closed its Ohio plant. I succeeded in this by bringing the shop stewards into the shutdown planning process from the outset and continually communicated with them regarding our outplacement and retraining efforts. I can bring experience with highly charged, emotional dealings to your firm.

Q: *Why should we hire you?*

This question is closely related to the preceding one. However, it is not quite as contentious and may not, therefore, require quite so specific a response.

My career has been marked by outstanding performance wherever I have been, and I will bring the same commitment and enthusiasm to this position. Moreover, I am very interested in assisting in implementing what I know about your mission and objectives from my review of your strategic plan/annual report/etc.

Q: *What are you looking for in a job?*

This question tends to elicit a vague response after an uncomfortable pause. A simple, succinct answer is best.

An opportunity to use my skills and knowledge, to perform well, to contribute to the organization, and to be recognized for my good work.

Q: *Why do you want to work here?*

This question is one that you should have answered for yourself long before you arrived at the interview. Your response should demonstrate interest in the employer's organization, some knowledge of what the employer is about, and a link between your skills and what the employer needs.

I have always been interested in the _____ industry and would like to be a part of _____ company's growth and globalization efforts. I think my background and interests would enable me to make a significant contribution to the success of the organization.

Q: *What skills or experience of yours would be useful in this position?*

Before the interview, write a detailed description of what you do well and practice talking about your strengths. Describe specific projects or assignments you feel proud about and that demonstrated those skills or experience. Don't forget to incorporate your "people skills" into your response.

Q: *What compensation are you seeking?*

Your response will depend to a large extent on what you have been able to learn about the salary structure of the employer's organization prior to your interview. If you respond with a salary range, understand that the interviewer will likely take strong note of the lower figure in the range and ignore the upper one. If you have not been able to learn anything about the employer's compensation scale, consider stating that your salary requirements are "flexible."

Another interesting and little-used counter to the salary question is to say something like this:

I don't want to disqualify myself by specifying a number at this juncture. Can you tell me how much you have budgeted for this position?

Whatever you do, do not state a figure that is likely to be totally out-of-line with the employer's salary structure. **Note**: In salary negotiations (and this question in an interview is the beginning of that process), a rule-of-thumb is that the person who mentions a specific dollar amount first loses. See also Chapter 37, "Negotiating the Employment Agreement."

The easy employer questions—the ones that, if asked, enable you to naturally shine—are ones that you will have no trouble with during the interview. Since they won't make you sweat, don't sweat them during your interview preparation.

Keep your preparation focused on the tough questions, the ones that make you nervous and uncomfortable. They will be the make-or-break moments of the interview.

Chapter 34

Bridging the Power Chasm

We tend to leave an interview believing that the interviewer is smarter than we are. Why? Because the interviewer was the one asking the questions.

Turn the scenario around. What if the candidate for the position was the one asking the questions? Who's smarter now?

With few exceptions, legal job interviews follow a predictable pattern. The interviewer goes first with his or her questions, followed by the candidate asking questions of the interviewer. This sequence is very much to your advantage as the candidate because it leaves a fresh and powerful impression of your intelligence with the interviewer when you walk out the door.

Virtually every legal job interview comes to a point where the interviewer asks the job applicant if he or she has any questions. The absolutely incorrect, toxic, job opportunity-killing response is something like: *"No, I think you have adequately answered all of my questions."* This opening is your opportunity to shine, to cement the interviewer's impression of you as a thoughtful, articulate individual with insight and foresight, and to *imprint* yourself favorably in the mind of the employer when you exit the interview room.

The "great questions to ask" that follow are general in nature. Certain questions, of course, will not be germane to or appropriate for every type of employer. These should be obvious from the context of the interview and the position for which you are applying. For example, you would not ask a government agency interviewer "how the legal department contributes to shareholder value." Specific questions geared to the particular position, employer, or industry are ones that you will need to devise for yourself, depending on the results of your pre-interview research.

Note: Do not ask any questions that are answered by either the job ad or vacancy announcement or that you should know by virtue of any other information you received from the employer, including information the interviewer just gave you during the interview. For example, do not—as one of my counseling clients did—ask the interviewer "why is this position open" if the job ad said that "this is a new position."

Great Questions to Ask

"Why is this position open?" Ask this question to determine what factors contributed to there being a vacancy, some of which may give you pause when considering a job offer from the employer, e.g., "The incumbent left after two months," or "We had to let her go because. . . ."

Conversely, the interviewer's response may give you cause for optimism about the position, e.g., "Ms. Doe was asked by the President to serve as Deputy Assistant Secretary of Energy for Fossil Fuels, so, despite her seven years with the firm, she felt that she could not pass up the opportunity."

"Which practice areas are growing and which are declining?" One of my counseling clients asked this question when interviewing for an associate position with a major national law firm. In her debriefing with me, she said, "The interviewer told me that I was

the only candidate who had ever asked this question." Two days later, she was offered the position.

This question may do more for you than any other you can ask—it accomplishes five key objectives favorable to your candidacy:

- It goes a long way toward "equalizing the interview power equation," leveling the playing field as much as anything can, and helping to make you feel more comfortable.
- It demonstrates your keen business sense and foresight.
- It sets a powerful tone for the rest of the interview.
- It answers a very important question that should be foremost in your mind.
- It "imprints" you on the interviewer, making you memorable once you depart and during the hiring decision process.

"How does the legal department contribute to increasing shareholder value?" This is a great question for corporate employers. It shows that you are bottom-line, business-oriented and that you understand, in an unusually sophisticated way, the role of the company legal department. Like the previous question, it is one that is rarely posed to interviewers and contributes to distinguishing you from other candidates, thereby making you memorable.

"What do you look for in a prospective employee?" The response to this question will give you an indication of the qualities and traits you will want to emphasize before the interview concludes. If the interviewer responds, for example, that the position requires strong organizational skills, you can make sure that you inject examples of how you have manifested such skills in the past.

"What are the likely challenges and difficulties that you foresee I might have to confront?" The answers may alert you to problems you may need to consider when determining whether or not to accept the position. If the interviewer tells you that everyone on the staff has to pitch in and do some fundraising when grants and donations to the nonprofit decline, you may hesitate to take the position, having reasonably concluded that something that might be distasteful to you occurs from time-to-time and might also threaten your job security.

"What is a typical day like for someone in this position?" "Day in the life" stories show the type of matters you'll work on and the amount of responsibility you'll get. Listen for descriptions of colleague, client, and staff interactions as well.

If the response is something like, "There is no such thing as a typical day," follow-up by asking what will be on the interviewer's "to do" list today. If the further response is, "I am interviewing candidates all day today," ask what the interviewer will face in a normal work schedule.

"How is performance evaluated?" You need to know how you are performing as soon as possible in advance of your (annual) review. Early notice will enable you to fix any problems and avoid surprises. You also need to know, in advance of accepting a position, that your employer both communicates his/her expectations and provides formal evaluations on a regular basis.

"For what activities do you engage outside counsel?" If you contemplate going to work for a corporation, you need to know which matters are handled in-house and which are farmed out so that you can recognize when it is timely to call in outside counsel.

"Would you describe your training program, please?" Formal, structured training programs are far and away the best. They include specific, measurable goals and assessments that can help you achieve them. Anything less than that will likely inhibit your professional development and make career advancement a dicier proposition.

"Do you have a mentoring program? If so, would you please describe it?" This is a follow-up question to the preceding one. A good mentor can be an invaluable part of the learning process. The more formal and structured the mentoring program, the better.

"What is the profile of a successful aspirant for promotion?" The response will enable you to model yourself after the ideal candidate for promotion.

"What are the short- and long-term goals of the organization?" It is important that every business have a plan for growth and sustainability and that its employees be cognizant of the plan.

"What is your staff turnover?" Naturally, you want to work for an organization that has low staff turnover, an indicator of stability and job satisfaction.

Caveat: There are certain organizations and practice areas in which low staff turnover may be a negative indicator. For example, attorneys who work for a golf law boutique firm may find that there are not many positions available outside of this rather narrow practice area and concentrated industry. Hence, there are not many places they can go.

"Who are your organization's internal clients?" If the response is preceded by a lengthy pause, then you are probably hearing that the legal office does not think of itself as having internal clients (good legal offices *do* think in those terms). You would not, of course, pose this question to a law firm interviewer unless you are seeking a position that supports the firm, such as general counsel (yes, a growing number of law firms now have their own general counsels), professional development, knowledge management, marketing, etc.

"What best demonstrates the organization's strengths?" Listen closely for information about organization values, culture, and priorities, in addition to expected information about specific matters handled by the firm. If the response includes information from outside the interviewer's own practice milieu, that will speak volumes about interrelationships, cross-selling, etc. The answer will tell you something about the cohesiveness of the firm and the feasibility of building your own practice through cross-marketing.

Follow-up question: Ask more about what the organization does best (and worst) to learn where your talents might best fit and how they might be valued. Will you have the opportunity to work on good and interesting cases?

"Did you achieve your office goals during the past fiscal year?" Both the content and the tone of the response could be revealing. The primary thrust of this question is to ascertain whether the organization *thinks* in terms of goals and objectives and plans ahead. If it does not, you may need to think twice about working there. Do not settle for a simple "yes, we did" answer. Probe enough so

that you pierce the organizational veil. You can do this by "drilling down" a bit, such as asking about more specific goals, such as client development, attorney training, expanding into new practice areas, etc.

"Can you give me an example of how your office has had to adapt to unanticipated change?" The response will give you an insight into the organization's agility and ability to react to changing events and circumstances.

"How would you describe the organization's personality?" The response can provide insight into whether your personality and the organization's align and possibly answer one of your most important unstated questions: "Will I be comfortable here?"

> If you cannot get good answers to what you consider your key questions, you should try to pose those questions to other attorneys or executives in the employer's organization. Also consider running any responses you receive from C-level executives, partners, senior associates, or senior legal staff by junior-level employees for confirmation and/or a different perspective.
>
> Before leaving this chapter, I want to reiterate the point that a set of great candidate questions is a tremendous boost that can set you head and shoulders above your competition.

Chapter 35

When to Explain a Termination

Explaining why you were let go by an employer is one of the most difficult hurdles for an attorney job seeker to overcome. Not only does the explanation have to satisfy a prospective employer; it also has to ring true.

If there is no way around revealing this negative information, timing becomes all important. After all, you do not want to kill your opportunity up front. It is always better to get to the interview stage at least, if at all possible.

Despite the unfortunate fact that you might be one of thousands of attorneys who is the victim of a layoff, that does not mean that employers will empathize with you. Employers understand that some attorneys must have been retained by your employer, which to them means that you might have been perceived as "tainted" in some way. You want to have the opportunity to get in front of potential employers in order to explain the layoff situation after they can see, and be impressed by, your good qualities.

What follows are various strategies you can employ to assist you in handling this problem.

- *Termination information has no place on a résumé, period.*
  Negative information on a résumé is almost always an ex-
  cuse for the employer's "first responders," which may be
  either the human resources office or the legal assistant or
  other operational office to which you are applying, to reject
  a résumé. Mentioning a layoff provides the recipient of a
  huge volume of résumés an opportunity to eliminate you
  from consideration early. Remember, the employer's initial
  résumé scan is often intended to reduce the pile of applications down to manageable proportions. Consequently, this
  is when the employer is the most risk-averse, which trans-
  lates into eliminating from consideration résumés that suggest a problem
- *Don't mention termination in your cover letter or transmittal e-mail if you can avoid the topic.* Don't say anything
  about termination until you absolutely have to reveal or
  acknowledge it. Again, addressing a termination up front
  reduces your chances of continuing further in the competitive battle for the position.
- *Ideally, wait until the interview to spill your guts, if then.*
  That will give you a chance to demonstrate your abilities,
  articulation, personality, likeability, and fitness face to face
  before having to introduce the termination.
- *Consider the precise moment when you will become officially unemployed.* How long will you remain on the pay-
  roll or receive remuneration from your employer? Until then,
  you are arguably still employed and can still contend on an
  equal footing with your still-employed competitors. The
  following considerations need to be factored into this delib-
  eration:
  - *The date of your final paycheck.* If you are paid monthly
    and your last day of work fell between pay periods, you
    may still be technically employed until you receive that
    last check.
  - *Accumulated vacation.* Will you receive compensation
    for unused annual leave?
  - *Accumulated sick leave.* Will you receive compensation
    for unused sick leave?

- *Continuing voice mail/e-mail service at your former place of work.* If you have arranged with your former employer to keep them active after your departure, this can provide you with some "cover" while you are job hunting.

If any of these factors are in play, then arguably you are still employed until they cease.

One additional factor also has to be considered. Is it likely that your potential employer knows about the layoff? If the prospective employer is local it increases this possibility, as is the case if you were part of a mass termination that made the national news or legal trade news. If your prospective employer is in the same industry as your former organization, then you will also have to consider carefully how to handle this.

If you feel that you have to say something about being laid off in your cover letter or transmittal e-mail, mention it at the end, as part of the closing. This will give a potential employer the opportunity to judge you on the merits of the case you make and not get distracted by hearing about your unemployed status up front. Otherwise, the interviewer may not notice the strengths you are trying to convey or may decide to read no further after discovering that you have been terminated. If there were extenuating or mitigating factors in your favor with respect to the termination, mention them, too. Here is an example that I recommended to some of my clients several years ago:

> I recently left my position at the U.S. Patent and Trademark Office as a result of a reduction-in-force (RIF) that eliminated 135 positions due to a sharp drop in trademark applications. The RIF was implemented on a straight seniority, last-in, first-out basis.

This chapter is closely related to Chapter 33, "Handling the Tough Questions." The central issue in this chapter is the proper time to address a termination. Hopefully, it impressed you with the notion that timing may be everything.

Part VI

Closure

Chapter 36
Due Diligence: Scoping Out Your Prospective Employer . . . 325

Chapter 37
Negotiating the Employment Agreement 339

Chapter 38
Epilogue: Connecting the Dots 347

Due Diligence: Scoping Out Your Prospective Employer

Perhaps nothing is more important to your career management success than knowing what you are getting yourself into. The road to legal career crises is littered with the shattered dreams of attorneys who either believed what the job ad, recruiter, or interviewer told them and/or did not bother to confirm the veracity of what they heard.

What makes employer due diligence so critical in the twenty-first century is a consensus prediction by those who study this sort of thing that job market volatility is not going away. It is likely that a law school graduate today will hold numerous jobs during his or her career. Performing due diligence on a prospective employer can cut down on this frenetic movement from job to job and provide some stability.

I always kept a full box of tissues in my conference room for use by the many attorneys—female and male—who broke down describing the horrific working conditions that confronted them once they were on the job. While I sympathized with them and, more often than not, became irate for them, I could not help but think that all of this pain and anguish might have been avoided had they bothered to do their homework beforehand.

The traditional definition of due diligence is the process whereby an acquiring company investigates and assesses a potential target acquisition—Company A scrutinizes Company B because Company A might be interested in buying Company B. Due diligence is a process that virtually every transactional lawyer becomes very familiar with in the course of his or her practice. However, you will be hard pressed to discover any seasoned transactional attorney who ever thought to apply due diligence techniques to his or her own career choices.

While I have run into a handful of attorneys who "got it" and actually attempted to find out what the employer and organization were really all about prior to accepting a position, I am still waiting to encounter someone who did this thoroughly. This despite the fact that taking a job is one of the most important life decisions a person ever has to make, a decision that affects everything else: family, health, happiness, location, finances, future.

Performing a due diligence investigation of your prospective employer is an essential component of the job-hunting process. While you will likely never get answers to every one of your questions before starting at a job, you will nevertheless be able to make a much more informed decision about your career direction if you're armed with as much information as you can muster.

If you are going to work for the government at any level (federal, state, local), you will find easy access to a huge assemblage of public record information about your prospective employer. Moreover, because government agencies and their law offices are, for the most part, funded either by tax dollars or fees they impose on the entities they regulate, they do not have to worry as much about finances from year to year. Thus, less due diligence on your part will be necessary than there would be with respect to non-governmental employers.

Similarly, if you want to work for a publicly traded company, you will find a great deal of information available to you about the company, due to regulatory filing requirements with agencies such as the Securities and Exchange Commission.

Nonprofits, too, must file annual reports/returns (Form 990) with the Internal Revenue Service. These documents are readily accessible online and provide solid information about the filers. In fact, beginning in 2009, Form 990 contains much more detail about non-profit filers than ever before.

There is usually a lot of material available about large law firms, both through Internet searches and in legal trade publications.

In addition to public record and publicly disclosed information, there are likely to be a variety of commercial directories and databases that collect information about larger or highly regulated employers. You will likely also find articles about larger employers in business and trade publications.

As a rule, the larger the employer, the more information is available to satisfy your due diligence requirements. In fact, you may be afflicted with "information overload."

Employers that are "household names" generally require less due diligence than smaller employers, since they are scrutinized much more closely by both their regulators and the media. This is, however, not the case with small law firms and solo practitioners. These employers are, by far, the most difficult ones to research. Information about them is spotty, if it exists at all. Nevertheless, it is small employers that necessitate the most intense due diligence.

Key Due Diligence Items

Here are the 10 key components of employer due diligence:

- *Financials*—You will want to ensure their accuracy.
- *Assets*—You will want to confirm their value and condition.
- *Employees*—You will want to ascertain how they are treated and how they feel about their employer.

- *Marketing*—What is being done to grow the business? What is working? What is not working? Are there plans to improve the marketing effort?
- *Industry trends*—Does management monitor and understand them?
- *Technology*—What is the state of the organization's technology systems?
- *Competition*—Is the organization competitive? What is it doing to keep up?
- *Legal Issues*—Make certain that there will not be any surprises if you come aboard.
- *Exposure*—Make sure you are not going to be exposed to any risks.
- *Clients*—Who are they? How loyal are they to the organization?

If possible, you should try to uncover as much of this information as possible about a company before accepting a position with them. Some will not apply to every business and it's likely you will not be able to find out every one. Some items can be ascertained by "eyeballing" the premises and people. Others will require deeper digging and a number will require you to pose good questions to your prospective employer at both the interview and the job offer stages of the process. Some of your due diligence can be initiated even before you and your prospective employer get serious about one another.

The following are some of the resources you can turn to in order to attempt to obtain useful information about smaller employers.

Internet Resources

- *Employer Web sites*—This should be your first online stop. Examine the employer's Web site(s) with your eyes wide open, mindful that this is information provided by the employer and, therefore, presumably is self-serving.

  Organizations, like individuals, love to talk about themselves. So much so that often they will reveal some gems that can contribute significantly to your due diligence. Their

Web sites often include press releases, firm history, regulatory filings, biographies of firm leaders, and other valuable information.

- *Internet search*—Conduct an Internet search for more objective information to compare with what you learned from the employer's Web site. Don't overlook social media sites, such as Facebook, LinkedIn, etc. Be alert to who posted the information and what their motives might be.

- *Corporate Counsel Directory* on Westlaw—While information is provided by the employer, the directory's real value is the ability to identify former employees of your prospective employer (if this information was provided to the publisher). You can contact former employees and pose some of your due diligence questions to them (see also People You Should Talk To, below).

- *State bar disciplinary bodies*—States that do not post lawyer discipline information on the Internet should be contacted directly by phone or e-mail.

- *American Lawyer Media's ALM Research Online* (http:// alacra.almresearchonline.com) can provide in-depth reports with detailed financial and business information for more than 300 law firms for a rather hefty fee ($249 for a one-year report). Note that the vast majority of these are large law firms. ALM Research Online also can provide lists and rankings for major firms in six states and the District of Columbia.

- *Law.com*, the American Lawyer Media Web site, runs many articles about law firms and other legal employers, although most of its attention is focused on the larger entities.

- *Lawyersweekly.com* publishes 15 commercial legal journals, mainly in the East, South and Midwest, and runs articles on law firms and other legal employers, including smaller employers.

- *Vault.com* (www.vault.com) offers research reports on legal employers. Again, Vault concentrates on the larger employers for which it is easier to compile information.

- *Wetfeet.com* (www.wetfeet.com) is another provider of such information.

- *National Association for Law Placement (NALP) Directory of Legal Employers* (www.nalpdirectory.com) contains information on more than 1,800 legal employers (law firms, corporations, government, public interest), including some smaller ones, with a heavy emphasis on law firms. The directory contains information on staff size, demographics, compensation, benefits, work/life balance (e.g., hours worked per week), and other useful information. There will be some holes, however, since the data is supplied to NALP by the employer. If you can locate past print editions of the directory, you can do some trends analysis by comparing the dated print data for the employer to the current online data.

Comparative Compensation Information

- *Altman Weil Pensa* (www.altmanweil.com) is a professional services consulting firm that conducts a rather exhaustive annual "Survey of Law Firm Economics," which the company sells for a hefty fee. You might be able to obtain just the specific firm information, if available, rather than having to purchase the entire survey report, by contacting Altman Weil and asking. These surveys and reports can give you a recent historical picture of firm finances, expectations of partners, partner compensation, etc. You may learn enough from these sources to make probing the firm directly about such sensitive matters unnecessary. **Note**: The vast majority of firms surveyed fall into the large firm category.
- *Researching small employer compensation.* While there are a number of good resources you can consult for information about compensation at major corporations, finding similar information about small companies is much more difficult. Compensation information for small companies is sometimes available from trade associations that represent such companies. Trade associations collect and maintain a great deal of information about their members businesses, often including compensation levels. One of the best free resources that you can use to identify trade associations is the "Gateway to Associations" at www.asaenet.org.

Questions for the Employer

A hiring decision is a two-way transaction. While the "power equation" is almost always skewed in favor of the employer, you can impress your prospective employer by asking good due diligence questions that manifest your business acumen.

The answers to the questions below should help you develop a better understanding of what you might be getting into with respect to a prospective employer. You may not feel comfortable posing all of these questions, likely depending on the rapport you have developed during your job interview. If you feel less than comfortable during the interview, you could defer some of the questions until after you receive an offer of employment.

All of the questions may not be relevant to your particular situation. Select only the ones that are germane to your due diligence requirements. Be careful not to pose questions to the employer to which you should already know the answers by virtue of the job ad, the employer's Web site, or your job interview(s).

Job Interview Due Diligence Questions

These due diligence questions have been divided into two parts. First, questions that you can ask at a job interview. Second, questions you may want to ask once you have received a job offer, but before you accept the position.

Note: The term "firm" below is intended to apply to any kind of organization, be it a law firm, a company, a nonprofit, etc.

- *What is the current client concentration and spread (including industry concentration and spread)?* Overreliance on just one or a handful of clients, or a disproportionate number of clients concentrated in one industry, carries some risk. If that industry might be adversely affected by external phenomena, such as interest rates, energy prices, or regulation, the risk is even greater.
- *What is the duration of your firm-client relationships?* Long-standing relationships are better than short-term ones.
- *How many firm attorneys engage in client development?* The legal world is littered with the corpses of law firms that had only a few partners engaged in client development.

- *Did the firm acquire any new major clients in the past year?* A positive response is a genuine positive.
- *Did the firm lose any major clients in the past year?* Such losses could severely impact the bottom line.
- *Describe the firm's relationships with other attorneys practicing in the community?* Naturally, you want those relationships to be positive and professional.
- *Does the firm have any near-term expansion plans? Firm-wide? Within your practice area?* Expansion is presumably a good thing, but beware of firms that might be overreaching or that have plans that do not appear to be well thought out.
- *Where does my practice area stand in the firm's value hierarchy?* If you cannot get a straight answer, that alone should speak volumes.
- *What is the firm's "unique selling proposition?"* A big plus if the answer comes quickly and easily, is sufficiently precise, and is stated with confidence. Anything else is "void for vagueness."
- *Does the firm have a marketing director?* This position is rapidly becoming a must for large and even mid-size law firms. While it is expected that a small firm could not afford to hire an individual for just this specific function, the firm should have given some thought to tasking someone with this responsibility.
- *If so, what does that person do?* The response to this question will tell you a great deal about how the firm goes about marketing its existence and services.
- *How does the marketing director/department work with the partners?* A flippant response, such as "great," is a non-answer. The reason for the question is the often controlling and micromanaging obsessions of many law firm partners.
- *How successful have the firm's marketing efforts been?* You will want some details, not just generalizations.
- *What were your firm's goals last year? Did you achieve them?* A well-run business—and yes, law firms are businesses—has a plan and a means of measuring success and failure.

- *Could you provide an example of how the firm has had to adapt to (unanticipated) change?* Say you are interviewing to be legal counsel to One Horse Shay & Co. a year after the introduction of the automobile. Naturally, you want to know One Horse Shay's plan to adapt to the new market reality.
- *What kind of turnover has the firm experienced? Among its attorneys? Support staff? Practice groups?* High turnover is never a good sign.
- *Why is this position vacant?* A positive response would be that this is a new position or that the incumbent was promoted, retired, or moved on to a bigger and better job.
- *How diverse is the firm?* A diverse workforce is increasingly important to corporate clients when they select outside law firms to represent them, so much so that many companies have established clear benchmarks to measure law firm diversity. Thus, diversity has become a bottom-line business consideration for law firms.
- *Has the firm done any succession planning?* The answer can loom large in your consideration if the firm is "senior-heavy," especially if the elders bring in most of the business and are, well, elderly.
- *What is the state of the firm's technology?* You don't want to find yourself in the position of being penalized because you have to rely on poor or dated technology or weak technological support.

Post-Job Offer Due Diligence Questions

Some employer due diligence questions are best left to the interregnum when your job offer is on the table and you have not yet accepted it.

- *What were the average billable hours last year per associate (and per associate in my practice group)?* A very rough norm these days would be 1,800 to 2,000 billable hours per year. If the response exceeds this figure by more than 100 billable hours, you are likely to find yourself in a "workaholic" setting. If the response is significantly under this range, you are likely to find yourself without enough work to do—and worse, with no justification for the firm keeping you on.

- *What qualifies as a billable hour?* What you are seeking to learn is whether work that you do on the client development side, such as writing for the firm newsletter or preparing remarks for a firm principal to deliver, counts toward your billable hour requirement.

- *What would my share be if I were to bring a new client to the firm? If it was a client in my practice area (where I would do—or collaborate in—the work)? If it was a client in another practice area (where I would not do the work)?* These formulas should be locked down before you begin work. Otherwise, you can get burned badly.

- *Is it possible for me to view the firm's partnership agreement?* This would only be of immediate importance if you would be entering the firm as a partner.

- *May I see the firm's employee handbook?* You need to become an expert on your organization's personnel policies as soon as you can.

- *What are the firm's short-term and long-term client development plans?* The reality of living in a highly competitive world mandates that organizations have such plans and that they be sufficiently detailed and realistic. While you may not find out all of the particulars, the organization should, at a minimum, be willing to share the broad outlines with you.

- *Does the firm have any plans to merge with or acquire another firm?* The number of law firm mergers, even involving mid-size and small law firms, is very much on the upswing. However, the American Bar Association reports that roughly half of all law firm mergers are unsuccessful, primarily resulting from a lack of adequate due diligence (there is that term again) on the part of the firms. Corporate mergers, on the other hand, have a much higher success rate. There needs to be a logic behind such initiatives, one that is plausible to you.

- *Does the firm have any plans to expand into other cities?* Such expansions are very popular, but sometimes law firms get ahead of themselves. Many firms that rushed headlong into Russia when it succeeded the Soviet Union, for example, were forced to close their Moscow and St. Petersburg offices within a few years. As with mergers, there has to be a compelling rationale for such expansion.
- *How does the firm gather competitive intelligence?* Lack of knowledge of one's competitors could be a serious problem in our highly competitive and rapidly changing economy.
- *How does the firm show appreciation to its good employees?* Bonuses, free trips, pats on the head?
- *What, if any, firm obligations would I be liable for if I accepted your job offer?* This is particularly important if you would come into a law firm as a partner.

People You Should Talk To

Firm/organization alumni/ae. Attorneys who are no longer working for your prospective employer may be very willing to share their impressions with you, provided they can be assured that you will keep the information confidential.

Opposing counsel. I was once asked by a friend to recommend the two best plaintiff's medical malpractice attorneys in our geographic area. Since U.S. Department of Veterans Affairs (DVA) field office lawyers defend the government in medical malpractice cases, I asked a former career counseling client (whom I helped land a job in a DVA field office litigating such cases) to name the two best plaintiff medical malpractice attorneys he had opposed during his tenure at DVA. He did not hesitate, and my friend interviewed both recommended attorneys, hired one, and ultimately won a very large judgment against a physician and hospital.

Identifying opposing counsel is a very good information-gathering method to employ in doing your employer due diligence. The strategy is not limited to litigators. It can be just as informative if you are pursuing a transactional position or even a regulatory job. Transactional lawyers have to negotiate with the lawyers representing the other party. Regulatory attorneys have to respond to attorneys who represent parties affected by a regulation, whether inside or outside the regulating agency. In short, the talk-to-opposing-counsel technique applies virtually across the board.

Former clients. Quite a few law firms list their representative clients in law directories (e.g., *West Legal Directory, Martindale-Hubbell*). If you can find a print edition of one of these directories from a few years ago, you may be able to identify former clients of the law firm, whom you can then contact.

Local law school career services office personnel. Law school career office staff should know quite a bit about the legal employers in their communities. They could be especially valuable when it comes to gathering or sourcing information about smaller employers, especially small law firms that post job ads through the law school.

If you run into a problem getting them to speak to you because you are neither one of their law students nor one of their alumnae, ask your own law school career office to make the request for you.

Other lawyers in the community. People who have spent their professional lives interacting with the organizations and attorneys you are considering will generally have very interesting information and insights about them. However, you need to tread very carefully down this path because your sources may have close business or personal relationships with your potential employer that they do not want to jeopardize.

Personal traits of your potential colleagues. Your employer due diligence should not be limited to finding out information about the firm. You should also apply the concept to the individuals within the firm. This is not easy to do, since your only personal contact with them will likely be the brief time you spend in a job interview and perhaps some telephone time. Nevertheless, be on the lookout for the following traits, while acknowledging that you are unlikely to be able to gather complete information.

- decisiveness
- risk acceptance
- persistence
- tough-mindedness
- perception by employees

- perception by co-workers
- real-world orientation
- common sense
- balance in personal lives
- money-sensitive

Questions you might ask about potential colleagues include:

- Do they like what they do?
- Do they take criticism and rejection well?
- Are they interested in the ideas of their subordinates and colleagues?
- Do they know their own strengths and weaknesses?
- Do they know when they need help?
- Are they ethical?
- How do they treat their people?

A Word about Practice Area Due Diligence

Your due diligence examination of your potential employer is also going to reveal good information about your contemplated practice area(s). In addition, be sure to incorporate the information about considering how external phenomena can affect your career (see Chapter 13 "The Career Impact of External Phenomena") into your practice area due diligence investigation.

> Employer due diligence is an often overlooked piece of the legal career transition puzzle. However, its importance cannot be overemphasized. If my conference room walls could speak, you would hear countless tales of woe from legal career transition counseling clients telling me, "If only I had known about what was going on there before I took the job."
>
> A lot of career regret, heartache, and Monday-morning quarterbacking can be obviated by performing the best employer due diligence that you can before accepting a position.

Chapter 37

Negotiating the Employment Agreement

One of my career counseling clients was offered a good position with a U.S. government agency's general counsel office. Before responding to the offer (and instead of asking me), she contacted a friend who was a corporate human resources director and asked for advice on negotiating an employment agreement. The HR chief told her that, since she was now in the driver's seat, she should raise all of her concerns about the job offer with the general counsel, including more compensation than what was offered, additional vacation time, expanded administrative leave, a flexible work schedule, and benefits for her partner. When she raised these issues in a phone call to the general counsel, the job offer was abruptly withdrawn.

My client was unaware that job offers from a government agency are non-negotiable, with only two narrow exceptions (see below). Nothing else is ever on the table. It was clear that the general counsel became skittish about

> hiring someone who (1) made what he perceived to be unreasonable demands and (2) was ignorant of the federal hiring process and had made no effort to find out about something so easy to determine.

Before diving into this matter in depth, it is important to note that entry-level law firm associates, particularly at major law firms, almost never have the opportunity to negotiate anything. Moreover, the law firm/associate employment relationship is only rarely memorialized in a written agreement.

If you are able to negotiate terms of employment, be very careful about (1) being reasonable in your demands and (2) maintaining friendly relations during the negotiations.

Here are some negotiation stories from my clients:

- One of my clients left his law firm and was offered a very nice position with a New York City investment banking firm at twice his law firm salary. The investment bank's policy was that junior equity shareholders were responsible for their own retirement plan contributions. Nevertheless, he insisted that the firm cover his entire annual contribution. The negotiations resulted in a splitting of the difference, but he began his investment banking career on a negative note that left a lingering bad taste in his bosses' mouth.
- A client was relocating as a "trailing spouse" from Washington, D.C. to Jackson, Mississippi. He had worked for an employment litigation boutique law firm in Washington and received a job offer in Jackson from a large corporate in-house counsel office that requested his salary expectations. Without doing any research (and prior to informing me of his job offer), he advised the company that he was aware that, given the cost of living differential between Washington and Jackson, he was willing to accept a lower salary than he had received in Washington.

The company was delighted at his modest salary demands and agreed to them on the spot. He later discovered that he had left $20,000 on the table.

- A client who had never brought in any business to her old firm demanded that her of-counsel agreement with her prospective employer (another law firm) include a much higher percentage share of such business than it was the law firm's policy to pay out. The firm withdrew its offer.

Employer Requests for Salary Requirements

The matter of salary requirements is a delicate issue in any job negotiation. You need to think very carefully about how you respond to an inquiry about your salary requirements. I have often been asked whether such a request from a prospective employer can be ignored. The answer is no. You must respond. Otherwise, the employer may reject your application as incomplete.

Don't respond before attempting to find out what the employer is currently paying similarly situated employees. Salary information is available for many employers, both in print and online. Think about what you are going to ask for if you are offered the position. You may want to consider responding with a salary range, mindful that the lower figure in the range is likely what the employer will hear and react to, while the higher figure is the most that you could expect.

What Can You Negotiate?

What is and is not negotiable varies with both the employment sector—law firm, major corporation, start-up business, government, nonprofit, etc.—and the specific employer. It may also depend on your employment status—partner, associate, of counsel, staff attorney, etc. Employment negotiations also often vary from industry to industry. More mature industries are generally less "negotiation-friendly" than new industries. And, of course, supply and demand plays a big role.

The larger the organization, the more likely it is that compensation and other terms of employment are pre-set, with little room for negotiation. This is especially true of government agencies. Large corporations are similarly disposed, with the exception of senior-level legal positions where there is some negotiation flexibility. Even large private organizations quickly become bureaucratic, and thus less flexible. Large law firms, mainly because they can hire lateral associates, equity and non-equity partners, staff attorneys who are not on the partnership track, and attorneys they can label "of-counsel" and define the meaning of that term as they please, have considerable negotiation flexibility. The only exception is with respect to new law school graduates. They are invariably locked into a pre-established compensation and benefits scheme.

Government agencies do not generally negotiate compensation or benefits because they are established by law and/or regulation and apply to every similarly situated employee across the board. There are some very limited exceptions in the federal government. Grade levels are negotiable if the job announcement cites more than one possible grade level at which the position could be filled. Salary steps within a federal grade level (each has 10 salary steps) are also often negotiable. It is always a good idea to try to negotiate the highest possible step for two reasons. First, the difference between Step 1 and Step 10 (the highest step) can be more than $20,000. Second, if you begin your job at a step higher than Step 1, that higher step means that, over time, you will earn considerably more money.

Otherwise, public-sector employment is almost always a "take-it-or-leave-it" proposition.

Once out of the large employer environment, all bets are off. As a rough rule of thumb, the smaller the organization, the more flexible it is likely to be regarding these matters. However, smaller organizations also do not have the resources of their larger counterparts, so the concept of "wiggle room" is relative.

Other employment sectors generally have considerably more flexibility than government agencies. That does not mean, however, that everything is always negotiable. If there are a hundred candidates out there like you, not very much will be negotiable. The rarer you are or can present yourself to be—more specialized, more educated, etc.—the more likely it is that you will be able to negotiate some of the terms of employment.

Finding Compensation Information

You cannot possibly be an effective negotiator without coming to the table armed with good information. This is especially true concerning compensation. Following are selected sources and source-types where you can find information about compensation.

General Information

- Pay scale—*www.payscale.com*
- National Association for Law Placement, *Annual Associate Salary Survey—www.nalp.org*
- Abbott, Langer & Associates, *Compensation of Legal and Related Jobs, 24th Edition (Non-Law Firms)—www.abbott-langer.com*
- Glassdoor.com—*www.glassdoor.com*
- Jobsmart—*www.jobsmart.org*
- Salary.com—*www.salary.com*
- Career Journal—*www.careerjournal.com*

Law Firm Positions

- Altman Weil Inc.—*www.altmanweil.com*
  - *Annual Survey of Law Firm Economics*
  - *Small Law Firm Economics Survey*
  - *Compensation Systems in Private Law Firms*

Corporations

- Altman Weil Inc., *Annual Law Department Compensation Benchmarking Survey—www.altmanweil.com*
- PricewaterhouseCoopers LLP, *U.S. Law Department Spending Survey—www.pwcglobal.com*

U.S. Government

- U.S. Office of Personnel Management, *Government Salary Schedules—www.opm.gov*
- Administrative Office of the U.S. Courts—*www.uscourts.gov*
- National Association of Assistant United States Attorneys—*www.nasusa.org*

State and Local Government Jobs

- National Center for State Courts, *Survey of Judicial Salaries (annual)—www.ncsconline.org*
- National Conference of State Legislatures *www.ncsl.org*
- Council of State Governments—*www.csg.org*
- National League of Cities—*www.nlc.org*
- National Association of Counties—*www.naco.org*

Colleges and Universities

- National Center for Education Statistics, *College and University Faculty—www.nces.ed.gov*
- National Education Association—*www.nea.org*

Trade and Professional Associations

- American Society of Association Executives, *Association Executive Compensation and Benefits Study* (biennial)—*www.asaenet.org*

Nonprofits

- Chronicle of Philanthropy, *Compensation Survey* (annual)—*http://philanthropy.com*
- GuideStar, *Nonprofit Compensation Report* (annual)—*www.guidestar.org*

Other Useful Sources

Salary information is sometimes available free of charge. Other, more extensive salary surveys and reports are available for a fee. Proxy statements filed by publicly traded companies with the U.S. Securities and Exchange Commission are often an excellent source of information about particular employers. See *www.sec.gov.*

Strategic Knowledge for Employment Negotiations

The following items are things you need to know before engaging in compensation and employment negotiations:

- *What you earned in your last job.* This is often a platform for salary negotiations. You are unlikely to make a huge leap in salary in a new position.
- *What does the competition earn?* This will often govern what you can reasonably expect.
- *What is your value to the new employer?* Make sure you have sufficient documentation to support an assertion of greater value than what the employer proposes to pay you. Are you adding something new to the employer that will benefit the organization? If you will be given your first supervisory responsibilities, these are also worth something.
- *How much do you need?* This could be very different from how much you *want*. How much money you need is likely to be your negotiating floor.
- *How much are you willing to accept in deferred compensation?*
- *What health, disability, life, long-term care, malpractice, and other insurances are available?*
- *What other benefits are available?* Possible benefits could relate to continuing legal (and other) education, training, bar dues, professional licenses, etc.?
- *What are the key features of the retirement plan?*
- *What credit will you receive if you bring in business?*
- *What kind of flexible work arrangements are available?*

This probably goes without saying, but negotiating terms of employment is not a proper subject during a job interview. Wait until you receive a job offer.

> The dreaded compensation question conundrum causes a lot of angst among legal job seekers. You can mitigate that angst if you come to this point in the job-hunting process armed with as much knowledge about compensation as possible.

Chapter 38

Epilogue: Connecting the Dots

Like so much else in life, job hunting and career changing are complex processes, replete with numerous elements that are part of a whole. Success in getting where you want to be means getting each element, as well as the whole, right. To do that, it is important to understand that every piece of the puzzle is related to every other piece, and also to understand how they are related.

Connecting all of these dots is much more difficult to do today than ever before. Life is fraught with increasing complexity and connections pulling against increased specialization. The webs that society weaves are much more difficult to sort out than they used to be. It is extremely rare when only one factor or variable affects a job search and is the reason for the decisions that you will have to make. In almost every case, a multitude of factors must be considered, including their influence on one another. You have only to examine major societal issues such as healthcare reform or financial regulation and the impossibly confusing legislation they are producing to see striking examples of that.

What this means for legal job seekers and career changers is that when you create, modify, or abandon one job-hunting puzzle piece, it has an effect—sometimes even a "cascade" effect—on the entire puzzle. You need to be cognizant of that in order to avoid the stumbles that this effect can cause. For example, if you decide to omit a position from your résumé that you held for only six weeks, you need to make sure that it does not show up in your Contacts Road Map, an inconsistency that will raise questions among your contacts, cause them to question their earlier very positive impression of your organizational skills, and diminish their enthusiasm for your campaign.

Accordingly, whenever you put together a document, decide on a reference, invoke and/or communicate with a contact, or pitch to a prospective employer, you need to perform a "regression analysis" to determine (1) if what you are doing is consistent with every other element of your campaign and (2) how your variable options will affect one another.

When you think about it, a successful legal job-hunting campaign is a wonderful training ground for the work you will be doing as an attorney for the rest of your career. Very few twenty-first century individuals—and fewer modern institutions—are good at connecting the dots. You have only to study the run up to the September 11, 2001, terrorist attacks or the failure of the government to respond timely or adequately to Hurricane Katrina to realize that. If you run a successful job search, you will have had to become adept at connecting the dots, and a lot of dots at that. Having achieved that, you will be able to apply that skill and talent in everything you do, professionally and otherwise.

Being able to connect the dots, to see and understand the interconnections and interactions of various phenomena, is an extremely rare talent, but one that often separates the peak performer from the crowd, and certainly the successful legal job seeker from his or her competition. While a rare talent, it is also one that, through effort, can be developed if you position yourself as (1) an "information sponge," and (2) a practitioner of dot connection in everything you do.

"Before" and "After" Résumés

Before—Traditional Reverse Chronological Résumé

Jane Doe
236 Eastwood Drive
Westwood, CA 90010
O: (213) 444-0000
H: (310) 555-1111
C: (310) 666-7777
E-mail: jdjd@vmail.com

Employment Counsel, Globalization Bancorporation
September 2003 – Present
Santa Monica, CA
- Responsible for all employment and employment-related matters of large, international financial institution.
- Advised General Counsel and C-level officers on all employment issues.
- Selected and managed outside employment counsel and strategized corporate defenses.
- Developed training materials and coordinated training of all employees.

Special Assistant to the Deputy General Counsel
January 1996 – August 2003
Federal Deposit Insurance Corporation, Washington, D.C.

- Advised Deputy General Counsel on the resolution of a myriad of labor, employment and corporate legal issues with legal, management, and political implications.

- Served on cross-divisional group tasked with developing various human resource initiatives to support c o r p o r a t e change, both organizational and cultural. Initiatives include the implementation of organizational mergers as well as the development of a "corporate university" and an executive compensation plan.

- Monitored sensitive employment cases on behalf of the Deputy General Counsel and review all settlement documents to ensure consistency and to ensure appropriate management action taken.

- Recognized by Senior Executive Diversity Steering Committee for two consecutive years for contributions to corporate-wide efforts in developing and implementing the FDIC's first diversity strategic plan including identifying strategic areas, goals, and objectives for the plan and devising a communications strategy. Legal representative on a Diversity Measurement working group tasked with measuring progress of diversity initiatives.

- Coordinated efforts on behalf of the Deputy General Counsel to revise the FDIC's Affirmative Employment and Procurement Plans to ensure compliance with current law and regulation. Prepared talking points for senior executives on affirmative employment and procurement as well as diversity.

- Participated in planning sessions to prepare for pay and benefits negotiations with union representing employees. Worked directly with outside counsel in preparing a legal brief for the arbitrator, which presented legal arguments as well as provided information about the FDIC and the environment in which it operates.

Management Analyst, Legal Division
March 1994 – December 1995
Resolution Trust Corporation, Washington, D.C.

- Conducted management study of the outside counsel management function and made recommendations, which were ultimately adopted to improve efficiency and productivity as well as to proactively address internal control issues.
- Prepared responses to a high volume of Office of Inspector General audits of outside counsel fee bills. Identified common audit findings and determined what measures to take to correct underlying issues whether through policy implementation or clarification of existing policy. OIG ultimately used the Legal Division outside counsel program as a model for effective internal controls.
- Prepared responses to Congressional inquiries on legal fees and expenses paid to minority and women-owned law firms as well as reports and briefing documents for use by the General Counsel.
- Served on a joint RTC/FDIC Legal Division team tasked with the development and implementation of a transition plan to minimize risk in the transition of legal matters to the FDIC at the RTC's sunset. Developed transition plans for sixteen substantive legal areas at Headquarters and comprehensive plans for the each of the five field Service Centers, which greatly contributed to a smooth transition with minimal disruption in legal services.

Management Analyst,
Division of Administration & Corporate Relations
May 1992 – March 1994
Resolution Trust Corporation, Washington, D.C.

- Managed project teams and participated as a member of project teams in conducting studies to evaluate management and administrative systems and policies, standards and procedures including a review of personnel management processes and of delegations of authority systems. Prepared written reports concerning findings and recommendations and presented to management officials.

- Coordinated a Division-wide management-by-objective system to ensure that all offices were meeting identified goals and objectives for priority projects within the Division and within established timeframes, which required establishing a reporting mechanism and format to ensure consistency.

Program Analyst, Office of the Ombudsman
November 1990 – May 1992
Resolution Trust Corporation, Washington, D.C.
- Served as liaison to the general public, industry, and trade organizations and other parties to facilitate resolution of issues arising in business dealings with the RTC. Effective resolution required extensive knowledge of RTC programs and operations.

Financial Specialist, Office of Corporate Funding
August 1989 – November 1990
Resolution Trust Corporation, Washington, D.C.
- At the inception of the RTC with an unprecedented number of savings and loan failures, monitored liquidity of savings and loan institutions that were placed in receivership and approved and monitored the disbursement of funds for those institutions with no other source of funds. Maintained lending documents to protect the RTC's interest. Forecasted agencies needs for funds for conservatorship and receivership activities and requested borrowings from the Department of Treasury and tracked those borrowings to ensure the statutory ceiling was not exceeded.

Education/Bar Admission
- University of Baltimore, Baltimore, MD, Juris Doctor, May 1995
- American University, Washington, D.C., Bachelor of Science (Business Administration-Finance), May 1989
- Bar Admission: Maryland, October 1995

After – Alternative "Hybrid" Résumé

Jane Doe, JD, BS (Finance)
236 Eastwood Drive • Westwood, CA 90010
O: (213) 444-0000 • H: (310) 555-1111 • C: (310) 666-7777
E-mail: jdjd@vmail.com

SUMMARY OF QUALIFICATIONS

Developed and implemented corporate and agency-wide policies and programs dealing with personnel and labor-management issues, outside counsel, and litigation management initiatives, diversity and EEO matters, consolidation and program transfers, and delegations of authority, among others. Strong and varied background in legal, management, and administrative considerations impacting decision-makers on labor, employment, and a wide range of other key issues. Handled highly sensitive matters under extreme pressure and critical time deadlines.

EMPLOYMENT HISTORY

Employment Counsel, **Globalization Bancorporation**, Santa Monica, CA 2003 – Present
Special Assistant to the Deputy General Counsel, **Federal Deposit Insurance Corporation**, Washington, D.C., 1996 – 2003
Resolution Trust Corporation, Washington, D.C. 1989-1995
   Management Analyst, Legal Division, 1994 – 1995
   Management Analyst, Division of Administration & Corporate Relations, 1992 – 1994
   Program Analyst, Office of the Ombudsman, 1990 – 1992
   Financial Specialist, Office of Corporate Funding, 1989 – 1990

PROFESSIONAL EXPERIENCE

Labor and Employment

- Responsible for all employment and employment-related matters of large, international financial institution.
- Advise General Counsel and C-level officers on the resolution of a myriad of labor, employment, and corporate legal issues, taking into consideration legal, management, and political implications.

- Monitor sensitive employment cases and review all settlement documents to ensure consistency and that appropriate management action taken.
- Participate in planning sessions to prepare for pay and benefits negotiations with employee union. Work directly with outside counsel in preparing a legal brief for the arbitrator, which presented legal arguments and provided information about the FDIC and its operational environment.
- Developed training materials and coordinated training of all employees.
- Coordinated efforts to revise the FDIC's Affirmative Employment and Procurement Plans to ensure compliance with current law and regulation. Prepared talking points for senior executives on affirmative employment, procurement, and diversity.
- Served on cross-divisional group tasked with developing various human resource initiatives to support corporate change, both organizational and cultural. Initiatives included the successful implementation of organizational mergers as well as the development of a "corporate university" and an executive compensation plan.
- Recognized by Senior Executive Diversity Steering Committee for two consecutive years for contributions to corporate-wide efforts in developing and implementing the FDIC's first diversity strategic plan, including identifying strategic areas, goals and objectives for the plan and devising a communications strategy. Legal representative on a Diversity Measurement working group tasked with measuring progress of diversity initiatives.

Litigation/Outside Counsel Management
- Selected and managed outside employment counsel and strategized corporate defenses.
- Conducted management study of corporate outside counsel management function and recommended efficiency, productivity and internal control improvements, which were adopted.

- Worked directly with outside counsel in preparing a legal brief for the arbitrator, which presented legal arguments and provided information about the FDIC and its operations.
- Prepared responses to a high volume of Office of Inspector General audits of outside counsel fee bills. Identified common audit findings and determined what measures to take to correct underlying issues, whether through policy implementation or clarification of existing policy. OIG ultimately used the Legal Division outside counsel program as a model for effective internal controls.
- Prepared responses to Congressional inquiries on legal fees and expenses paid to minority and women-owned law firms as well as reports and briefing documents for use by the General Counsel.

Crisis Management
- At inception of the RTC, confronted with an unprecedented number of savings and loan failures, monitored liquidity of savings and loan institutions placed in receivership, and approved and monitored the disbursement of funds for institutions with no other source of funds. Maintained lending documents to protect RTC's interest. Forecasted agencies needs for funds for conservatorship and receivership activities, requested borrowings from the Treasury Department, and tracked those borrowings to ensure statutory ceiling was not exceeded.
- Served as liaison to the public, industry and trade organizations and other parties to facilitate resolution of issues arising in business dealings with the RTC. Effective resolution required an extensive knowledge of rapidly expanding and evolving RTC programs and operations.

Transition Planning and Implementation
- Served on a joint RTC/FDIC Legal Division team tasked with developing and implementing a transition plan to minimize risk in the transition of legal matters to the FDIC at RTC's sunset.

- Developed transition plans for 16 substantive legal areas at Headquarters and comprehensive plans for the each of the five field Service Centers, which greatly contributed to a smooth transition with minimal disruption in legal services.

EDUCATION/BAR ADMISSION

- University of Baltimore, Baltimore, MD, Juris Doctor, 1995
- American University, Washington, DC, Bachelor of Science (Finance), 1989
- Bar Admission: Maryland, 1995

Appendix B

Maximizing Your Contacts

Direct Networking Contacts	Networking Contacts' Contacts	Employers in Reach of Contacts
Friends		
Relatives		
Friends of friends		
Friends of relatives		
Neighbors		
Friends of neighbors		
Fellow academic alumni/ae		
Teachers & school administrators		
Law school		
Graduate school		
College		
Other		
Current classmates		
Current employer (if he or she knows about your job search)		

Direct Networking Contacts	Networking Contacts' Contacts	Employers in Reach of Contacts
Colleagues at work		
Current Job		
Former Jobs		
Workplace alumni/ae		
Current job		
Former jobs		
Former employers		
Other professional colleagues		
Job interviewers you impressed		
Political contacts (if any)		
Members of your clubs/ organizations (e.g., bar associations, community and cultural groups, church/synagogue/mosque, PTAs, athletic teams, etc.)		
Other individuals		
Postal carrier		
Barber/beautician		
Tradesmen		
Vendors		

Representative Legal/ Law-Related Credential Enhancement Programs

Less expensive alternatives to LL.M. programs are proliferating. Some programs have eligibility requirements that must be met prior to registration. An increasing number are offered online. In other cases, certain organizations offer programs and examinations in multiple locations nationwide and via more than one delivery system.

The following is a highly selective list (taken from my list of almost 500 programs) designed to give you an idea of the vast array of possibilities and offering organizations available.

Alternative Dispute Resolution

Hamline University School of Law (*www.hamline.edu/law*)— Certificate in Dispute Resolution

Association for Conflict Resolution (*www.acrnet.org*)—Family Mediation Training Programs

Art & Museums

Harvard College (*www.harvard.edu*)—Certificate in Museum Studies

DePaul University College of Law (*www.law.depaul.edu*)— Certificate in Intellectual Property: Arts & Museum Law

Banking & Finance

Credit Union National Association (*http://training.cuna.org*)—
Regulatory Training & Certification

Association of Certified Anti-Money Laundering Specialists
(*www.acams.org*)—Anti-Money Laundering Specialist Certificate

Bankruptcy Law

American Board of Certification (*www.abcworld.org*)—Business
& Consumer Bankruptcy Certificates

Bioethics

Union Graduate College—Mount Sinai School of Medicine
(*www.bioethics.union.edu*)—Certificate in Bioethics—
Specialization in Health Policy & Law

Bioterrorism Preparedness

Penn State University (*www.worldcampus.psu.edu/certificates.
shtml*)—Certificate in Bioterrorism Preparedness (online)

Child Welfare Law

National Association of Counsel for Children (*www.
naccchildlaw.org*)—Child Welfare Law Specialist

Climate Change

University of California—Irvine (*http://unex.uci.edu*)—Decision
Making for Climate Change (online)

Compliance

Seton Hall University School of Law (*www.law.shu.edu*)—Health
Care Compliance Certificate

Sheshunoff (*www.sheshunoff.com*)—Regulatory Compliance
Certification Program

Society of Corporate Compliance & Ethics (*www.corporate
compliance.org*)—Certified Compliance & Ethics Professional

Consulting

Kaplan University (*www.kaplan.edu*)—Legal Nurse Consulting
Certificate

Contracts & Procurement

National Contract Management Association (*www.ncmahq.org*)—
Certified Federal Contracts Manager

Corporate Governance

University of North Carolina—Greensboro (*www.uncg.edu*)—
Corporate Governance & Ethics Certificate

Corporate Restructuring

Association of Certified Turnaround Professionals
(*www.actp.org*)—Certified Turnaround Professional

Counseling

Capella University (*www.capella.edu*)—Graduate Certificate in
Professional Counseling

Creditors' Rights

American Board of Certification (*www.abcworld.org*)—Creditors'
Rights Law Certificate

Criminal Justice

National Board of Trial Advocacy (*www.nbtanet.org*)—Criminal
Trial Certificate (online)

Disability

National Board of Trial Advocacy (*www.nbtanet.org*)—Social
Security Disability Certificate (online)

Domestic Relations

National Board of Trial Advocacy (*www.nbtanet.org*)—Family
Law Certificate (online)

E-Commerce

University of Virginia (*www.uva.edu*)—Graduate Certificate Program in E-Commerce

E-Discovery/Records Management

California State University at Fullerton (*www.csufextension.org*)—Certificate in Electronic Discovery

Economic Development

Penn State University (*www.worldcampus.psu.edu/certificates.shtml*)—Certificate in Community and Economic Development (online)

Education

National Alliance for Insurance Education and Research (*www.scic.com/CRM/CRMmain.htm*)—Certified School Risk Manager (CSRM) [California and Texas only]

Elder Law and Affairs

National Elder Law Foundation (*www.nelf.org*)—Certified Elder Law Attorney

Emergency Management

Emergency Management Institute (*http://training.fema.gov*)—Fifty Different Certificate Programs

Employee Benefits

Georgetown University Law Center (*www.law.georgetown.edu*)—Employee Benefits Law Certificate

Employment Law

Expert Rating (*www.expertrating.com*)—Employment Law Certification (online)

Energy & Natural Resources

University of Denver, Sturm College of Law (*www.law.du.edu*)—Certificate of Studies (CS) in Natural Resources Law and Policy

American Association of Professional Landmen (*www. aapl.org*)—Certified Professional Landman

Entertainment, Sports & Media

UCLA Anderson School of Management (*www.anderson. ucla.edu*)—Summer Intensive Certificate Program in Entertainment/Media Management

United States Sports Academy (*www.ussa.edu*)—Sports Law and Risk Management Certificate (online)

National Football League Players Association (*www.nflplayers. com*)—Agent Certification

Environmental Law & Regulation

Harvard University (*www.extension.harvard.edu*)—Certificate in Environmental Management (online)

Estate Planning, Planned Giving & Trusts

National Association of Estate Planners & Councils (*www. naepc.org*)—Estate Planning Law Specialist

Ethics

University of New Mexico (*www.unm.edu*)—Health Care Ethics Certificate Program

University of Florida (*www.ufl.edu*)—Pharmacy Law and Ethics Certificate Program

Food & Drugs

Michigan State University (*www.msu.edu*)—International Food Law Internet Certificate Program;

Northeastern University (*www.spcs.neu.edu*)—Medical Devices Regulatory Affairs (online option)

Fraud Investigation

Association of Certified Fraud Examiners (*www.acfe.com*)—
Certified Fraud Examiner

Globalization

Thunderbird School of Global Management (*www.thunderbird. edu*)—Globalization Certificate

Grants Management

Management Concepts (*www.managementconcepts.com*)—Grants Management Certificate Program

Guardianship

Center for Guardianship Certification (*www.guardianshipcert. org*)—Registered Guardian Certification

Health Law & Administration

Mountain States Employers' Council (*www.msec.org*)—HIPAA: Privacy Rules and Portability
Cleveland State University (*www.csuohio.edu/ce*)—Patient Advocacy Certificate Program (online)

Historic Preservation

University of Hawaii (*www.hawaii.edu*)—Graduate Certificate in Historic Preservation

Human Resources

Villanova University (*www.villanove.edu*)—Master Certificate in Human Resource Management (online)

Human Rights

Center for International Humanitarian Cooperation (*www.cihc.org*)—Humanitarian Negotiators Training Course

Insurance & Risk Management

Kaplan University (*www.kaplan.edu*)—Risk Management Certificate (online)

American Institute for CPCU & Insurance Institute of America (*www.aicpcu.org*)—Associate in Risk Management (ARM)

Intellectual Property

Licensing Executives Society (*www.usa-canada.les.org*)—Intellectual Asset Management Certificates

Franklin Pierce Law Center (*www.piercelaw.edu*)—Intellectual Property Diploma

University of California, Berkeley Extension (*www.unex.berkeley.edu*)—Certificate in Technology Transfer and Commercialization

World Intellectual Property Organization (*www.wipo.int*)—Biotechnology and Intellectual Property

Intelligence, Homeland Security, & National Security

Michigan State University (*www.msu.edu*)—Online Certificate in Homeland Security Studies

International Affairs & Business

IIT Chicago-Kent College of Law (*www.kentlaw.edu*)—Certificate in International Law & Practice

International Maritime Law Institute (*www.imli.org*)—International Law of the Sea Certificates

Thunderbird (*www.thunderbird.edu*)—Doing Business in China Certificate (online)

Investigations

Center for Legal Studies (*www.legalstudies.com*)—Graduate Certificate in Legal Investigation

Investment Banking

New York University (*www.nyu.edu*)—Certificate in Investment Banking

Labor & Employment

Rutgers University (*www.rutgers.edu*)—Public Sector Labor Relations Certificate Program

Law Office Management

Florida International University (*www.fiu.edu*)—Law Office Management Certificate

Legal Administration

Association of Legal Administrators (*www.alanet.org*)—Certified Legal Manager Certification Program

Legal Marketing

University of Miami (*www.educationmiami.edu*)—The UM Marketing Program for Lawyers

Legislation

Georgetown University (*http://gai.georgetown.edu*)—Certificate Program in Legislative Studies

Licensing

International Licensing Industry Merchandisers Association (*www.licensing.org*)—Licensing Certificate

Life Sciences

American Health Lawyers Association (*www.healthlawyers.org*)—Life Sciences Law Institute

Negotiation

University of Notre Dame (*www.nd.edu*)—Executive Certificate in Negotiation (online)

Nonprofit Management

Duke University (*www.learnmore.duke.edu*)—Nonprofit Management Certificate

Privacy

International Association of Privacy Professionals (*www.iapp. org*)—Certified Information Privacy Professional (CIPP)

Professional Liability

American Board of Professional Liability Attorneys (*www. abpla. org*)—Legal Professional Liability Certificate

Public Administration

Brookings Institution (*www.brookings.edu/execed/certificate programs.aspx*)—Certificate in Public Leadership

Real Estate

University of Wisconsin (*www.wisc.edu*)—Real Estate Certificate Program

Regulatory Affairs

San Diego State University (*www.ces.sdsu.edu/regulatoryaffairs. html*)—Advanced Certificate in Regulatory Affairs

Securities

Financial Industry Regulatory Authority (*www.finra.org*)—Compliance Boot Camp

Tax

New York University School of Law (*www.law.nyu.edu*)—Advanced Professional Certificate in Taxation

Trial Advocacy

National Board of Trial Advocacy (*www.nbtanet.org*)—Civil Trial Certificate (online)

Training

International Import-Export Institute (*http://expandglobal.com*)—Certified U.S. Export Compliance Officer

Victims' Rights

Center for Legal Studies (*www.legalstudies.com*)—Graduate Certificate in Victim Advocacy

Water Law

UNESCO (*www.unesco.org*)—Water & Environmental Law and Institutions

Appendix D

Résumé Addendum: Significant Highlights

This device is your opportunity to escape the constraints of your résumé and show your prospective employer what a star you really are. I have yet to encounter a legal or law-related employer who told me that a résumé addendum violated any perceived rule about résumé length. An addendum is your chance to shine, to engage in storytelling, and to set yourself apart from the competition. The following example is one that one of my clients used successfully to move from government to the private sector.

Significant Highlights
Executive Summary

The following describes my approach to resolving major issues that I faced as an attorney at the Federal Deposit Insurance Corporation. It describes how I handled an issue that arose in the context of closing down hundreds of failed financial institutions and disposing of their assets.

Establishing a National Environmental Program
Problem

As a result of the banking crisis of the early 1990s, I was asked to establish and lead several major new programs during a time of rapidly changing law and business operations at the FDIC. During this period, the FDIC was confronted with record numbers of bank failures and the sale of large volumes of assets—the majority being real estate assets from failed banks. We needed to resolve failed banks with minimum disruption to the banking system and to millions of depositors (the public) while maximizing revenues from sales of assets from failed banks in order to repay the Bank Insurance Fund.

I was assigned the responsibility of supervising environmental legal services nationwide. I was challenged to develop an environmental program and quickly provide essential legal services at the same time that the FDIC was absorbing staff transferred from a closed agency—the Federal Savings and Loan Insurance Corporation—and establishing many new field offices nationwide.

Analysis

In examining the matter, it became readily apparent that environmental issues had to be factored into the disposition of tens of billions of dollars of real estate assets assumed by the FDIC from failed institutions, and that this had to be accomplished as soon as possible. If not, the FDIC risked the likelihood of having to defend hundreds of lawsuits as well as potential liability for environmental cleanups costing billions of dollars.

Proposed Solution

I mapped out a far-reaching national program that included a proposed budget, an estimate of manpower requirements, a strategy for incorporating environmental considerations into real estate dispositions, a template for analyzing environmental risks associated with real estate assets, and a timeline for implementation of my proposal.

Implementation

My success in persuading the FDIC of the importance and urgency of environmental laws and issues—and in proposing a systematic agency-wide program to manage them—is reflected by the fact that the FDIC established environmental policies and procedures nationwide and by the fact that the FDIC hired environmental attorneys and program specialists in all of its 26 field offices.

Results

The nationwide program that I designed proved so successful that the FDIC was *never successfully challenged regarding any environmental matters* it inherited when it took over hundreds of failed banks and thrifts during this time period.

I received an FDIC Meritorious Service Award—the highest honor the agency can confer—for this achievement, along with a substantial cash bonus.

Appendix E

Selected Legal and Law-Related Networking Organizations

The following list is a sampling of some of the hundreds of legal and law-related membership organizations that provide extensive networking opportunities to attorneys.

- American Academy of Criminal Defense Attorneys (*www.ameracadcrimdefattys.org*)
- American Academy of Estate Planning Attorneys (*www.aaepa.com*)
- American Agricultural Law Association (*www.aglaw-assn.org*)
- American Association of Attorney-Certified Public Accountants (*www.attorney-cpa.com*)
- American Association of Nurse Attorneys (*www.taana.org*)
- American Association of Visually Impaired Attorneys (*www.visuallyimpairedattorneys.org*)
- American Bar Association (Sections and Committees) (*www.abanet.org*)
- American College of Bankruptcy (*www.amercol.org*)
- American College of Legal Medicine (*www.aclm.org*)
- American Health Lawyers Association (*www.healthlawyers.org*)

- American Immigration Lawyers Association (*www.aila.org*)
- American Inns of Court (*www.innsofcourt.org*)
- American Intellectual Property Law Association (*www.aipla.org*)
- American Masters of Laws Association (*www.amola.org*)
- American Society for Healthcare Risk Management (*www.ashrm.org*)
- American Society for Pharmacy Law (*www.aspl.org*)
- American Society of Corporate Secretaries (*www.ascs.org*)
- American Society of International Law (*www.asil.org*)
- Association of Attorney-Mediators (*www.attorney-mediators.org*)
- Association of Certified Fraud Examiners (*www.acfe.com*)
- Association of Corporate Counsel (*www.acc.com*)
- Association of Insurance & Risk Managers (*www.airmic.com*)
- Association of Legal Administrators (*www.alanet.org*)
- Association of Life Insurance Counsel (*www.alic.cc*)
- Association of Student Judicial Affairs (*www.asjaonline.org*)
- Association of Trial Lawyers of America (*www.atla.org*)
- Association of University Technology Managers (*www.autm.org*)
- Black Entertainment & Sports Lawyers Association (*www.besla.org*)
- Center for Telehealth & E-Health Law (*www.ctel.org*)
- Christian Legal Society (*www.clsnet.com*)
- Council of School Attorneys (*www.nsba.org/SecondaryMenu/COSA.aspx*)
- Council on Litigation Management (*www.litmgmt.org*)
- Customs and International Trade Bar Association (*www.citba.org*)
- Cyberspace Bar Association (*www.cyberbar.net*)
- Education Law Association (*http://educationlaw.org*)
- Energy Bar Association (*www.eba-net.org*)
- Environmental Law Institute (*www2.eli.org*)

- Ethics and Compliance Officers Association (*www.theecoa.org*)
- Federal Bar Association (*www.fedbar.org*)
- Federal Communications Bar Association (*www.fcba.org*)
- Food and Drug Law Institute (*www.fdli.org*)
- Health Care Compliance Association (*www.hcca-info.org*)
- Hispanic National Bar Association (*www.hnba.com*)
- International Association of Entertainment Lawyers (*www.iael.org*)
- International Association of Facilitators (*http://iaf-world.org*)
- International Association of Privacy Professionals (*www.privacyassociation.org*)
- International Association of Sports Law (*http://iasl.org*)
- International Center for Not-for-Profit Law (*www.icnl.org*)
- International Legal Technology Association (*www.iltanet.org*)
- International Masters of Gaming Law (*www.gaminglawmasters.com*)
- International Media Lawyers Association (*www.internationalmedialawyers.org*)
- International Municipal Lawyers Association (*www.imla.org*)
- International Society of Certified Employee Benefit Specialists (*www.iscebs.org*)
- International Tax Planning Association (*www.itpa.org*)
- International Technology Law Association (*www.itechlaw.org*)
- International Trademark Association (*www.inta.org*)
- Internet Bar Association (*http://lawyers.org*)
- Judge Advocates Association (*www.jaa.org*)
- Lawyers' Committee for Civil Rights Under Law (*www.lawyerscommittee.org*)
- Lawyer Pilots Bar Association (*www.lpba.org*)
- Legal Marketing Association (*www.legalmarketing.org*)
- Lesbian and Gay Law Association (*www.le-gal.org*)
- Licensing Executives Society (*www.usa-canada.les.org*)

- Lithuanian-American Bar Association (*http:// javadvokatai.org*)
- Maritime Law Association of the United States (*www.mlaus.org*)
- National Academy of Elder Law Attorneys (*www.naela.org*)
- National Asian Pacific American Bar Association (*www.napaba.org*)
- National Association for Athletics Compliance (*www.nacda.com*)
- National Association of Blind Lawyers (*www.blindlawyer.org*)
- National Association of Bond Lawyers (*www.nabl.org*)
- National Association of College and University Attorneys (*www.nacua.org*)
- National Association of Counsel for Children (*www.NACCchildlaw.org*)
- National Association of Guardians ad Litem (*www.nagalro.com*)
- National Association of Legal Fee Analysis (*www.thenalfa.org*)
- National Association of Legal Search Consultants (*www.nalsc.org*)
- National Association of Women Lawyers (*www.abanet.org/nawl/*)
- National Bar Association (*www.nationalbar.org*)
- National Contract Management Association (*www.ncmahq.org*)
- National District Attorneys Association (*www.ndaa.org*)
- National Employment Lawyers Association (*www.nela.org*)
- National Legal Aid and Defender Association (*www.nlada.org*)
- National Lesbian and Gay Law Association (*www.nlgla.org*)
- National Native American Bar Association (*www.nativeamericanbar.org*)

- National Organization of Social Security Claimants' Representatives (*www.nosscr.org*)
- National Organization of Veterans Advocates (*www.vetadvocates.com*)
- Natural Resources Defense Council (*www.nrdc.org*)
- Risk Management Association (*www.rmahq.org*)
- Sarbanes-Oxley Compliance Professionals Association (*www.sarbanes-oxley-association.com*)
- Society of Corporate Compliance and Ethics (*www.corporatecompliance.org*)
- Sports Lawyers Association (*www.sportslaw.org*)
- State and Local Bar Associations (Sections and Committees)
- Transportation Lawyers Association (*www.translaw.org*)
- United States Ombudsman Association (*www.usombudsman.org*)
- University Risk Management & Insurance Association (*www.urmia.org*)
- Women in Government Relations (*www.wgr.org*)

Appendix F

Contacts Road Map

The example below is typical of the type of contacts road map that any job or career transition candidate should be able to put together. While it is based on an actual road map that I crafted for one of my legal career transition counseling clients who left a high-level position, the concept is appropriate for every legal job seeker at any level.

Positions of Interest

Corporation
- General Counsel
- Senior Regional Counsel
- Division Counsel
- Litigation Manager

Law Firm
- Law Firm Partner/ Shareholder
- Law Firm Of Counsel

Examples of Prospective Employers

Representative Food Industry Companies
- ConAgra
- Campbell Soup
- Del Monte
- Dean Foods
- Wrigley
- Kraft
- Nestle
- Safeway
- Wegman's
- Hershey
- PepsiCo
- Procter & Gamble
- Coca-Cola
- Anheuser-Busch Companies
- McCormick & Company
- Kellogg Company

Representative Consumer Products Companies
- Clorox
- Wal-Mart
- Costco
- Colgate-Palmolive
- Avon Products
- Estee Lauder
- Alberto-Culver

Law Firms with a Food Industry or Consumer Products Industry Practice
- Abel & Cain
- Smith & Jones
- Dewey, Cheatem & Howe
- Lex & Legis
- Jordan & Gallilee
- Holdem & Scoldem
- Barracuda, Serpent & Squid

Supporting Rationale
(Why I Fit Into These Positions and Organizations)
Food Industry and Consumer Products Companies
- 10+ years at Berner North America as Division Counsel
- Member, Legal Committee, Grocery Manufacturers Association (members represent virtually all the major U.S. food manufacturers)
- Managed $20-$30 million per year outside counsel budget
- Negotiated license agreements, purchase and sale agreements, and settlements related to advertising disputes with many of the other U.S. food companies.
- Selected, directed and supervised outside counsel in M&A, litigation and employment matters
- Member, Advisory Board, Chief Legal Officer magazine

Law Firms—Food Industry/Consumer Products Practice
Fifteen years of experience with every aspect of food industry law, including litigation, major transactions, due diligence, regulatory matters, government relations, etc.

Excellent business development contacts and potential
- Strong personal relationships with numerous Berner in-house counsel, including:
    - Group General Counsel in Austria,
    - Regional General Counsels
    - Head of Market lawyers around the world

- Senior Vice President of Mergers and Acquisitions
- Intellectual Property General Counsel
- Director of captive Berner Oberland Investment Fund (which will be making significant equity investments in the U.S. and elsewhere
- Vice President-Government Affairs-U.S.
- Strong personal relationships with former Berner executives now at ConAgra, Campbell Soup, and other businesses
- Strong personal relationship with Grocery Manufacturers Association General Counsel
- Member, Executive Committee, Corporate Law Section, Los Angeles County Bar Association—work closely with fellow members who are primarily General Counsels at companies such as Avery Dennison Corporation, Mattell, Inc., Sempra Energy, Southern California Edison, Hilton Hotels, IndyMac Bank, University of Southern California, Paramount Pictures, US Telepacific, KCET, Northrop Grumman, Harman Industries, and Trust Company of the West, as well as members of the Bank of America and Wells Fargo legal departments, among others.
- Recently coordinated and co-chaired four roundtable programs with guest speakers from in-house counsel offices at companies such as Unum Provident, Forest Lawn, and State Farm Insurance Company.
- Good relationships with other members of the Bay Area General Counsel and the Southern California Chapter of the Association of Corporate Counsel
- Delivered numerous presentations sponsored by The Rutter Group (CLE), bar associations, and the Institute for Corporate Counsel
- Worked on deals with numerous investment banks and bankers

Appendix G

Reference List

A. Spiring Advocate, ESQ.
22 Peninsula Gap · Atoll, CA 92999
Home: (310) 555-2468 · Cell: (310) 555-4321
lawyerabc@hotmail.com

REFERENCES

Clare Obscura, Esq., Deputy U.S. Attorney, United States Attorney's Office, Southern District of California, 123 Faultline Precipice, San Andreas, CA 92998. O: (310) 555-1111.
Ms. Obscura was opposing counsel in several criminal matters in which my clients prevailed.
Contact information: Ms. Obscura can be contacted at her office phone number (listed above) between 9:00 a.m. and 5:00 p.m. Monday through Friday.

Henry Hammerhead, Esq., Shareholder, Great, White & Hammerhead, 333 Chum Court, Chasm, CA 92555.
H: (310) 555-6666; O: (310) 555-7000
Mr. Hammerhead was my practice group leader at Great, White & Hammerhead, and my co-counsel in several successful jury trials.
Contact information: Mr. Hammerhead can be contacted either at his office or at home in the evening, Monday through Thursday.

Honorable Hang. M. High, Terminator County Superior Court, 122 Abbey Lane, No Problemo, CA 92111. O: (310) 555-8888.
I clerked for Judge High after graduation from law school.
Contact information: Judge High can be contacted in his chambers between noon and 2:00 p.m. at the listed phone number.

Appendix H

Interview Rating Scale

Note: This is typical of what some *Fortune* 500 corporations use to rank candidates at their job interviews.

Candidate: _____

Position: _____

	Strong	Acceptable	Weak
FIRST IMPRESSIONS			
1. Entrance			
2. Introduction			
3. Handshake			
4. Posture			
5. Eye contact			
6. Listening skills			
7. Appropriate dress			
8. Appropriate grooming			
9. Appears self-confident			
10. Positive attitude			

	Strong	Acceptable	Weak
JOB READINESS IMPRESSIONS			
11. Interest in job & company			
12. Knowledge of company			
13. Knowledge of job			
14. Manner of answering questions			
15. Description of background			
16. Points out job-related skills & abilities			
PERSONAL IMPRESSIONS			
17. Explains any problems credibly			
18. Appears dependable & honest			
19. Appears well-mannered			
20. Appears cooperative			
21. Appears easy to get along with			
22. Maturity			
23. Realistic goals & future plans			
24. Smiles & appears friendly			
FINAL IMPRESSIONS			
25. Handles salary/benefits well			
26. Asks good questions			
27. Closes interview well			
28. Seems qualified			
29. Seems enthusiastic			

I would hire this person: Yes ☐   No ☐   Not Sure ☐

Appendix I

Networking Contacts Record

Name of Contact:_____

Title: _____

Organization:_____

Address:_____

_____

_____

Telephone(s): (O)_____ (H)_____ (C)_____

E-mail:_____

Fax:_____

Preferred Contact Mode: _____

Date(s) contacted by phone or e-mail:_____

Date(s) met in person:_____

Information learned, or other names suggested as further contacts:

1. _____

2. _____

3. _____

4. _____

5. _____

Notes:_____

_____

_____

_____

_____

Follow-up:

By letter:_____   Date sent:_____

By phone:_____   Date sent:_____

By e-mail:_____   Date sent:_____

Appendix J

Sample Cover Letter/ Transmittal E-mail

Dear Ms. _____:

I have enclosed my résumé for consideration for the Associate General Counsel position available in your office, in response to your ad at www.AttorneyJobs.com.

My wide-ranging law firm experience resolving complex legal issues, counseling companies in a variety of industries, my ability to quickly resolve novel issues, and my extensive experience mentoring young associates, are consistent with the qualities that the Office of General Counsel seeks.

I am currently a Senior Business Associate at Hamilton & Burr, where I advise, counsel, and represent clients on a wide range of corporate issues and interact well with people at all levels of my clients' organizations. In this capacity, I provide detailed guidance on executive compensation disclosure mandated by recent Securities and Exchange Commission rules and structure and negotiate private company mergers and acquisitions. In recent years, a large part of my practice involves counseling corporate boards and senior executives on various corporate governance and compliance issues. In addition to my corporate practice, I also have experience with commercial litigation.

I am a quick study and am the "go-to" attorney in my firm with respect to first impression issues that require a fast response and rapid resolution. Whether participating in strategic decisions on legal issues, managing submissions to government agencies, or simply answering a frantic late afternoon request for advice, it is the day-to-day human counseling aspect of my job that I value the most. In that regard, I am seeking a position where I can continue to resolve complex issues while working with others.

I believe my broad-based legal experience, my ability to quickly understand new issues and work independently, and my strong interpersonal skills suit this position. I would appreciate the opportunity to meet with you at your convenience and look forward to hearing from you soon.

Sincerely,

Enclosure: Résumé

Index

A

academic institutions, 109–15
academic performance, unimpressive, 171–73
ACCL (American College of Construction Lawyers), 28
accountability, 44
accounting firms, 88, 90
acquaintances, casual, 5
Acquired Immune Deficiency Syndrome (AIDS), 130
Administrative Conference of the United States, 121–22
administrative law judge (ALJ), 206
administrative litigation, 190–91
ADR (alternative dispute resolution), 30
ageism, 176, 223–27
AIDS, 130
ALJ (administrative law judge), 206
alternative dispute resolution (ADR), 30
Altman Weil Inc., 343
American Association of Petroleum Landmen, 68
American Bar Association (ABA), 35, 48, 109, 117
   Rule of Law Initiative, 117
   Standing Committee on Specialization, 35
American College of Construction Lawyers (ACCL), 28
American Dental Association, 109
American Express, 90
American Health Lawyers Association, 81

American Immigration Lawyers Association, 81
American Institute of Architects, 109
American Institute of Certified Public Accountants, 109
American Medical Association, 109
American Psychological Association, 109
American Recovery and Reinvestment Act of 2009, 197
Americans with Disabilities Act of 1990, 123, 232
Ameriprise, 90
annual reviews, 157, 166–67
Annual Source of Employment Survey (March 2008), 4
appellate litigation, 191
application documents, lack of interest and enthusiasm and, 16
Arab oil embargo (1973–74), 128
art recovery practice, 78–79
Asia Foundation, 117
Association Executive Compensation and Benefits Study (ASAE), 344
Association of Attorney-Mediators, 81
Association of Corporate Counsel, 81
Association of University Technology Managers, 91
attitudinal barriers
   bitterness and negativity, 16
   defined, 13
   disrespect, 18–19
   hubris, 18
   lack of energy, 17–18

389

lack of interest and enthusiasm,
    16–17
lack of self-esteem, 13–15
self-pity, 15–16
attorney membership organizations,
    70–71
Aviation and Transportation
    Security Act of 2001, 96, 124

B

banking and financial services
    industry, 87
bankruptcy courts, 198
behavioral interviews, 294–95
Bioterrorism Preparedness and
    Response Act of 2001, 124
bitterness and negativity, 16
Board of Veterans Appeals, 55
British Petroleum, 121, 127
bursting bubbles, 130
business and marketing plans for
    solo practices, 149–52
business press releases, 70

C

Capp, Al, 46
carbon transactions practice, 79
Carborundum Corporation, 127
Cardinal Health, 90
career credential enhancement, 31–
    35
career paths, parallel, 27–30
career progression, 45, 175
career transition. *See* job hunting;
    legal careers
Careers and the Disabled Magazine,
    231, 241
Carefusion, 90
Carter Center, 117
Carter, Jimmy, 41
case study interviews, 293
casual acquaintances, 5
CBS, 90

certificate programs
    finding, 35
    LL.M versus, 32
    pursuing, 11
    state specialty, 34
Certified Federal Contracts Manager,
    136
charitable organizations, 117–18
Chemonics International, 117
Chevron, 121
China National Petroleum Company,
    121
Chipotle, 90
Chronicle of Higher Education, 112
Cold War ending, 124
College and University Faculty
    (NCES), 344
college and university jobs
    application forms for, 162
    charitable giving officers, 136
    compensation information for,
        344
    law-related jobs in, 58
    real estate positions, 193
    risk management positions, 30
    technology transfer offices, 90–91
    types of jobs, 109–15
Commercial Law Development
    Program, 117
commodities finance practice, 78
commodity price volatility, 128
common sense, 41–42
compensation and other terms of
    employment, 330, 341–45
compensation, comparative, 330
*Compensation of Legal and Related
    Jobs* (Abbott, Langer &
    Associates), 343
Compensation Survey (Chronicle of
    Philanthropy), 344
conflicts checks, 157, 167
Congress
    legislative action, 96–97, 122
    support offices and legislative
        assistants for, 99

Congressional Research Service, 91
connections/contacts, job hunting
    and, 23–25
consulting firm jobs, 9, 30
contacts. *See* networking contacts;
    references
Contacts Road Map, 157, 265, 284,
    285
contracting and subcontracting,
    104–5
Contracts Road Map, 157, 158–59
Cornell School of Industrial and
    Labor Relations, 236
corporations
    business expansion, 89
    compensation information for,
        343
    emerging, 90–92
    hidden corporate legal niches,
        85–88
    new product announcements of,
        88–89
    real estate departments, 193
    résumés for, 177–80
    spin-offs, 89–90
    terms of employment at, 341–42
Council of State Governments, 344
courts, bankruptcy, 198
courts, federal, 100, 343
courts, state, 102, 344
cover letters
    ageism and, 225
    candidates with disabilities and,
        234
    example, 165
    lack of interest and enthusiasm
        and, 16
    to mitigate résumé weaknesses,
        171
    out-of-town candidates, 252
    overview, 157, 164
    persuasive ability demonstrated
        on, 43
CPA firms, 88, 90
criminal law, 198

D

deal sheets, 157
Deloitte Touche, 88
Department of Homeland Security
    Act of 2002, 97
*Directory of Executive & Profes-
    sional Recruiters* (Kennedy
    Information), 277
disabilities
    accommodations, 235–38
    cover letters and, 234, 242
    employers and candidates with
        disabilities, 230–33
    impact on employment, 229–30
    interviews and, 234–35
    résumés and, 234, 242
    special hiring programs, 238–41
Disability Coordinators, 239
disabled veterans, 239–41
disrespect, 18–19
dissecting legal job ad form, 157–58
dollar depreciation, 129
Dow Jones Industrial Average (DJIA)
    companies, 14–15
Du Pont, 236
due diligence for prospective
    employers
    importance of, 325–26, 337
    information sources, 326–27,
        328–30
    key items, 327–28
    people to talk to, 335–37
    post-job offer questions, 333–35
    practice area due diligence, 337
    questions for the employer, 331–
        33
    See also employers

E

e-mail résumés, 157, 162
e-mails
    lack of interest and enthusiasm
        and, 16

persuasive ability demonstrated in, 43
The Economist, 125
elder law, 79, 142–43
eminent domain practice, 196–97
employers
  candidates with disabilities and, 229–33
  current employer as reference, 263–64
  desired candidate attributes, 39, 46
    accountability, 44
    being a quick study, 42
    career progression, 45
    common sense, 41–42
    fit, 40–41, 298
    intelligence, 41–42
    likeability, 39–40, 299
    organizational skills, 42–43
    persuasive ability, 43
    stable job record, 45–46
    well-roundedness, 44
  interviews and, 295
  making a positive impression on, 13
  reading of résumés, 177–82
  references from terminating employer, 303–4
  references not provided by, 268
  storytelling and, 211–12
  understanding of résumé terminology, 201–3
  See also due diligence for prospective employers; *specific types of employers*
employment agreements, 339–45
employment gaps, 173
employment law, 80
EnableAmerica, 241
energy, lack of, 17–18
energy and telecom boutique law firms, 82
Energy Bar Association, 81

energy costs, 120–21
energy law, 68, 76, 121, 193–94, 199
Enron and related corporate scandals, 97
enthusiasm and interest, lack of, 16–17
environmental law, 55, 80
Environmental Protection Agency (EPA), 55, 121
EPA (Environmental Protection Agency), 55
Equal Employment Opportunity Commission, 232
Ernst & Young, 88
ethics offices, 85–86, 109
executive branch jobs, state and local, 100–102
Executive Order 13, 518, 240
Expedia, 90
Exxon, 121

F

face-to-face interviews, 291
Facebook, 282, 283
Family and Medical Leave Act of 1993, 114
Family Educational Rights & Privacy Act (1974), 114
family law, 80
federal courts, 100
federal government jobs. *See* public sector jobs
Federal Laboratory Consortium for Technology Transfer, 91
Fifth Amendment, 196–97
Financial Industry Regulatory Authority, 97
Financial Services Modernization Act of 1999, 87, 113
Food and Drug Law Institute, 81
food and drug regulation, 76
for-profit corporations, 9

Fortune 500 companies, 251
Fortune 1000 companies, 85
Foundation Center, 112, 118
foundations, 117–18
Fourteenth Amendment, 196–97

G

global politics, 123–25
globalization and legal process
    outsourcing, 128–29
goals, identifying, 8
golf practice, 79
Good cop–bad cop interviews, 292
gotcha interviews, 293
Government Accountability Office,
    91
government contracts, 104–5, 135–
    36, 198
government employers. *See* public
    sector jobs
Government Performance and
    Results Act of 1993, 103
government research and develop-
    ment (R&D) initiatives, 91
Government Salary Schedules, 343
*Graduate Law Degree Program
    Directory* (Thomson Reuters),
    35
Gramm-Leach-Bliley Act, 87, 113
Granovetter, Mark, 4
Great Recession, 55, 75, 83, 86, 130,
    223, 227
Gulf, 121

H

headhunters
    criteria for candidates, 272–73,
        277
    defined, 271–72
    finding, 277
    law firms' use of, 274
    non-legal, 28–29, 276–77
    number of placements using, 274

search process, 274–76
three-way relationship, 276
health law, 76, 80, 126
healthcare providers, 115
hidden job market
    competition for the positions in
        the, 118
    identifying opportunities in the,
        65–71
    nonprofits
        academic institutions, 109–
            15
        overview, 107–8
        trade and professional
            organizations, 108–9
    predicting the government future,
        103
    private sector
        corporations, 85–92
        law firm, 75–85
    profile of, 64–65
    public sector
        contracting and subcontract-
            ing, 104–5
        federal government, 93–100
        state and local government,
            100–103
    resources for information regard-
        ing, 71–73
    See also legal job market
Higher Education Opportunity Act
    of 2008, 114–15
homeland security, 59, 77, 96–97,
    124–25
hospitals, 115
hubris, 18

I

in-house counsel positions, 29, 51–
    53, 88
Indian legal outsourcing services,
    128–29
industry reorganizations and area
    changes, 121

insurance industry, 87
intellectual property law, 79–80,
    198
intelligence, 41–42
InterActive Corp., 90
interest and enthusiasm, lack of, 16–
    17
interest rate fluctuations, 120
intermediaries, 210–11
Internal Revenue Code, 86, 237–38
Internal Revenue Service, 76
International Boundary and Water
    Commission, 54
International Masters of Gaming
    Law, 81
international politics, 123–25
international trade law, 80
Internet Bar Association, 81
Internet job advertisements, 4
Internet job boards, 4
Interstate Commerce Commission
    (ICC), 122
Interviewing Guidelines (EEOC),
    232
interviews
    accountability demonstrated
        during, 44
    ageism and, 226
    being likeable during, 39–40
    bitterness and negativity during,
        16
    candidate's questions during,
        313–18
    candidates with disabilities and,
        234–35
    company "fit" and, 40–41, 298
    demonstrating intelligence
        during, 42
    demonstrating quick study ability
        during, 42
    disrespect during, 18–19
    due diligence questions, 331–33
    employer's thoughts during, 295
    goals for the candidate during,
        297–300

hubris during, 18
interviewers, 291
lack of energy during, 17–18
lack of interest and enthusiasm
    during, 17
medium used, 291–92
negotiating terms of employment
    during, 345
number of, 292
organizational skills demon-
    strated during, 43
out-of-town candidates, 250, 252
payment for travel to, 244–46
résumé's weaknesses and, 169–70
self-pity during, 15
termination discussion during the,
    319–21
tough questions during, 301–11
types of, 292–95
unpredictable nature of, 289–90
invention and innovation, 126–27
Iranian oil embargo (1979), 128
IRIS Center at the University of
    Maryland, 117

J

*JD Preferred: 600+ Things You Can
    Do with a Law Degree*
    (Thomson Reuters) 57–58
Job Accommodation Network, 236
job advertisements, 4, 68–69, 183–
    87
job-hopping history, 174–75
job hunting
    applying for unrealistic jobs, 22–
        23
    applying to one job at a time, 21–
        22
    attitudinal barriers and, 13, 19
        bitterness and negativity, 16
        disrespect, 18–19
        hubris, 18
        lack of energy, 17–18

lack of interest and enthusiasm, 16–17

lack of self-esteem, 13–15

self-pity, 15–16

connections/contacts and, 23–25

credential enhancement for, 31–35

documents for, 157–67

employers' desired candidate attributes, 39, 46

accountability, 44

being a quick study, 42

career progression, 45

common sense, 41–42

fit, 40–41

intelligence, 41–42

likeability, 39–40, 299

organizational skills, 42–43

persuasive ability, 43

stable job record, 45–46

well-roundedness, 44

hidden skill sets, 189–99

interconnections and interactions, 347–49

job advertisements, 68–69, 183–87

long-term career interests and, 133–35

myths and facts regarding, 3–6

organization skills and, 156–57

organizing principles for, 168

out-of-town

distance job-hunting tips, 249–52

employers' concerns, 243–49

parallel career paths, 27–30

psychological preparation for, 155

record-keeping, 168

time management and, 155–56

tunnel vision and, 22

See also specific types of employers

job market. *See* legal job market

job offers, evaluating, 133–35

job titles, undistinguished, 175

Jobvite, 282, 283

JSC Gazprom of Russia, 121

K

Kennecott Copper, 127

knowledge, skills, and abilities (KSA) statements, 157, 162–64

KPMG, 88

KSA (knowledge, skills, and abilities) statements, 157, 162–64

L

lack of energy, 17–18

lack of interest and enthusiasm, 16–17

The Land Trust Alliance, 195

land trusts, 116, 195–96

landman positions, 68, 193–94

law firms

ancillary businesses (subsidiaries) of, 84–85

Boutique Law Firm Trends, 82–83

changing practice areas, 76–77

compensation information for, 343

entry-level associates at, 340

expanding existing practice areas, 75–76

headhunter use by, 274

law firm lawyer analysis, 81

legal careers in, 9, 49–51

new practice areas, 77–79

new skills for lawyers in, 83–84

résumés for, 177–80

spin-off practice areas, 79–81

technology and, 77

terms of employment as, 342

writing topics of, 81–83

legal careers

alternative dispute resolution, 30

consulting firms, 30

external influences on, 119, 131
bursting bubbles, 130
dollar depreciation, 129
energy costs, 120–21
global politics, 123–25
globalization, 128–29
government actions and
legislation, 121–23
industry reorganizations and
area changes, 121
interest rate fluctuations, 120
invention and innovation,
126–27
professional personnel
shortages, 130–31
technological paradigm
shifts, 125–26
unfortunate coincidences,
130
government employers, 29
in-house counsel positions, 29
law-related, 9
long-term career interests, 133–35
mainstream, 9
mergers and acquisitions, 127–28
multiple job over career, 7–8
parallel career paths, 17–30
private practice, 29
resource shortages, 128
sector list, 9–10
self-awareness questions related
to, 8–12
trade associations, 30
transitions strategies, 135–37
university risk management
positions, 30
*See also specific sectors and types
of employers*
legal job market
demographics, 48–49
mainstream legal careers
demographics, 48–49
government law offices, 53–
56

in-house counsel offices, 51–
53
law firms, 49–51
profit versus non-profit, 51
non-mainstream legal careers
education and work experience as asset for, 59–60
pluses and minus of working
in the, 60–61
proliferation of, 58–59
types of, 56–58
See also hidden job market
legislation, monitoring of, 96–97
legislative branch jobs
federal, 98–99
state, 101–2
legislative or regulatory threats,
121–22
letters of recommendation, 157,
166, 263
likeability as desired attribute,
39–40, 299
"Lil' Abner" comic strip, 46
LinkedIn, 282, 283
litigation, administrative, 190–91
litigation, appellate, 191
litigation management, 191–92
litigation practice, 141, 190–92
LL.M. degrees
choosing, 33–35
enhancing career credentials with,
11, 31–32
local government jobs. *See* public
sector jobs
longevity law practice, 79
Lotus, 90

M

mainstream law, 9
manufacturing industry, 87
March of Dimes, 126
marketing and business plans for
solo practices, 149–52
McDonald's, 90

mealtime interviews, 294
membership organizations, attorney,
    70–71
mergers and acquisitions, 127–28
MIT laboratories, 90
Mobil, 121
multitasking, 27–30
Mutt and Jeff interviews, 292

N

NALSC (National Association of
    Legal Search Consultants), 277
NASA, 91
The National Academy of Elder Law
    Attorneys, 142
National Aeronautics and Space
    Administration (NASA), 127
National Association for Law
    Placement, 343
National Association of College and
    University Attorneys, 81
National Association of Counties,
    344
National Association of Legal
    Search Consultants (NALSC),
    277
National Association of Realtors,
    109
National Conference of State
    Legislatures, 102, 344
National Contract Management
    Association, 136
National Education Association, 344
National Employment Lawyers
    Association, 81
National Iranian Oil Company, 121
national security law, 80
National Technology Transfer
    Center, 91, 127
National Venture Capital Associa-
    tion, 90
networking
    hidden job market and, 65–67, 71
    importance of, 279, 280
    as job-finding strategy, 3–6
    organization membership and, 28
    social networking Web sites and,
        282–84
    networking contacts
    building a network, 281–84
    galvanizing contacts, 167–68
    information sharing with, 279,
        284–85
    references and, 261
    self-pity and, 15–16
    storytelling and, 210–11
    when to communicate with, 280
    whom to contact, 281
networking contacts forms, 157, 158
networking contacts records, 157,
    158
new-hire and promotion announce-
    ments, 69–70
NGOs (non-governmental organiza-
    tions), 116–17
non-governmental organizations
    (NGOs), 116–17
non-profit versus profit organiza-
    tions, 51
Nonprofit Compensation Report
    (GuideStar), 344
nonprofit sector jobs, 9–10, 49, 193,
    344, *See also* college and
    university
jobs; trade and professional associa-
    tions/organizations
Northern Virginia Technology
    Council, 73

O

Obama administration, 68, 76
Office of Attorney Recruitment and
    Management (OARM), 280
Office of Disability Employment
    Policy, 241
Office of Science and Technology
    Policy, 91

Office of Technology Assessment, 122
Office of the Consumer Advocate at the Postal Rate Commission, 54
Offices of the United States Trustee, 198
offshore outsourcing, 128–29
oil embargoes, 128
online applications, 205–8
Oracle of Delphi, 7
Organizational Sentencing Guidelines, 85
organizational skills, 42–43
outsourcing, 128–29
Overseas Private Investment Corporation, 124

P

Pascal, Blaise, 203, 220
Pension Benefit Guaranty Corporation, 97
performance appraisals, 157, 166–67
personnel shortages, 130–31
persuasive ability, 43
Petrobras of Brazil, 121
Petroleos de Venezuela, 121
Petronas of Malaysia, 121
Philippine legal outsourcing services, 129
political appointments, lower level, 97–98
presentation interviews, 293–94
press releases, 70
PricewaterhouseCoopers, 88
private practice careers, 9, 29, 241, See also corporations; law firms; solo
practices
private-sector job résumés, 177–80
product announcements, 88–89
professional associations. See trade and professional associations/ organizations

professional personnel shortages, 130–31
profit versus non-profit organizations, 51
promotion and new-hire announcements, 69–70
Public Company Accounting Oversight Board, 97
Public Health Security and Bioterrorism Preparedness and Response Act of 2002, 96
public interest organizations, 115–16
public sector jobs
candidates with disabilities and, 238–41
compensation information for, 343–44
contracting and subcontracting, 104–5, 135–36
federal government, 29, 93–100
legal careers in, 53–56
real estate practice, 194
résumés for, 180–81
state and local, 100–103
terms of employment at, 341, 342
types of, 10

R

real estate associations, 194–95
real estate attorneys, 192–98
real estate distress law, 193
reference lists, 43, 157, 166, 266–67
references
current employer, 263–64
dual-use, 261
employers that do no provide, 268
from terminating employer, 303–4
initial contact with, 167, 265–66
letters of recommendation, 263
lining up, 167
number needed, 258–59
on-going information for, 167, 266

reference management importance, 255, 269
selecting, 259–61, 262–63
storytelling and, 210–11
when to find, 256–58
when to provide, 267–68
Regan, Ronald, 82, 147
Regional ADA Technical Assistance Center, 236
Rehabilitation Act of 1973, 239
relocation expenses, 246
Representative Matters List, 157, 160–61
research and development (R&D) initiatives, 91
Resolution Trust Corporation, 121
resource shortages, 128
résumés
  ageism and, 176, 224–25
  basic considerations, 159–60
  candidates with disabilities and, 234
  career progression demonstrated on, 45
  e-mail, 157, 162
  employers' reading of, 177–82
  headhunters and, 272, 273
  hidden job market and, 64
  intelligence and, 41
  for job search and career transitions, 157
  language used on, 201–3
  mitigating weaknesses on, 169–76
  negative "stick out" résumés, 25–26
  online applications, 205–8
  online résumé banks, 64
  organizational skills demonstrated on, 42–43
  out-of-town candidates, 252
  persuasive ability demonstrated on, 43
  purpose of, 159

quick study skills demonstrated on, 42
references and, 265
Representative Matters List, 160–61
résumé addendum, 157, 160
résumé substitutes, 157, 161–62
self esteem and, 14
stabile job record and, 46
video, 157, 162
well-roundedness demonstrated on, 44
Royal Dutch Shell, 121

S

Sabin, Albert, 126
salary requirements, requests for, 341
Salk, Jonas, 126
Sara Lee, 90
Sarbanes-Oxley Act of 2002, 51, 58, 78, 85, 86, 97
Saudi Aramco, 121
Scientific American, 126
screening interviews, 292
scripted interviews, 292
search consultants. *See* headhunters
Securities and Exchange Commission, 90, 97
securities law, 198
Selective Placement Coordinators, 239
Selective Placement Program for Individuals with Disabilities, 231
self-awareness, 7–12
  questions, 8–12
self-destruction, avoiding, 21–26
self-esteem, lack of, 13–15
September 11, 2001 terrorist attacks, 59, 77, 96, 124–25
Seven Sisters companies, 121
skill sets, hidden, 189–99
social media networks, 4
social networking Web sites, 282–84
software industry, 72

Sohio, 127
solo practices
  business and marketing plans,
    149–52
  considerations when starting
    business failure, 148–49
    client pitch, 148
    competition, 144–45
    components/characteristic of,
      140–41
    fee collection, 148
    goals and objectives, 140
    location of, 142–43
    markets for the practice and
      how to reach them, 146,
      147–48
    personal strengths and
      weaknesses, 145–46, 146–
      47
    practice areas, 140–42
    pricing services, 148
    resources required, 144
    secondary markets and
      services, 143–44
    time allocation, 144
  ease of launching, 152
  number of, 139
stable job record, 45–46
state government jobs. *See* public
  sector jobs
state specialty programs, pursuing,
  11
Stimulus Package. *See* American
  Recovery and Reinvestment
  Act of 2009
storytelling, 209–15
street smarts, 41–42
subcontracting and contracting,
  104–5
support groups, hidden job market
  and, 65
Survey of Judicial Salaries (NCSC),
  344

T

tax law, 76, 86
teaching positions, 109–15
technological paradigm shifts, 125–
  26
technology corridors, 73
technology, new, law firm practice
  and, 77, 83–84
Technology Review, 126
telecom and energy boutique law
  firms, 82
Telecommunications Reform Act of
  1996, 82
telephone interviews, 291–92
Texaco, 121
3Com, 90
trade and professional associations/
  organizations
  careers in, 30, 108–9
  compensation information for,
    344
  networking and, 66–67
  publications and Web sites of, 72
  real estate, 194–95
  traditional interviews, 292
transactional law, 192
transcripts, 157, 165
transferable skills lists, 157
transmittal e-mails. *See* cover letters
Transportation Security Act of 2001,
  124
Transportation Security Administration (TSA), 96
trends analysis, 10, 67–68
tribal finance practice, 78
trusts and estates, 198
TSA (Transportation Security
  Administration), 96
tunnel vision and job hunting, 22
Twitter, 282, 283–84

U

unemployment, 173–74, 302–5
United States Access Board, 236
university jobs. *See* college and
    university jobs
university risk management posi-
    tions, 30
U.S. Bankruptcy Court Staff Attor-
    ney Offices, 198
U.S. Bureau of Labor Statistics, 130,
    139
U.S. Commerce Department, 117
U.S. Commerce Department's Office
    of General Counsel, 54
U.S. Commodity Futures Trading
    Commission, 128
U.S. courts, 100
U.S. Department of Defense, 239
U.S. Department of Energy, 120
U.S. Department of Homeland
    Security, 124
U.S. Department of Justice, 97, 198,
    280
U.S. Department of Labor, 97, 231
U.S. Department of Veterans Affairs,
    239
U.S. Interior Department, 121
U.S. International Trade Administra-
    tion, 54
U.S. Justice Department, 121
U.S. Minority Business Develop-
    ment Agency, 54
U.S. National Institute of Standards
    and Technology, 54
U.S. National Oceanic and Atmo-
    spheric Administration, 54
U.S. Nuclear Regulatory Commis-
    sion, 121
U.S. Office of Personnel Manage-
    ment, 343
U.S. Office of Personnel Manage-
    ment (OPM), 206
U.S. Patent and Trademark Office,
    54, 127
U.S. Sentencing Commission, 97
U.S. Small Business Administration,
    139
U.S. Technology Administration, 54
U.S. Trademark Office, 55
U.S. Treasury Department's Office of
    Technical Assistance, 117
USA PATRIOT Act of 2001, 96, 114,
    124
USAID, 117

V

values, identifying, 8–9
venture capital firms, 90
veterans, disabled, 239–41
Viacom, 90
video résumés, 157, 162
videoconference interviews, 292

W

Web-based information
    for candidates with disabilities,
        231, 236, 239, 241
    for comparing cost-of-living and
        compensation scales, 251
    on compensation information,
        343–44
    for elder law, 142
    for emerging companies, 90–92
    for employment surveys, 4
    for energy landman information,
        68
    for federal court jobs, 100
    for federal government contracts,
        104
    for finding headhunters, 277
    for foreign news, 125
    for foundations and charitable
        organizations, 118
    for information on prospective
        employers, 328–30
    for innovation and invention
        tracking, 127

on land trusts, 116
for legal education information,
     35
for new technology, 126
for NGOs, 117
for the software industry, 72
for state jobs, 102, 105
for tax law, 76
for teaching positions, 111–12
for technology companies, 73
on mergers and acquisitions, 128
well-roundedness, 44
White House Office of Science and
     Technology Policy, 91
World Intellectual Property Organi-
     zation, 127
writing samples, 43, 157, 165–66,
     217–21

About the Author

Richard L. Hermann is a professor at Concord Law School, teaching the only full-semester course in legal career management in the United States. His *Future Interests* blog appears twice a week on www.legalcareerweb.com, and he is the author of many books on legal careers. He was the co-founder of Federal Reports Inc., the leading U.S. provider of legal career information, and of AttorneyJobs.com and Law Student Jobs Online, as well as a principal in Nationwide Career Counseling for Attorneys and Sutherland Hermann Associates, a legal outplacement and disability insurance consulting firm. He is a graduate of Yale, the New School University, Cornell Law School, and the U.S. Army Judge Advocate General's School. He also served with the U.S. Army NATO Atomic Demolitions Munitions Team.

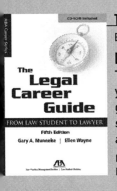